the PRINCIPLES of SUSTAINABILITY

the PRINCIPLES of SUSTAINABILITY

Simon Dresner

London • Sterling, VA

First published by Earthscan in the UK and USA in 2002

Reprinted 2003, 2004, 2006, 2007

Quotations from *Our Common Future* © World Commission on Environment and Development (1987) reprinted by permission of Oxford University Press.

ISBN   978 1 85383 842 2 paperback
   978 1 85383 841 5 hardback

Printed and bound in the UK by Cromwell Press, Trowbridge
Cover design by Yvonne Booth

For a full list of publications please contact:

Earthscan
8–12 Camden High Street, London, NW1 0JH, UK
Tel: +44 (0)20 7387 8558
Fax: +44 (0)20 7387 8998
Email: earthinfo@earthscan.co.uk
Web: **www.earthscan.co.uk**

22883 Quicksilver Drive, Sterling, VA 20166-2012, USA

Earthscan is an imprint of James & James (Science Publishers) Ltd and publishes in association with the International Institute for Environment and Development

A catalogue record for this book is available from the British Library

Library of Congress Cataloging-in-Publication Data

Dresner, Simon.
 The principles of sustainability / Simon Dresner.
   p. cm.
 Includes bibliographical references and index.
 ISBN 1-85383-841-1 — ISBN 1-85383-842-X (pbk.)
  1. Sustainable development. 2. Economic development—Environmental aspects. I. Title.

HD75.6 .D735 2002
338.9'27—dc21

2002004127

The paper used for this book is FSC-certified and totally chlorine-free. FSC (the Forest Stewardship Council) is an international network to promote responsible management of the world's forests.

Mixed Sources
Product group from well-managed forests and other controlled sources
www.fsc.org Cert no. TT-TOC-2082
© 1996 Forest Stewardship Council

Contents

Acknowledgements

This book is based on research I conducted for my PhD at Edinburgh University, funded by the Economic and Social Research Council. I would like to thank my supervisors, Robin Williams and Tony Clayton (now at the University of the West Indies) for their advice and encouragement during the course of my studies. I would particularly like to thank Tony for suggesting this topic for my PhD and subsequently encouraging me to publish a book based on the research.

The research included interviews with dozens of people involved in the issues discussed. Many of those not mentioned in the text provided me with valuable insights. I remain grateful to all those I interviewed for having been generous enough to give me their time and their thoughts.

My thanks to the people at A SEED Europe for their assistance with my research in the Netherlands. I thank Jackie Roddick for her help and advice about my attendance at the Commission on Sustainable Development in New York. I would also like to thank Pratap Chatterjee for his help and advice during the time I spent in Washington DC.

The course from PhD thesis to published book has been long and arduous. I would like to thank a number of people. Nigel Gilbert was very supportive and provided invaluable advice about book proposals. Ragnar Lofstedt helped in getting Earthscan interested. Stuart Parkinson and Katie Begg gave me a great deal of useful information about the climate negotiations. Stuart provided advice, suggestions and encouragement about the book more generally for which I am particularly grateful.

At Earthscan, I thank Jonathan Sinclair-Wilson, Pascale Mettam, Andrew Luck, Victoria Burrows, Frances MacDermott and Akan Leander and for their advice and suggestions.

Finally, I would like to thank my parents and my partner Afrodita for their support, encouragement and assistance. This book is dedicated to them.

Acronyms and Abbreviations

AOSIS	Alliance of Small Island States
BCSD	Business Council for Sustainable Development
BSE	bovine spongiform encephalopathy
CDM	Clean Development Mechanism
COP	Conference of the Parties (to the Framework Convention on Climate Change)
CSD	Commission on Sustainable Development
DDT	dichlorodiphenyltrichloroethane
ECOSOC	UN Committee on Economic and Social Affairs
ETR	ecological tax reform
EU	European Union
GATT	General Agreement on Tariffs and Trade
GCI	Global Commons Institute
GEF	Global Environment Facility
GM	genetically modified
GMO	genetically modified organism
GNP	gross national product
HDI	Human Development Index
IMF	International Monetary Fund
IPCC	Intergovernmental Panel on Climate Change
ISEW	Index of Sustainable Economic Welfare
JUSSCANNZ	Japan, United States, Switzerland, Canada, Australia, Norway and New Zealand
LETS	Local Economic Trading System
MIT	Massachusetts Institute of Technology
NGO	non-governmental organization
ODA	official development aid
TQM	Total Quality Management
UN	United Nations
UNCED	United Nations Conference on Environment and Development
UNDP	United Nations Development Programme
UNEP	United Nations Environment Programme
US	United States
VAT	value added tax
VCR	video cassette recorder
WCED	World Commission on Environment and Development
WTO	World Trade Organization

Introduction

Why should I care about posterity? What's posterity ever done for me?
                                                                    – Groucho Marx

What is sustainability?

The idea that we should live 'sustainably' has become central to environmental discussions. When an environmental issue is discussed in the media, there is frequently a quotation from a scientist or an environmental activist saying that the trend in question is 'unsustainable'. Even the slogan of the publishers of this book is 'delivering sustainability'.

Why has this idea of sustainability become so important in recent years? One reason is because it is much more powerful rhetorically than an idea like being 'environmentally friendly'. Not caring about the environment has a long history and is still regarded as acceptable in some circles, but publicly saying that you don't care that what you are doing is unsustainable sounds tantamount to admitting that you are intellectually incoherent. That cannot be the entire explanation, though. After all, the term sustainability was hardly heard until the late 1980s, 20 years after the contemporary environmental movement got going.

The concept of sustainability in something like its modern form was first used by the World Council of Churches in 1974.[1] It was proposed by Western environmentalists in response to developing world objections to worrying about the environment when human beings in many parts of the world suffer from poverty and deprivation. The concept of sustainable development was put forward by the International Union for Conservation of Nature and Natural Resources in 1980.[2]

Sustainability and sustainable development finally came to prominence in 1987, when the United Nations' World Commission on Environment and Development, chaired by former and later Norwegian prime minister Gro Harlem Brundtland, published its report *Our Common Future*.[3] The central recommendation of this document, usually known as the Brundtland report, was that the way to square the circle of competing demands for environmental protection and economic development was through a new approach: sustainable development. They defined it as development that 'meets the needs of the present without compromising the ability of future generations to meet their needs.'[4] They wrote that sustainable development was about both equity between generations and equity within generations.

The slogan 'sustainable development' was quickly taken up by governments and international agencies. At the United Nations Conference on Environment and Development (UNCED), which took place in Rio de Janeiro in 1992, the world's political leaders pledged their support for the goal. However, the sight of such unanimous support from politicians has encouraged the suspicion among some environmentalists that sustainable development is a meaningless concept. Different people use the term in different ways, some emphasizing development through economic growth, and others emphasizing sustainability through environmental protection.

Some environmentalists have claimed that sustainable development is a contradiction in terms, and can be used merely as a cover for continuing to destroy the natural world.[5] On the other side of the debate, some economists have argued that sustainable development is too cautious about the future, potentially leading to sacrifices of economic growth for the sake of excessive concern about depletion of natural resources. Defenders of the concept argue that disagreement about sustainable development does not show that it is meaningless. Rather, it is a 'contestable concept' like liberty or justice. Most people support these goals but disagree about what exactly constitutes liberty or justice.[6] It is also sometimes argued by environmentalists that the compromises inherent in combining 'sustainable' with 'development' were a necessary price to pay to get the idea of sustainability into the political mainstream at all.

Sustainability and equity

The sustainability debate is not just about 'environment versus growth'. The Brundtland Commission originally used the idea of sustainable development to try to get round that polarized debate which had already run from the early 1970s. Although sustainability is often presented as a matter of prudence, even of common sense – that you should not destroy the basis of your own existence – it is really more a question of *equity*. Concern about sustainability must be based on moral obligations towards future generations – not just personal self-interest. A crucial sentence in the Brundtland report stated: 'Even the narrow notion of physical sustainability implies a concern for social equity between generations, a concern that must logically be extended to equity within each generation.'[7] In this way, the Brundtland Commission's conception of sustainable development brought together *equity between generations* and *equity within generations*.

Bringing these two ideas together was a political masterstroke. From the late 1960s, when the present-day environmentalist movement was starting, leftists and representatives of the developing countries had frequently accused environmentalists, with their concerns about 'the population bomb' and 'the limits to growth', of being unconcerned about the plight of the poor. They saw all this talk of 'limits' as a cover for traditional conservative arguments that wealth was too scarce for everyone to share in it – a thinly disguised justification for inequality.

Malthus and Marx

The historical precedent for this view was Marx's critique of the argument put forward by Malthus at the end of the 18th century. Malthus had claimed that uncontrolled population growth among the poor meant that wealth could not be distributed more equally, as some supporters of the French Revolution wanted. The numbers of poor would quickly grow to eat up any surplus and reduce everyone to a state of bare subsistence.

Marx and Engels argued that Malthus' argument was false and was simply an excuse for inequality. The poor could learn the same 'moral restraint' against large families that apparently had kept the rich from breeding themselves into poverty. More importantly, they argued that Malthus' concept of natural limits was oppressive and conservative. It justified social injustice and ignored the potential for scientific and technical progress.

Ironically, today it is free market economists who most enthusiastically echo Marx and Engels' faith in growth and progress. In the 1990s, environmentalists took up Brundtland's idea of the connection between equity within generations and equity between generations. Using the concept of 'environmental space', many environmentalists now claim that sustainability requires people in the industrialized countries to reduce their consumption of resources per head to a level that everyone in the world would be able to live on indefinitely.

Defining sustainability

Environmental economists define sustainability in terms of non-depletion of capital. It is argued that we are presently depleting the 'natural capital' of the Earth and, as the green economist Herman Daly put it, treating the world 'as if it were a business in liquidation.'[8] However, there is disagreement around the extent to which advancing technology enables human-made capital to replace natural capital, and how far the idea of non-depletion of natural capital should be taken. Oil is currently being consumed at a million times the rate at which the reserves were laid down. Should we immediately reduce our consumption a millionfold in order to be sustainable?

Even the most radical Greens see the absurdity of that line of thinking. The debate between 'strong' sustainability and 'weak' sustainability is about whether, in general, the proceeds from running down natural capital like oil reserves, that can be substituted for, should be invested directly in substitutes for those resources – such as solar power technology, or can be invested in other forms of capital – such as education. Another debate is about whether there is such a thing as 'critical' natural capital that cannot be substituted for by technology, and must be preserved absolutely.

Risk and inequality are two sides of the same coin

The dispute between environmentalists and economists over sustainability is not just about the capacity of technological progress to substitute for natural resources. In the absence of sufficient understanding of the natural environment and of the capacities of future science and technology to deal with any problems, it involves disputes about how to deal with indeterminate risks. Economists tend to average out such risks in their calculations, burying worst-case possibilities in the average, or often even ignoring the possibility that things might turn out worse than they expect, so tending to advocate risky approaches to environmental futures. Environmentalists instead highlight worst-case outcomes and suggest that extra efforts should be taken to avoid them.

There are parallels between the risky approach that economists take with the future and their lack of support for egalitarianism in the present. Both are a result of the assumptions of the utilitarian philosophy underlying mainstream economics, which is indifferent to the risk of very bad outcomes for some individuals in the present or everyone in some alternative futures. Most contemporary environmentalists are more left wing, and it turns out that there is a real philosophical parallel between their interest in equity to future generations and equity within generations. Drawing on the theories of the philosopher John Rawls, I will suggest that there are very severe tensions between the utilitarian basis of mainstream economics and sustainability's concern for equity within and between generations.

More broadly, the liberal objection to limiting each individual's material consumption only applies if you accept the 17th century philosopher John Locke's justification for private property rights – that my expropriation of natural resources does you no harm as there is enough for you. If we live in a world with environmental limits, then that argument does not hold. Resources have to be shared so that there is enough for everybody, both now and in the future.

In this way, sustainability is an idea with a certain amount in common with socialism. In an irony of history, the rhetoric of sustainability was adopted on to the political agenda in the 1990s at precisely the same time that the classical political philosophies that could support its concerns (democratic socialism and social democracy) were being abandoned.

The ecological economist Richard Norgaard[9] has argued that the concept of sustainable development actually marks the beginning of a break by the dominant strand of Western culture from an idea it has been firmly wedded to for the past two centuries – faith in Progress. When people believed in Progress they did not worry about taking care of the environment for the sake of their children and grandchildren. Progress was seen in terms of the mastery of nature. People assumed that advancing science and technology, by increasing human mastery over nature, would decrease our dependence on it. In recent years, faith in human beings' capacity to successfully master nature or even to collectively control our own destiny has been diminished.

Will sustainability be like socialism?

I will argue that the present debate about sustainability is part of a wider re-evaluation of many of the modernist values that have been passed down to us from the Enlightenment. It is the ideas of the Enlightenment that inspired Western culture's optimism about science and progress. For a long time, that optimism appeared to be amply borne out. Only in the last few decades has widespread doubt set in about the direction that our path of development is taking us.

However, the environmental movement shares many Western post-Enlightenment values, while criticizing others – it has an ambivalent relationship to modernity itself. The commitment to equity that is crucial to the idea of sustainability comes straight out of the values of the French Revolution. The concept of sustainability is also an extension of the sort of commitment to large scale social reform that the Enlightenment brought to the Western world. So sustainability combines much of the social optimism of the Enlightenment with disillusion about the means by which its goals were pursued.

The sociologists Ulrich Beck[10] and Anthony Giddens[11] have claimed that we are living in the era of 'reflexive modernization', where modernity has turned on itself and is subjecting itself to the same kind of critique that it brought to pre-industrial society. However, the socialist movement also believed that it was about the human race consciously taking control of its historical destiny, rather than allowing capitalist development to proceed blindly into the future. Socialism ultimately failed in its attempt to consciously transform the world to bring about a new society. The idea that we can achieve sustainability implies that we will this time be able to consciously take control of our destiny. To try to achieve sustainability is really to set ourselves a goal at least as ambitious as any of the aims of the Enlightenment or socialism.

Jean-Luc Godard once said that although he agreed that every story should have a beginning, a middle and an end, he did not think they should necessarily be in that order. But in order to describe the complicated story of thinking about sustainability, I think it is best to start by going back to the beginning.

Part One
PAST

1

Progress and its Discontents

Man had always assumed that he was more intelligent than dolphins because he had achieved so much... the wheel, New York, wars, and so on, whilst all the dolphins had ever done was muck about in the water having a good time. But conversely the dolphins believed themselves to be more intelligent than man for precisely the same reasons.

– Douglas Adams

The Enlightenment

It was the development of Western science that allowed human beings to break free of the technological limits which had constrained earlier civilizations, leading to the emergence of belief in Progress.[1] The rediscovery of Greek science from the Arabs and information gleaned from the Arabs themselves launched European science at the end of the Middle Ages. The invention of the printing press enabled ideas to spread quickly. In the 17th century, European scientists began to make dramatic new breakthroughs. The invention of the telescope and Galileo's discovery of moons orbiting Jupiter led to the overthrow of the old Earth-centred view of the universe. The discrediting of the authority of the Catholic Church's teachings about astronomy precipitated the development of rationalism as an ideology for scientists. The power of reason was demonstrated by Isaac Newton when he developed his laws of motion to explain the movement of the heavenly bodies in mechanical terms.

Francis Bacon was a particularly important ideologist of science. In his utopian novel *The New Atlantis*, published in 1627, he introduced the idea that science would enable the domination of nature.[2] It had previously been believed that man had permanently lost his dominion after the expulsion from the Garden of Eden. Bacon proposed that it could be regained through a scientific understanding of nature's workings. His startling idea was that scientific men could gain powers that had been believed to belong to God. His imagery was striking and not at all politically correct: 'I am come in very truth leading to you Nature with all her children to bind her to your service and make her your slave.'[3]

Another important early ideologist was René Descartes. In *A Discourse on Method*, he put forward the idea that nature could be understood by the use of Reason.[4] He firmly separated 'man', who possessed rationality, from the rest of the natural world, which did not and could be regarded as a machine. Even animals, which appeared to be conscious, were in fact mere automata. There were no longer any ethical restraints on what could be done to other living things or the Earth. The first great success of Descartes' vision of scientific progress through the analogy of Nature as a machine was Newton's discovery of the laws of motion. It was followed in the late 17th and the 18th century by rapid advances in many fields of science.

In the 18th century, the Enlightenment and the Age of Reason looked for the rationality that was being applied so successfully in science to be turned to other fields. In England, the philosopher John Locke outlined a political theory based on a deduction of the rights to life, liberty and property.[5] Locke inspired Thomas Jefferson's American Declaration of Independence. The idea of a rational political order took an even more powerful hold in the French Revolution, inspired by *philosophes* like Voltaire and Rousseau.

In Britain, rationality was applied in the field of economics. Early capitalism began to break down the semi-feudal order and the factory system was created. Intellectual support for capitalism and the market came from the Scottish political economist Adam Smith, as exemplified in his description of the division of labour in a pin factory.[6] He showed how a complex and difficult task had been rationally broken down into a series of tasks, which could be completed much more quickly when divided up in this way. Smith also reasoned counter-intuitively that efficient economic coordination could be achieved through competition in markets. If each individual acted to maximize their own economic self-interest, the 'invisible hand' of the market would bring about the most efficient distribution of resources.

Unlike Locke, Smith and the English tradition of liberalism, who based their theories on the idea that self-interest was natural, but could be harnessed for the general good, Jean-Jacques Rousseau argued that man was born good, but was corrupted by society.[7] Adam Smith welcomed the creation of new desires that followed from economic development. Rousseau thought that human desires beyond the need for food and shelter contributed to *unhappiness*. Possessions are not essential for happiness, Rousseau wrote, and the desire for them arises out of comparison with others, and sense of vanity, which Rousseau called *amour-propre*. The result is that people are unhappy in civilized societies, not because they are unable to fulfil their basic needs, but because they cannot fulfil socially created desires. Economic development continually creates a gap between new wants and their fulfilment. Rousseau held that the route to happiness lay in abandoning society and returning to life as a natural being in a natural world. His ideas inspired the Romantic movement in the early 19th century, and are echoed today by the Green movement.

It was Smith, rather than Rousseau, who captured the spirit of the future. At the end of the 18th century, the application of the steam engine, starting in England but soon spreading across Europe and America, led to a sudden explosion of manufacturing activity that Engels later named the 'Industrial Revolution'. Within two generations it had led to the most profound changes in the nature of people's lives since the invention of agriculture several millennia earlier. The technology and social organization that flowed out of the Industrial Revolution gave human beings a degree of control over nature unparalleled in previous history.

Malthus on population

Just as the Industrial Revolution was starting to expand the limits of material progress, the English country parson Thomas Robert Malthus published his *Essay on Population* in 1798. He argued that the tendency of population towards geometric growth meant that it would always outstrip the growth in food supply. The population was controlled by 'misery' (rising mortality rates due to food shortages) and 'vice' (prostitution and contraception). The standard of living of the labouring classes always hovered around the minimum necessary for subsistence. This tendency towards population increase meant that any improvement in the conditions of the labouring classes could be only temporary and would soon be eaten up by population growth. The poor laws, which provided relief for unemployed labourers, only encouraged them to have more children than they could support. Those laws should be abolished. The 'iron law of population' would also prevent any permanent improvement in the lot of the masses, making futile any attempt at a more just and egalitarian society, as proposed by Godwin and Condorcet after the French Revolution. Malthus claimed to have come to this view reluctantly: 'I have read some of the speculations on the perfectibility of man and society with great pleasure. I have been warmed and delighted with the enchanting picture which they hold forth. I ardently wish for such improvements, but I see great, and, to my understanding, unconquerable difficulties in the way to them.'[8]

William Godwin had proposed a utopian anarchist society where property and self-interest had disappeared. People would instead act rationally in the interests of the whole. One of Malthus' first critics was Godwin himself. In 1801, he responded to Malthus and pointed out that if the birth rate could be reduced through 'moral restraint' (delayed marriage) then 'misery' and 'vice' could be avoided.[9] Godwin pointed out that such restraint must exist among the rich, or else they would have bred to the point of poverty themselves, so it could be acquired by the poor. Malthus accepted this point in the second edition of the essay, published in 1803. This marked something of a retreat from the position in the first edition that any improvement in the condition of the masses would automatically be eliminated by increases in population. He came to the view that the condition of the poor could be gradually improved by education about the benefits of delayed marriage. Combined with economic growth, it would slowly raise their living standards. But he continued to argue that redistribution of wealth could not work. It would only mean that the misery and poverty of the masses would be made general.

Unlike Godwin, Condorcet could not respond to Malthus – he had died in the Jacobin Terror of 1794. Condorcet had been a liberal Frenchman who believed in sexual freedom and advocated contraception as the means to curb population growth. Malthus, like nearly all his English contemporaries, considered contraception to be 'vice'. Malthus argued that contraception discouraged prudence and took away the pressure to support a family that encouraged people to work. Malthus was not, as is often imagined, against population growth. He thought that it was a good thing. What he thought was a bad thing was that the population grew faster than the means to support it. Malthus was not the extreme conservative he is often remembered as having been, either. He was a moderate Whig who supported civil rights for the lower classes, and even the eventual extension of the vote to them once they had become educated.

Not surprisingly, socialists in particular hated what Malthus said. There were very few in Britain at that time, but there were a number of socialist thinkers in France. They generally agreed that there was a danger of overpopulation, but they tended to see the solution in improved social and economic organization, more advanced technology and a consequent rise in the standard of living. They believed that as more varied pleasures became available, people would turn away from unbridled sexuality. They rarely saw value in contraception. The exception was Fourier, who regarded even abortion as legitimate in order for people to enjoy a good sex life.

Fourier believed that a socialist regime would result in a rapid increase of wealth to four times the level it was then. Nonetheless, he was worried about the physical limits of resources. He said the world was finite, and in two centuries would probably have a population of 5.5 billion. Even though the deserts might be reclaimed, the human species would become overcrowded and suffocate through excessive numbers. But he hoped that new conditions of life in a socialist society would humanely limit the population.[10]

What actually happened was that the population of Britain rose from around 10 million to around 50 million in the following 100 years. But thanks to the mechanization of agriculture and food imports from the outside world, particularly the Empire, food shortages grew less rather than more. A similar pattern was repeated in the rest of Europe. Even so, the population eventually grew to a point that locally available fertilizer was no longer sufficient and it had to be supplemented to maintain the rise in yields (first with guano from Chile, later with artificial fertilizer manufactured from fossil fuels). Britain remains a net importer of food today.

The 19th century European population explosion was eased by the emigration of 60 million people from Europe to other parts of the world, especially the Americas. As living standards rose and urbanization continued, the size of European families gradually became smaller. Population growth levelled off in Europe in the 20th century. In the past decade, the average fertility rate in most European and other industrialized countries has fallen well below two children per woman. However, population growth began to increase in the non-industrialized countries of the world as death rates began to fall in the middle of the 20th century. By 1992 the world had a population of 5.5 billion, rising at 1.7 per cent each year, and it reached 6 billion in 1999.

Marx's critique of Malthus

Malthus had been dead for ten years before his fiercest and ultimately most influential critics began their attacks on his ideas. Karl Marx and Friedrich Engels did not deny the phenomenon that Malthus was describing, of the wages of agricultural labourers falling to subsistence levels, but they explained it as a 'reserve army of labour' necessary for capitalist accumulation. The law referred to an excessive number of labourers relative to the means of employment, not subsistence.

Their argument had two parts; firstly, that Malthus' 'law' of population was not universal or necessary, and, secondly, that relative surplus population was not an inevitable effect of the human condition, but of the dynamics of capital accumulation. Their intention was to show that the cause of the prevailing poverty and misery in society was not overpopulation, but oppressive economic and political structures. Marx and Engels' view of Malthus was connected to their perceptions of the political consequences of his theories. Marx wrote in 'Critique of the Gotha Program':

> But if this theory is correct, then again I cannot abolish the law even if I abolish wage labour a hundred times over, because the law then governs not only the system of wage labour but every social system. Basing themselves directly on this, the economists have been proving for fifty years and more that socialism cannot abolish poverty, which has its basis in nature, but can only make it general, distribute it simultaneously over the whole surface of society![11]

Engels repeated many familiar arguments against Malthus. He gave Godwin's point about the role of sexual restraint in response to Malthus' warnings:

> We derive from it the most powerful economic arguments for a social transformation. For even if Malthus were completely right this transformation would have to be undertaken straight away; for only this transformation, only the education of the masses which it provides, makes possible that moral restraint of the propagative instinct which Malthus himself presents as the most effective and easiest remedy for over-population.[12]

Engels went on to say that it was absurd to talk of overpopulation when only a third of the Earth's land surface was cultivated and the application of agricultural improvements already known could raise the production of this third six-fold. Moreover, he added, the geometrical rise in population was matched by a geometrical increase in science and its application: 'And what is impossible to science?'[13]. That phrase was a denial of any problem with natural limits – because human scientific ingenuity was such that essentially *nothing* is impossible. In reference to Malthus' theory, Engels says: 'our attention has been drawn to the productive power of the earth and mankind; and after overcoming this economic despair we have been made for ever secure against the fear of over-population.'[14]

The apparent limits to the fertility of land had led the early economists to conclude that there were limits to the growth of the economy. As science and technology began to make possible many things previously unimagined, and mechanization enormously increased agricultural productivity, the idea put forwards by Marx and Engels, that this kind of growth could continue for ever and that any apparent natural limits were not real, began to take hold. Their criticism of Malthusian natural limits was influential well beyond those who accepted their views generally, and today, paradoxically, is held at least as forcefully by mainstream economists as by the few surviving orthodox Marxists.

Ted Benton[15] has analysed Marx and Engels' rebuttal of Malthus' natural limits conservatism. He argues that their 'social constructivist' response that the limits are purely social goes beyond what is necessary to rebut Malthus and, ironically, goes against the materialist spirit of their philosophy. He distinguishes between 'utopian' and 'realist' emancipatory perspectives. 'Utopian' perspectives seek to deny the existence of limits to human emancipation. 'Realist' perspectives accept that there may be limits to what is possible, and seek to achieve transformation within those boundaries.

He goes on to criticize their characterization of production in terms of material transformation from raw material to product. He points out that many aspects of production, such as farming, are not really examples of such transformation. By such a characterization, Marx overlooks the extent to which human existence is dependent on the operation of natural ecological cycles, and he overstates both the transformative aspect of praxis and the extent to which praxis is based on domination of nature.

Benton argues that each form of social life does indeed have its own specific material constraints and limits. However, it is possible to adopt social and technical strategies to deal with these limits. For example, recycling is a means of effectively transcending natural limits to the availability of non-renewable resources. The emphasis is instead on adaptive technologies rather than directly transformative ones.

Benton points to some evidence that Marx and Engels acknowledged the trans-historical necessity of human dependence upon naturally given conditions and limits to social activity. There are two passages representing the 'ecological Marx' that he quotes. One is Marx's discussion of the deleterious effects of capitalist agriculture on soil fertility:

By this action it destroys at the same time the health of the town labourer and the intellectual life of the rural labourer. But while upsetting the naturally grown conditions for the maintenance of that circulation of matter, it imperiously calls for its restoration as a system, as a regulating law of social production, and under a form appropriate to the full development of the human race.[16]

The other is from Engels:

Thus at every step we are reminded that we by no means rule over nature like a conqueror over foreign people, like someone standing outside nature – but that we, with flesh, blood and brain, belong to nature and exist in its midst, and that all our mastering of it consists in the fact that we have the advantage over all other beings of being able to know and correctly apply its laws.[17]

However, Rainer Grundmann[18] responded to Benton by criticizing his claim that Marx overemphasized the transformative potential of technology. Grundmann argued that Benton had made too much of the distinction between different kinds of interventions in nature. Farming and recycling are also transformations of nature, just ones that Benton approves of. Grundmann went on to criticize the ecological critique of the domination of nature: '... a society that does not take into account the repercussions of its transformation of nature can hardly be said to dominate nature at all.'[19] He sees the theme of conscious control over human affairs as the Archimedean point from which Marx levels his critique of capitalism and derives his perspective of what a communist society would be like. For Marx, a communist society would be one that institutionalizes conscious human control over its own fate.

Grundmann does see a problem in Marx's ideas about the relationship between technology and nature. He writes that Marx conceived the development of technologies and social relations within an evolutionary perspective: a new social formation or a new productive force emerges out of a prior formation – the old is pregnant with the new. But this model poses a dilemma in the case of technology because either the liberating form of technology is already present under capitalism, or it has not yet developed. The former position would mean that capitalism and technology were aligned. The latter position was a philosophically impossible one for Marx to take, since this would amount to an *idealistic* hope for a better future. Marx's solution to the dilemma, says Grundmann, was to attribute all negative effects of machine technology to its capitalist *use*, and to attribute all positive aspects to machine technology *as such*: 'No matter how we view this theoretical trick, it enables us to solve the dilemma in a satisfactory way. That is to say that technology, in so far as it has a detrimental impact on the natural environment, has to be changed and replaced by a technology that meets the criteria that it be consciously controlled and worthy of human nature. At the same time, the view that capitalism is the main cause of ecological problems must be abandoned.'[20]

I cannot find Grundmann's solution entirely satisfactory. Although Marxism's materialism implies the possibility of accepting limits to human power, Marx's own emphasis on the conscious control of nature and social relations led him into a voluntaristic dismissal of any suggestion of limits to control. The tragedy of 20th century Communism was that it ruthlessly pursued both forms of control and in doing so ran into limits to the control of society and of nature that Marx had denied the possibility of finding. Grundmann implies that such problems could be avoided in future by a more intelligent approach to the domination of nature. Today, many people think that the problem lies in the goal itself.

Mary Shelley and the Frankenstein myth

Even in the 19th century, the goal of human domination of nature was not universally shared among political radicals. The Romantics were an important intellectual movement at the beginning of the Industrial Revolution. They reacted against what they saw as the increasing estrangement of human beings from nature as the Industrial Revolution took place. They were opposed to the prevalent mechanistic approach to science, to the humanist separation of human beings from nature, and to the Christian separation of God from nature. It was a Romantic, Mary Shelley, who reworked the old Biblical myth of the danger of eating from the tree of knowledge in a modern secular form which underlies many present-day fears about out-of-control technology – the Frankenstein myth.

In Shelley's novel, the eponymous Dr Frankenstein created a being that destroyed all his family and friends and ultimately himself as well.[21] In the novel the monster was a consequence not just of Frankenstein's egotistical single-mindedness, but also Frankenstein's masculine desire to father a creature entirely his own with no female aid (clearly a severe case of uterus envy). Shelley presents his search in sexual terms reminiscent of Bacon's language: 'They [scientists] penetrate into the recesses of nature, and show how she works in her hiding places,' Frankenstein says. Later, 'With unrelaxed and breathless eagerness, I pursued nature to her hiding places... a resistless, and almost frantic impulse, urged me forward; I seemed to have lost all soul or sensation but for this one pursuit.'[22] Frankenstein's science is shown as an obsessive quest for power over nature and for public glory – an example of hubris with ultimately tragic results.

Frankenstein is one of the most famous books ever written, but it is much less well known that Mary Shelley later wrote *The Last Man*, the first book warning of global environmental catastrophe.[23] The arrogant male scientists of the 22nd century believe that they now understand Nature and can control it. They are proved disastrously wrong when there is a sudden and inexplicable climatic change, leading to famine and then a plague that wipes out the human race. Mary Shelley's bizarre imaginings about the dangers of scientific and technological hubris were not taken seriously for over a century, but her ideas were re-invented in the late 20th century.

John Stuart Mill's stationary state

John Stuart Mill, who was widely regarded as the greatest English philosopher of his time, was also concerned about the human domination of nature. In his epic *Principles of Political Economy*, Mill devoted a short chapter to the idea of a 'stationary state economy', one which in today's language was not growing. He noted that according to classical political economy, profits and economic growth would ultimately decline over time as the limits to the productivity of land were reached. Classical political economists, following Adam Smith, had believed that population growth was unavoidable, so therefore an end to economic growth would lead to increasing hardship for the population. Mill pointed out that population growth must be restrained anyway and went on:

> I cannot, therefore, regard the stationary state of capital and wealth with the unaffected aversion so generally manifested towards it by political economists of the old school. I am inclined to believe that it would be, on the whole, a very considerable improvement on our present condition. I confess I am not charmed with the ideal of life held out by those who think that the normal state of human beings is that of struggling to get on; that the trampling, crushing, elbowing, and treading on each other's heels, which form the existing type of social life, are the most desirable lot of human kind, or anything but the disagreeable symptoms of one of the phases of industrial progress...

> There is room in the world, no doubt, and even in old countries, for a great increase in population, supposing the arts of life to go on improving, and capital to increase. But even if innocuous, I confess I see very little reason for desiring it... It is not good for man to be kept perforce in the presence of his species. A world from which solitude is extirpated, is a very poor ideal... Nor is there much satisfaction in contemplating the world with nothing left to the spontaneous activity of nature; with every rod of land brought into cultivation, which is capable of growing food for human beings; every flowery waste or natural pasture ploughed up, all quadrupeds or birds which are not domesticated for man's use exterminated as his rivals for food, every hedgerow or superfluous tree rooted out, and scarcely a place left where a wild shrub or flower could grow without being eradicated as a weed in the name of improved agriculture. If the earth must lose that great portion of its pleasantness

which it owes to things that the unlimited increase of wealth and population would extirpate from it, for the mere purpose of enabling it to support a larger, but not a better or a happier population, I sincerely hope, for the sake of posterity, that they will be content to be stationary, long before necessity compels them to it.[24]

Reflections

Many of the themes that are debated today around the issue of the environment would be recognizable to a Victorian intellectual. The concern about limits to growth in today's environmentalism would be familiar from Malthus. The discussion today about the dangers of technology and the limits to scientific certainty would remind them of Mary Shelley. The present-day Green agenda would strike them with its similarity to John Stuart Mill's concerns about the destruction of nature in pursuit of economic growth.

On the other hand, they would find some aspects of the present debate rather different. The argument made originally by Marx and Engels that natural limits could always be overcome by science and progress comes today more from the right than the left. A Victorian would also be struck by the extent to which we, who live in a world that has seen so much progress in the last century or so, have lost faith in the ideal of a better world in the future. Unlike Victorians, who generally looked to the future optimistically, we tend to look to the future with the feeling that optimism is passé. The slogan 'sustainable development' is an attempt to sound optimistic which reveals a degree of doubt about the future that most Victorians did not share. Our intellectual mood would strike them as very similar to Romanticism. They would wonder quite why that has happened.

2

From Muir to Meadows

I think that God in creating man somewhat overestimated his ability.

– Oscar Wilde

John Muir and the Sierra Club

The organized environmental movement was started by John Muir, a Scottish emigrant to America. In 1864, as a young man of 26, he disappeared into the Great Lakes wilderness. There, he discovered an awe for nature similar to that of the Romantics earlier. Muir later walked across much of North America, eventually going to California, where he settled and focused his energy on preserving the Sierras.

Muir's first book, *The Mountains of California*, describes the natural wonder of the state and also the loss of biological diversity in California already apparent due to the pressure of development:

> But of late years plows and sheep have made sad havoc in these glorious pastures, destroying tens of thousands of the flowery acres like a fire, and banishing many species of the best honey-plants to rocky-cliffs and fence-corners, while, on the other hand, cultivation thus far has given no adequate compensation, at least in kind; only acres of alfalfa for miles of the richest wild pasture, ornamental roses and honeysuckles around cottage doors for cascades of wild roses in the dells, and small, square orchards and orange-groves for broad mountain-belts of chaparral.[1]

Muir's greatest personal achievement against the forces of development was the establishment of Yosemite as a National Park in 1890. Within two years development pressures were so severe that a group of Californians led by Muir founded the Sierra Club to defend the park. The final years of Muir's life were dominated by the unsuccessful 1908–13 campaign to prevent the building of a dam in Hetch Hetchy Valley, the next valley north of Yosemite.

Gifford Pinchot's Conservationism

A very different tradition of conservation also appeared in the United States at the turn of the century, personified by Gifford Pinchot. He was the most prominent advocate of 'sustained yield' forestry, in contrast to the rapacious practices of the 'robber barons'. The Conservationist approach he put forward was implemented under the presidency of Teddy Roosevelt in the first decade of the 20th century. Roosevelt appointed Pinchot the first director of the US Forest Service. His Conservationism sought to conserve natural resources as it saw the destruction of resources such as forests as wasteful. The justification for conservation was that the resources could be more economically efficiently exploited. Pinchot said that the aim of conservation, echoing Jeremy Bentham's formulation of utilitarianism, was 'the greatest good for the greatest number for the longest time.' The Conservationist position was known as 'wise use' and became the cornerstone of official thinking about the environment in the United States. It was criticized even from the start by more radical thinkers, often called Preservationists, led by John Muir. The Conservationists believed that *not* utilizing natural resources was wasteful. When it was suggested that hydroelectric development of Niagara would spoil the river's beauty, Conservationists responded that it would be a crime to let so much energy go to waste.[2] The two groups fought over the Hetch Hetchy dam, intended to provide water for the rapidly growing city of San Francisco. It was a battle that eventually the Preservationists lost. The Conservationists had supported the dam, claiming it was a wise use of nature for human ends. The Preservationists argued against its construction as it would destroy one of the most beautiful valleys in the world. John Muir personally believed that the crime in building the dam was the destruction of nature more than the loss of aesthetic value. At that time, though, the use of this non-anthropocentric argument was not politically viable.

The Conservationists invented the profession of forestry, which they saw as tree farming. They created America's National Forests, areas of public land set aside primarily to provide for the need for timber. To obtain the maximum 'sustained yield' of timber, foresters grow only one species of tree in neat rows to make for easier harvesting and operate a system of rotation every few decades. The result lacks all the biological diversity of natural forests.

The practical problems with Conservationism lay in its lack of understanding of ecology. The Conservationists brought about the adoption by the US government of the policy of exterminating all predators. It became apparent to some people that this was not necessarily a good idea when it led to the population of deer in the Kaibab Forest near the Grand Canyon exploding, then crashing after they destroyed their food supply in the 1920s.[3] One response to these problems was the development of ecology as a science.

Aldo Leopold's land ethic

Aldo Leopold decided that the problem lay deeper than insufficient scientific knowledge. Leopold had been trained by Conservationists in the Yale Forestry School, and for the early part of his professional life he accepted Conservationist teaching. Gradually, however, he became disillusioned. The issue that precipitated this change of heart was predator control.[4] In his book *A Sand County Almanac*, Leopold called for a 'land ethic'.[5] Leopold's intuition was that the earth was an indivisible living being, each species playing its part in an indivisible whole, and human beings were just one part of that community. The land ethic stated that 'a thing is right when it tends to preserve the integrity, stability, and beauty of the biotic community. It is wrong when it tends otherwise.'[6] He said that the land ethic 'changes the role of *Homo sapiens* from conqueror of the land-community to plain member and citizen of it.'[7]

Yet Leopold justified the land ethic in anthropocentric terms – essentially that the long term human interest was best served by a healthy ecosystem, even if the short term interest was best served by purely economic criteria. That is the argument given for adopting criteria of 'sustainability' in decision making today. Leopold argued that it was not sensible from our point of view to remove a species from an ecosystem without knowing what the long term consequences would be: 'To keep every cog and wheel is the first precaution of intelligent tinkering.'[8] That is another argument that is familiar today, in the form of the precautionary principle.

Rachel Carson's *Silent Spring*

The new environmental movement that emerged in the 1960s was sparked off by Rachel Carson and her book *Silent Spring*.[9] Carson was a respected writer and scientist who wrote *Silent Spring* to draw attention to the destruction of wildlife by the use of the pesticide DDT. What was new about Carson's book was that it criticized a technology intended to better the condition of the human race, rather than a specific development, and that her book revealed *unintended and unpredicted* consequences of this technology.

Carson revealed that our actions could lead to seriously damaging environmental consequences when we interfered with natural systems we did not fully understand. She criticized the unthinking use of the technological 'quick fix' of employing synthetic chemicals to control insects. She warned that these chemicals contained the prospect of a dying world in which springtime would no longer bring forth new life, only silence. Carson concluded that 'the "control of nature" is a phrase conceived in arrogance, born of the Neanderthal age of biology and philosophy, when it was supposed that nature exists for the convenience of man.'[10] Carson's challenge to pesticides was implicitly a challenge to science and the idea of technological progress.

Modern environmentalism has two key concerns: the limits to control that were emphasized by Leopold and Carson, and also the idea of a global environmental crisis – limits of scale on a small planet. Atmospheric nuclear testing was banned in 1963 after the discovery of strontium-90 from nuclear fallout in mother's milk and in the fat of Antarctic penguins. Not long afterwards, traces of DDT were also found in Antarctic penguins. The notion that the world was not large, but relatively small, began to gain currency.

'Spaceship Earth'

The metaphor of the earth as a spaceship was coined by the American presidential candidate Adlai Stevenson in a campaign speech as far back as 1952.[11] It was taken up by the British journalist Barbara Ward in her 1966 book *Spaceship Earth*.[12] The concept was developed simultaneously by the economist Kenneth Boulding. In his essay 'The Economics of the Coming Spaceship Earth' Boulding put forward the idea that previous human history had taken place against a background where the scale of human activities was tiny compared to the environment.[13] In this situation, there was always somewhere 'out there' to expand to or put your wastes. He called this a 'cowboy' economy because the idea of an endless frontier was embodied by the American cowboy. What was now happening was that human activity was growing to a size where there was no 'out there' left. In this situation it was no longer possible to try to put problems somewhere else. They would always return to you. He wrote that it would require a 'spaceman' economy because frontiers had shrunk to zero, there was nowhere to expand to, nothing could be simply thrown away and all waste would have to be recycled. Boulding's essay was influential, but the metaphor did not catch on immediately.

In the 1960s there was a growing sense that Western technology had reached every corner of the earth and that with improved communication the world was growing smaller and closer together. This was the time of Marshall McLuhan's 'global village'.[14] It was also the time when a global nuclear holocaust seemed a real possibility. What really brought the metaphor alive was the photographs of the Earth that the Apollo astronauts took from the Moon at the end of the 1960s. The pictures were of a small and beautiful blue-white planet with oceans and clouds, against the blackness of space and the grey of another, lifeless, world. The photograph perfectly visualized the metaphor 'Spaceship Earth' and the environmental movement seized on it. Within a few years the metaphor had become a tiresome cliché, but while it lasted it was extremely powerful. In 1970 the first Earth Day was held. In 1972, at the UN Conference on the Human Environment, the official slogan was 'Only One Earth'.

The metaphor has two different connotations. One is of limits to human activities. The other is of the need for human management of the environment. The two meanings are not entirely incompatible, but there is clearly a tension between them. One implies that we are overcrowding passengers. The other implies that we are the new commander about to bravely go where no species has gone before, presumably replacing God.

The Costs of Economic Growth

In 1967, the prominent economist Edward Mishan shook up the economics profession with the publication of *The Costs of Economic Growth*.[15] He argued that calculations of Gross National Product (GNP) were seriously misleading as a measure of human welfare because they included the costs of defensive measures such as anti-pollution expenditure and failed to count negative effects of affluence like aircraft noise against growth. A decade earlier, John Kenneth Galbraith had made fairly similar arguments against GNP as a measure of welfare, but without the emphasis on environmental externalities.[16] Mishan's argument was sound, but embarrassing to economists. One of my interviewees, Hans Opschoor, now a professor of economics, was inspired to specialize in the then non-existent discipline of environmental economics by reading *The Costs of Economic Growth*.

The Population Bomb

The era of 'Spaceship Earth' was the time when fear of global environmental limits began to emerge. Environmentalism came together with a renewed Malthusianism. Concern about exponential population growth, this time in the developing world, came to the fore with the publication of Paul Ehrlich's *The Population Bomb*.[17] Paul and Anne Ehrlich (who co-wrote the book but was denied credit by the publisher) were animal population biologists who had developed these opinions after personally witnessing the hunger and overcrowding in India. The Ehrlichs argued that population growth would lead to massive famines in Asia and Africa in the 1970s. Most controversially, they proposed that some countries, such as India, were such hopeless cases that resources should not be wasted on helping them. This ruthless position was very reminiscent of Malthus himself, the first person to suggest that exponential growth would lead to an imminent collision with natural limits.

   The Ehrlichs' terrible predictions of famine and imminent ecological collapse failed to come true. Famines had occurred quite often in India until the 1970s, but have not happened since (although the Ehrlich's point out that the present population of India is being fed by methods that cause massive soil erosion[18]). The large famines of the 1970s and 1980s in Africa took place mostly in war torn countries. It seems, though, that at the time the self-proclaimed alarmism of *The Population Bomb* was very influential in raising concern. The theologian and environmentalist John Cobb told me that it was *The Population*

Bomb's alarmism that motivated him to become an environmental activist. Cobb said that although the book had been wrong in its predictions and contained 'gross exaggerations', he wanted to acknowledge that it was *The Population Bomb* that shook him into action. The environmental economist John Pezzey was also scared into environmentalism by *The Population Bomb* and other alarmist books of the late 1960s. He told me that he now felt cheated by the alarms that were raised about problems that had not turned out so bad as he had been led to believe then. This kind of alarmism was an easy target for John Maddox, the editor of the journal *Nature*, in his anti-environmentalist polemic *The Doomsday Syndrome*.[19] Today, his optimism appears as wide of the mark as the Ehrlichs' pessimism. Maddox did not believe that there were ecological limits. For example, he argued that there was no shortage of land for cultivation in the world and pointed to the Amazon and Congo basins as large areas suitable for agricultural development.

Ehrlich went on to develop his ideas to consider the overall environmental impact of the human population, rather than sheer numbers. It was expressed in the equation I=PCT, where I is the environmental impact, P is the population size, C is per capita consumption and T is the environmental impact of the productive technology.[20] Although many of Ehrlich's early ideas are regarded with embarrassment by most environmentalists today, the I=PCT equation opened up the way to many of the ideas that environmentalists campaign on today because the levels of material consumption in Western countries are several times the global average and fifty times those in the poorest countries. I=PCT actually suggests that increasing consumption is a greater cause of the growing environmental impact of the human race than population growth.

The Limits to Growth

The crystallization of the concerns of the first wave of environmentalism that ran from around 1966 to 1972 was *The Limits to Growth*.[21] A report by a group of young scientists from the Massachusetts Institute of Technology (MIT), it immediately took the world by storm, gaining enormous media coverage. It was translated into 28 languages and sold 9 million copies. *The Limits To Growth* was based on computer models that appeared to show that if the current trends of exponential growth in population and demand for non-renewable resources continued, the world would face severe shortages of food and non-renewable resources by the middle of the 21st century. The modellers concluded that 'the limits to growth on this planet will be reached some time in the next hundred years.'[22]

The model assumed that there are finite amounts of fossil fuels and minerals available on the Earth. It did not simply assume that you use a certain amount and then run out, but modelled the price behaviour of an increasingly scarce and difficult to obtain resource. The estimates of availability given could be challenged but, the MIT team argued, because of the nature of exponential growth, even if resources were several times larger than the current estimates, they would still become extremely scarce and expensive only a few decades later. According to the model, population growth was happening too fast for demographic transition before collapse unless population control measures were introduced. The authors admitted they had no idea of the pollution absorption capacity of the environment, but they felt that with exponential growth in pollutants it would be reached relatively quickly. They modelled pollution as a single long-lived chemical that in high concentrations would shorten human life and interfere with food production.

The authors explicitly stated that their model was not a definite prediction of what would happen – it was an exploration of the consequences of current trends. They ran versions of the model which assumed various changes, such as enormous potential increases in agricultural productivity, the availability of cheap nuclear power, extensive mineral recycling and very strict pollution control standards. Even with all these running in the model, exponential growth still caused an overshoot of what could be sustainably supported by the planet and a collapse of civilization before the end of the 21st century. When they modelled a future with zero population growth and zero capital growth, and assuming a fourfold increase in the technological efficiency of production, and investment in agriculture to end malnutrition, the model gave an ultimately stable state at a European average standard of living: 'It is possible to alter these growth trends and to establish a condition of ecological and economic stability that is sustainable far into the future.'[23]

Criticism of *The Limits to Growth*

Critics pointed out that the output of the computer model was determined by the assumptions the programmers had made. The project had been funded by the Club of Rome, an international grouping of prominent scientists, business people and civil servants concerned about environmental problems. They were of an essentially Malthusian persuasion. The late Donella Meadows stated that she and her husband were Malthusians when they started the project. In fact, they started work on the project two weeks after returning from a year in Asia. Donella Meadows told me about the conclusions of the model:

We had kind of intuited it in India, but it was just a feeling to go from one of the world's richest places to one of the world's poorest and to see the soil erosion and to see the children, the burgeoning cities and the disappearing forests. You just somehow knew all of this was inconsistent, was offensive, was morally intolerable and furthermore it was physically impossible to continue doing things this way. We knew that, but we couldn't put a case for it. It was something *any* intelligent observer knows anywhere they go in the world. So the computer model helped us to put numbers, to put time frames, to get a much neater mental model of the problem and the possible solutions.

It can be argued that they already knew what they were expecting to find and wrote the model in that way. There is perhaps truth in that. Because of the status computers had at that time, there was a tendency for the public to believe any computer model was correct. The reality was that it all depended on the validity of the assumptions.

The best developed critique of *The Limits to Growth* came from a team at Sussex University's Science Policy Research Unit.[24] They pointed out that the computer model was no less subjective or ideological than the mental models on which it was based. They criticized several aspects of the model, but concentrated on the Malthusian pessimism of the assumptions underlying it. The Sussex team examined the model and argued that the assumptions about the rate of technological progress and the availability of physical resources were too pessimistic. They accepted that physical growth cannot continue indefinitely on a finite planet, but held that any physical limits were much more distant. The Sussex team more generally criticized the determinism of the model as it did not include the feedbacks that would allow for resource substitution, new inventions and changing ways of life. They accused *The Limits to Growth* of discounting the potential for adaptation in human society and putting forward a counsel of despair in proposing an immediate end to growth. The Sussex team claimed that the concentration on disaster in 100 years' time distracted from what could be done to solve urgent existing problems, such as the distribution of the world's wealth.

Herman Daly's *Steady-State Economics*

The ideas in *The Limits to Growth* did not go away, though. They were instead taken up and elaborated. Herman Daly used the law of entropy to attempt to demonstrate that the scale of the economy was limited.[25] Economic activity is about the creation of order (low entropy) in one place. The entropy law demands that a larger amount of entropy is created elsewhere. Daly's former professor Nicholas Georgescu-Roegen had already used that argument.[26] He had concentrated on the irreversibility of the use of non-renewable fossil fuels as a source of energy. Daly made the point that economic activity (or rather energy and material throughput) necessarily creates pollution and wastes. More activity means more pollution and waste. There is a limit to how much the biosphere can absorb. Daly concluded that the entropy law set a limit to the scale of the economy. His claim that entropy sets a limit to the physical scale of the economy is now widely accepted, but his conclusion that there is an absolute limit to economic growth is still very controversial.

Global 2000

Ideas about limits to growth even influenced the 1977–81 Carter administration in the United States. President Carter was concerned about the 'energy crisis' and promoted research into renewable energy sources. He commissioned a report on the state of the global environment up to 2000. The report's conclusion was:

> If present trends continue, the world in 2000 will be more crowded, more polluted, less stable ecologically and more vulnerable to disruption. Serious stresses involving population, resources, and environment are clearly visible ahead. Despite greater material output, the world's people will be poorer in many ways than they are today.
>
> For hundreds of millions of the desperately poor, the outlook for food and other necessities of life will be no better. For many it will be worse. Barring revolutionary advances in technology, life for most people on earth will be more precarious in 2000 than it is now – unless the nations of the world act decisively to alter current trends.[27]

The finding from the *Global 2000* study which came as a surprise to many people was a calculation that habitat destruction was likely to lead to the extinction of 500,000 to 2 million species, mostly in tropical forests. Concern about loss of biodiversity, first raised by the biologist Norman Myers, quickly moved up to become a major environmental concern.[28]

At the end of 1980, Carter lost power to Ronald Reagan, who was a determined anti-environmentalist. Campaigning for the Presidency, he claimed: 'Approximately 80 per cent of our air pollution stems from hydrocarbons released by vegetation. So let's not go overboard in setting and enforcing tough emissions standards for man-made sources.' Once elected President, he went on to say: 'Trees cause more pollution than automobiles do.'[29] These beliefs were reflected in the policies that his administration followed.

As a consequence, environmental leadership passed from the United States to Europe in the 1980s. The environmental movement had already spread in the early 1970s, first to Scandinavia, then to the rest of western Europe, and particularly to Germany. European environmentalism was less concerned with the wilderness issues that have always remained crucial to North American environmentalism, and was more concerned with the problems of industrialism.

In the 1970s, though, environmentalism was a Western idea of little interest to the developing world. The next chapter describes how environmentalists invented the concept of sustainability in an attempt to overcome hostility to their concerns in the developing world.

3

Sustainability Emerging

This is the first age that's paid much attention to the future, which is a little ironic since we may not have one.

– Arthur C. Clarke

UN Conference on the Human Environment – Stockholm, 1972

The poverty of the developing world was a key issue at the UN Conference on the Human Environment, held in Stockholm in 1972. The Swedish government had been concerned about the damage that pollution from other European countries was doing to their lakes. Initially, developing country governments regarded environmental concern as a luxury for the rich, and argued that the environments of people in the developing world were blighted by poverty. They regarded it as hypocritical of Western countries to warn them about pollution. Indira Gandhi, prime minister of India, was the only national leader to attend the conference apart from the Swedish prime minister. She told the conference: 'Poverty is the worst pollution.' The same kind of polarization and misunderstanding between the West and developing countries was evident two years later in Bucharest at the first World Population Conference.

However, the idea that the environment was a critical development issue was accepted to some extent and was included in the Stockholm Declaration on Human Environment that was agreed at the conference. The Stockholm Conference did succeed in placing environmental problems on the international agenda for the first time. It led to the establishment of the United Nations Environment Programme (UNEP). It was based in Nairobi and had as its first Executive Director Maurice Strong, the Canadian who had chaired the Stockholm Conference. Strong coined the term 'ecodevelopment' as a way of verbally reconciling the desire for development and environmental protection. UNEP succeeded in establishing itself as a global environmental conscience, encouraging countries to develop environmental policies and agencies. However, based in Nairobi, far from the centres of power in the UN system, UNEP has always been short of funds and one of the weakest agencies in terms of institutional power.

Small is Beautiful

In the 1970s, the idea of ecodevelopment was often combined with the idea of 'appropriate technology'. The guru of the appropriate technology movement was the dissident economist Fritz Schumacher. In his bestseller *Small is Beautiful* he linked concern about pollution and depletion of natural resources to development issues.[1] Schumacher claimed that conventional development strategies promoted islands of Western modernity in the cities, while doing nothing for the vast majority in the countryside. These development projects were dependent on imported technology and experts. Schumacher's solution was rural development that would be on a 'human scale', and based on 'appropriate technology'. Appropriate technology would be small scale technology that could be understood and controlled by ordinary people, rather than dependent on experts. In the end the downfall of ecodevelopment was its association with Schumacherian views. Rural ecodevelopment did not allow developing countries to create modern economies. The urban elites, who actually controlled the governments of developing countries, were not content to accept the idea that they could not follow the path to Western modernity.

The sustainable society

The seeds of the approach the Brundtland Commission was to successfully take in the 1980s were laid as early as 1974. The concept of a 'sustainable society' emerged at an ecumenical study conference on Science and Technology for Human Development that was convened by the World Council of Churches. They defined it as follows:

> First, social stability cannot be obtained without an equitable distribution of what is in scarce supply or without common opportunity to participate in social decisions. Second, a robust global society will not be sustainable unless the need for food is at any time well below the global capacity to supply it and unless the emission of pollutants are well below the capacity of the ecosystems to absorb them. Third, the new social organization will be sustainable only as long as the use of non-renewable resources does not out-run the increase in resources made available through technological innovation. Finally, a sustainable society requires a level of human activities which is not adversely influenced by the never-ending large and frequent natural variations in global climate.[2]

The 'sustainable society' concept is notable because it starts with the principle of equitable distribution, which was to be a cornerstone of the Brundtland Report's approach. Still more remarkably, it involves the concept of democratic participation, which became important at the Earth Summit nearly 20 years later. The second and third conditions of the definition are similar to the definitions of physical sustainability used today. What is most interesting is that the original definition started, not with environmental conditions, but with social conditions for sustainability: the need for equity and for democracy. The debate about sustainability could be defined as the ideas that emerge when concern for the global environment and concern for global social justice meet.

John Cobb told me that the idea of the sustainable society emerged in the World Council of Churches in the aftermath of the Stockholm Conference. Like the United Nations, the World Council of Churches was very much influenced by the developing world. Many developing world clergymen thought that the environment was a distraction from justice and development. They saw environmentalism as a 'bourgeois' concern. The idea of a sustainable society – one that would not self-destruct – sounded more serious and also had less tension with the concern for justice. The environmentalists, led by the anthropologist Margaret Mead, managed to get the World Council of Churches to adopt the phrase 'a just, participatory and sustainable society' as an official slogan in 1975.

Very few people were aware of the work in the World Council of Churches. Even Dennis Pirages, who edited *The Sustainable Society*[3] in 1977, had not heard of it. Among some academic environmentalists, though, the idea of sustainability was beginning to catch on. *The Sustainable Society*, the first book with the word in its title, explored the issue of how to reconcile limits to growth with concern for social justice. The book concluded that less growth would make equality more difficult. In a period of growth, it is much easier to direct more of the benefits to those at the bottom. Without growth, improving the lot of the poor would require bringing down the rich, which is politically very difficult.

Sustainable development

The term 'sustainable development' emerged in the World Conservation Strategy of 1980, published by the International Union for Conservation of Nature and Natural Resources. Sustainable development was defined as 'the integration of conservation and development to ensure that modifications to the planet do indeed secure the survival and well-being of all people.'[4] Development was defined as 'the modification of the biosphere and the application of human, financial, living and non-living resources to satisfy human needs and improve the quality of human life.'[5] Development could, however, be a threat unless resources were effectively conserved. Development had to be combined with conservation, which was defined as 'the management of human use of the biosphere so that it may yield the greatest sustainable benefit to present generations while maintaining its potential to meet the needs and aspirations of future generations.'[6] The definition of conservation included elements of Gifford Pinchot's old definition as 'the greatest good for the greatest number over the longest time' and the new definition of sustainable development that was to emerge out of the Brundtland Report.

The World Conservation Strategy foreshadowed many of the ideas associated with Brundtland. It emphasized the importance of incorporating conservation into development planning at the beginning. It identified the main causes of habitat destruction as poverty, population pressure, social inequity and terms of trade that worked against poorer countries. It called for a new international development strategy that would redress inequity, stimulate economic growth and counter the worst poverty.

The problem the World Conservation Strategy had was that it was written by a group identified as being Northern environmentalists. Its concern for habitat conservation was ultimately based on a moral framework that was not universal. The emphasis on the environment in the document did not go down well with development agencies. Worse, the World Conservation Strategy did not discuss political and economic changes that would be needed to bring about the goal of sustainable development, so it lacked practical credibility as well. The task of making the idea of sustainable development politically acceptable fell to the Brundtland Commission.

The Brundtland Report

In 1983, the UN General Assembly set up the World Commission on the Environment and Development (WCED) with the Norwegian Labour Party leader, formerly and latterly prime minister, Gro Harlem Brundtland as the chairperson. The outcome of their efforts, *Our Common Future*,[7] was published in 1987. They came to focus on one central theme:

> many present development trends leave increasing numbers of people poor and vulnerable, while at the same time degrading the environment. How can such development serve next century's world of twice as many people relying on the same environment? This realization broadened our view of development. We came to see it not in its restricted context of economic growth in developing countries. We came to see that a new development path was required, one that sustained human progress not just in a few places for a few years, but for the entire planet into the distant future.[8]

They called this new path 'sustainable development', and defined it as 'development which meets the needs of the present without compromising the ability of future generations to meet their own needs.'[9] That phrase has been repeated, misquoted and rewritten countless times since. Its strength is that it is both simple and vague. That is also its weakness. However, the Brundtland

Commission's own conception of what sustainable development would be was more complicated than simply that one-sentence definition. They went on to say:

> The concept of sustainable development does imply limits – not absolute limits but limitations imposed by the present state of technology and social organization on environmental resources and by the ability of the biosphere to absorb the effects of human activities. But technology and social organization can be both managed and improved to make way for a new era of economic growth. The Commission believes that widespread poverty is no longer inevitable. Poverty is not only an evil in itself, but sustainable development requires meeting the basic needs of all and extending to all the opportunity to fulfil their aspirations for a better life. A world in which poverty is endemic will always be prone to ecological and other catastrophes.
>
> Meeting essential needs requires not only a new era of economic growth for nations in which the majority are poor, but an assurance that those poor get their fair share of the resources required to sustain that growth. Such equity would be aided by political systems that secure effective citizen participation in decision making and by greater democracy in international decision making.
>
> Sustainable global development requires that those who are more affluent adopt life-styles within the planet's ecological means – in their use of energy, for example. Further, rapidly growing populations can increase the pressure on resources and slow any rise in living standards; thus sustainable development can only be pursued if population size and growth are in harmony with the changing productive potential of the ecosystem.
>
> Yet in the end, sustainable development is not a fixed state of harmony, but rather a process of change in which the exploitation of resources, the direction of investments, the orientation of technological development, and institutional change are made consistent with future as well as present needs. We do not pretend that the process is easy or straightforward. Painful choices have to be made. Thus, in the final analysis, sustainable development must rest on political will.[10]

I have quoted at some length because that passage, immediately following the single sentence so often quoted, summarizes well much of what the Brundtland Commission meant by 'sustainable development'.

The Brundtland report set much of the subsequent agenda for both academic debate about sustainability and international political debate about environment and development. Why was the Brundtland report so influential? Many people have claimed that what it said was not very intellectually innovative. It was, after all, the unanimous report of a group of establishment politicians and diplomats from all over the world. But for such a body, the Brundtland report was remarkably innovative politically.

The basic political problem the Brundtland Commission was faced with was how to reconcile concern for environmental protection with the desire for economic development in the South and economic growth in the North. Environmental protection had been seen as a threat to development and growth. Fifteen years earlier, at the UN Conference on the Human Environment in Stockholm, many developing countries had argued that environmental protection was a luxury for the rich. The Brundtland report drew on thinking in environmental economics and argued that there was a mutual interlinkage between the economy and the environment. A healthy economy required a healthy environment:

> We have in the past been concerned about the impacts of economic growth upon the environment. We are now forced to concern ourselves with the impacts of ecological stress – degradation of soils, water regimes, atmosphere, and forests – upon our economic prospects. We have in the more recent past been forced to face up to a sharp increase in economic interdependence among nations. We are now forced to accustom ourselves to an accelerating ecological interdependence among nations. Ecology and economy are becoming ever more interwoven – locally, regionally, nationally, and globally – into a seamless net of causes and effects.[11]

Environmental resources were often undervalued and overexploited. The Brundtland Commission stressed the importance of the integration of environmental decisions into central economic decision making. They gave the example of the way that industry ministries would be responsible for promoting production targets, while the resulting pollution would be the responsibility of the environment ministry. The consequence was that environmental costs were often ignored in economic planning. These costs were later paid by society.

At the same time, they argued, a healthy environment was not possible in a world marked by the existence of extreme poverty. Environmental degradation often affected the poorest groups in society most severely, as they were unable to protect themselves from the environmentally destructive activities of richer and more powerful people. The Brundtland Commission also argued that extreme poverty often forced people to practice environmentally destructive activities as a desperate means of ensuring short term survival:

> Environmental stress has often been seen as the result of the growing demand on scarce resources and the pollution generated by the rising living standards of the relatively affluent. But poverty itself pollutes the environment, creating environmental stress in a different way. Those who

are poor and hungry will often destroy their immediate environment in order to survive: They will cut down forests; their livestock will overgraze grasslands; they will overuse marginal land; and in growing numbers they will crowd into congested cities. The cumulative effect of these changes is so far-reaching as to make poverty itself a major global scourge.

On the other hand, where economic growth has led to improvements in living standards, it has sometimes been achieved in ways which are globally damaging in the longer term. Much of the improvement in the past has been based on the use of increasing amounts of raw materials, energy, chemicals and synthetics and on the creation of pollution which is not adequately accounted for in figuring the costs of production processes. These trends have unforeseen effects on the environment. Thus today's environmental challenges arise both from the lack of development and from the unintended consequences of some forms of economic growth.[12]

Further on, the Brundtland report says:

As indicated earlier, development that is sustainable has to address the problem of the large number of people who live in absolute poverty – that is, who are unable to satisfy even the most basic of their needs. Poverty reduces people's capacity to use resources in a sustainable manner; it intensifies pressure on the environment... A necessary but not sufficient condition for the elimination of absolute poverty is a relatively rapid rise in per capita incomes in the Third World. It is therefore essential that the stagnant or declining growth trends of this decade be reversed.[13]

The Brundtland Commission emphasized that sustainable development was a matter of equity both between and within generations, saying in a crucial sentence: 'Even the narrow notion of physical sustainability implies a concern for social equity between generations, a concern that must logically be extended to equity within each generation.'[14] However, the Brundtland Commission trod very carefully when discussing what sustainable development would mean for the North:

Meeting essential needs depends in part on achieving full growth potential, and sustainable development clearly requires economic growth in places where such needs are not being met. Elsewhere, it can be consistent with economic growth, provided the content of growth reflects the broad principles of sustainability and non-exploitation of others... Hence sustainable development requires that societies meet human needs both by increasing productive potential and by ensuring equitable opportunities for all.[15]

So the Brundtland Commission broadly supported economic growth, although with the proviso that there are indeed limits to physical growth:

> Growth has no set limits in terms of population or resource use beyond which lies ecological disaster. Different limits hold for the use of energy, materials, water, land. Many of these will manifest themselves in the form of rising costs and diminishing returns, rather than in the form of any sudden loss of a resource base. The accumulation of knowledge and the development of technology can enhance the carrying capacity of the resource base. But ultimate limits there are, and sustainability requires that long before these are reached, the world must ensure equitable access to the constrained resource and reorient technological efforts to relieve the pressure.[16]

The Brundtland report is not always a consistent document. For example, it is critical of the way that income as currently measured fails to take account of the depletion of natural capital, but otherwise uses current measures of GNP growth as real measures of increasing income. At one point it says that raising living standards in the South requires growth in GNP per capita of at least 3 per cent. It then goes on to say that for enough capital to be available, the economies of the North (which have only very slowly growing populations) must grow at a minimum of 3–4 per cent a year. This would seem to give little possibility for increasing equity between North and South. With such a rate of economic growth in the North, it would take very much higher rates of per capita growth in the South to catch up in any reasonable time. Even if there was no growth in the industrialized North, the income gap the Commission reports between the industrialized market economies and the low income economies is so great that at 3 per cent a year it would take about 150 years to bridge the gap.

The report points out that bringing living standards in the South up to current levels in the North would involve expanding the world economy by a factor of 5–10. It goes on to state that an expansion of energy consumption on that scale with current technologies would be an ecological impossibility. With current energy mixes, even a doubling would probably be impossible. So the need is for increased efficiency. However, elsewhere the Commission points out that the earlier stages of industrialization that many Southern countries are going through tend to involve the development of industries that are particularly energy intensive. This is a problem that they mention in passing, but do not go on to address.

There are also many signs within the report of disagreements among Commission members. On the issue of nuclear power, the report actually admits to these disagreements, although in tone the report is predominantly anti-nuclear. On other issues there is more of an attempt to paper over the divisions, for example on consumption patterns. Nitin Desai, now UN Under-Secretary General for Economic and Social Affairs, was the member of the Brundtland Commission secretariat largely responsible for the drafting of the first section of the report. When I spoke to him, he said: 'The Brundtland report, I admit, is a little careful in its formulations on the issue of consumption.' He implied that was because of the need to maintain consensus among members of the Commission. Evidently, some of the Northern members had been wary of a more explicit discussion of the consumption issue.

The significance of the Brundtland report for environmentalists was that it reflected many of their concerns, even if it did not put forward proposals as radical as they would have liked. And, in particular, the Brundtland report accepted the idea of environmental limits. On the other side, governments and industry could accept the idea of environmental limits because these limits were not seen in the report as a brake on economic development or growth (this approach is now sometimes rather grandly called 'ecological modernization theory'). In this way the Brundtland report cleverly balanced environmental and economic considerations. Or as the environmental economist John Pezzey put it to me less kindly: 'It's a very attractive message. You can have your cake and eat it, there's not a conflict... But it's a very tricky message because I think it was jumped on by all sorts of politicians who didn't like confronting people with choices or trade-offs and wanted to pretend they could have everything.'

It is this seeming desire of the Brundtland Commission to tell people they could have everything they wanted and that nobody would have to make sacrifices that explains both its political popularity for squaring a circle and the suspicion it is viewed with by the more sceptical.

Another cause of the attention paid to the Brundtland report was probably that it was in the right place at the right time. The Commission was formed by the UN General Assembly in 1983, a time when the profile of environmental issues was quite low. The reception of the Brundtland report should be judged against the background of increasing concern about environmental issues in the late 1980s as the Cold War drew to an end and environmental problems became seen as a new global threat to survival. The discovery in 1985 of a large hole in the ozone layer over Antarctica had come as a complete surprise. Evidence was rapidly found supporting the theory that chlorofluorocarbons, chemicals used in refrigeration and aerosols, were responsible. The drama of the Chernobyl nuclear accident in 1986, which spread radioactive fallout across Europe, drew the attention of the world. Over the next few years, the environment moved to near the top of the agenda of journalists and politicians. Unlike the first wave of environmental concern in the late 1960s, which was confined to Western countries, the environmental wave of the late 1980s and early 1990s was felt almost everywhere in the world.

The Brundtland report had an important legitimizing role, particularly among Southern governments. After Brundtland, few governments continued to dismiss environmental concern as merely a Western or 'bourgeois' luxury. By emphasizing the connections between the environment and more traditional concerns with economic development, the Brundtland report forced governments and international agencies such as the World Bank to begin to think and talk about the issues. Real action, however, tended to be much less forthcoming.

4

From Rio to Kyoto and Later Disappointments

There is a fatality about all good resolutions. They are invariably made too soon.

– Oscar Wilde

The Earth Summit

The most obvious direct consequence of the Brundtland Commission's work was that in 1992 the United Nations Conference on Environment and Development (UNCED), often called the Earth Summit, took place in Rio de Janeiro. Such a conference had been one of the concrete proposals made in the Brundtland report. UNCED was the largest international conference held up to that time, including over a hundred heads of government. The intention of UNCED's organizers was to provide a focus for global concern about the environmental and development crises. It was also hoped that the end of the ideological divisions of the Cold War and the demands that it had made upon Western budgets would yield a large 'peace dividend'. Maurice Strong, who was Secretary General of the conference, had a plan for what he wanted to achieve:

• Conventions on climate, biodiversity and forests;

• An Earth Charter;

• Agenda 21, a global action plan outlining the sustainable development priorities for the 21st century;

• An agreement on new financial resources to implement Agenda 21, and progress on agreements to transfer environmentally sound technologies from North to South;

• A strengthening of UN institutions, including an Earth Council.

Strong had some success with all these, except for a forest convention, which did not emerge at all. However, the content of the agreements reached was rather less impressive.

The Framework Convention on Climate Change

The main impetus for the Climate Convention came from the 1990 report of the Intergovernmental Panel on Climate Change (IPCC), a body of leading scientists advising the United Nations.[1] They had predicted that, if carbon dioxide emissions continued to rise, a global average temperature rise of 1.5 to 4.5°C could be expected over the next century. The global average temperature today is only 3°C higher than in the depths of the last Ice Age. According to the IPCC, a 60 per cent reduction in carbon dioxide emissions from present levels would be needed to stabilize the climate and prevent levels building up in the atmosphere indefinitely. They proposed that a 60 per cent reduction should take place by 2040 to avoid dangerously rapid climate change.

The Climate Convention was inspired by the success in reaching agreement to reduce the production of the ozone-depleting chlorofluorocarbons in the 1987 Montreal Protocol. The difference was that the Montreal Protocol had dealt with a class of chemicals that threatened the very existence of life on Earth, yet were economically marginal and could relatively cheaply be substituted with less damaging alternatives. The Climate Convention would instead be dealing with limits on the use of fossil fuels, the economic lifeblood of industrialized societies.

In the climate negotiations, it became clear that the best that could be broadly agreed was that the governments of industrialized countries would set a target to return carbon dioxide emissions to 1990 levels by 2000, while there would be no target for Southern countries. The United States, which emits more carbon dioxide than any other country, refused to accept a *binding* target even for stabilizing carbon dioxide emissions, saying that it would be economically damaging. President Bush notoriously said: 'The American way of life is not up for negotiation.'

The Framework Convention on Climate Change signed at Rio reflected that. The convention did accept that climate change was a serious problem and that action could not wait for resolution of scientific uncertainties. It also accepted that industrialized countries should take the lead. As a result of American pressure, it had no binding targets or dates, although it indicated that a first step would be for industrialized countries (the 'Annex 1' countries in the convention) to stabilize carbon dioxide emissions at 1990 levels by 2000. The framework convention also included arrangements for the future negotiation of a binding convention – a process that led to the Kyoto Protocol five years later.

The Convention on Biological Diversity

In the biodiversity negotiations, the US administration of President Bush took an even more obstructive line and eventually refused to sign the Convention on Biological Diversity. This was despite the fact that the biodiversity convention dealt more with ensuring access to biodiversity (predominantly in the South) for countries with biotechnology (predominantly in the North) than with actually protecting biodiversity. President Bush regarded the framework for access to biodiversity as a threat to the American biotechnology industry, which wanted no restrictions.

The convention affirmed that countries have 'sovereign rights' over biological resources in their territory, which should be shared internationally on mutually agreed terms. These terms included recognition of indigenous knowledge as intellectual property due royalties. Countries which signed the convention had to develop plans to protect biodiversity and submit information on them. However, there was no requirement for new plans, no presentation of standards for the plans to meet and no international action plan for the preservation of biodiversity.

The Statement on Forest Principles

The Statement on Forest Principles emerged after negotiations on a forests convention collapsed. Pressure for a forests convention had come from Western countries concerned about tropical deforestation. Countries with tropical forests, particularly Brazil, regarded the idea of international intervention in their use of forests as intolerable. In order to avoid the embarrassment of producing nothing, a document based on the lowest common denominator was agreed, emphasizing national sovereignty over forests. Many environmentalists felt that it was worse than no agreement at all.

The hope for some years afterwards was that a real forests convention could be negotiated. It was to eventually become apparent that the issue was too sensitive for the countries with tropical forests to agree to anything substantive. They saw the forests as a natural resource they had the sovereign right to exploit and resented being lectured on the matter by industrialized countries which had already destroyed most of their own native forests.

The Rio Declaration

The Rio Declaration on Environment and Development was the substitute for Maurice Strong's 'Earth Charter'. The name was changed at the insistence of Southern countries which objected to the environmental emphasis in the proposed name. Strong had intended a brief and inspiring statement of a new global environmental ethic. What actually emerged was a lengthy and uninspiring piece of diplomatic jargon.[2] A sign of the lack of a new environmental ethic is the first four principles of the 27 in the declaration. The first principle stated that 'Human beings are at the centre of concerns for sustainable development. They are entitled to a healthy and productive life in harmony with nature.'[3] The second principle of the Rio Declaration affirmed the sovereign right of states to exploit resources according to their own environmental and development policies. The third principle asserts the 'right to development'. The fourth principle makes environmental protection 'an integral part of the development process'.

The important environmental principles that the Rio Declaration included which were absent from the Stockholm Declaration are the precautionary principle (Principle 15) and the 'polluter pays' principle (Principle 16). However, both principles were heavily qualified. In general, the Rio Declaration was less progressive than the Stockholm Declaration 20 years earlier. The Rio Declaration emphasized development and national sovereignty, while the Stockholm Declaration had emphasized environmental protection and international cooperation.

Agenda 21

Agenda 21 was intended to be a framework of action for achieving sustainable development. Over 500 pages long, it is a document of mind-boggling complexity. There are some important recurring themes. Perhaps the most important is the bottom-up approach, emphasizing the role of citizens (particularly women), communities and non-governmental organizations (NGOs). Development, for perhaps the first time in an international agreement, is seen as something built by people, rather than from the top down through large state projects. The entire tone of Agenda 21 is about participation and open government. UNCED had an unprecedented degree of NGO involvement, and this was institutionalized in the document. Agenda 21 also emphasizes the role of the market, trade and business in bringing about sustainable development. Both these features of Agenda 21 can partly be attributed to the demise of state socialism and the general disillusionment with bureaucratic approaches to problems. However, the emphasis on participation is also the result of intensive lobbying from NGOs. Even regimes which clearly did not believe in democratic participation did not feel strong enough to oppose the principle.[4]

Agenda 21 emphasizes the importance of creating adequate knowledge and institutions, known in UN jargon as 'capacity building'. Almost every chapter includes references to education and the development of 'human resources'. Agenda 21 is also full of references to the importance of integrated approaches to environment and development. It calls for institutions that transcend traditional sectoral divisions and attempt to deal with the linkages underlying specific problems.

Missing from Agenda 21 was adequate discussion of several important, but controversial, issues known as 'black holes'. These include consumption patterns, population, international debt and militarism. Chapter 4 of Agenda 21 is devoted to consumption patterns, and does include a reference to 'unsustainable patterns of production and consumption', particularly in industrialized countries, as a matter of grave concern. The chapter also calls for national strategies and policies to encourage 'sustainable consumption patterns'. The chapter is extremely weak on specifics, though. Industrialized countries, especially the United States, resisted the entire theme and had the text toned down considerably.[5]

Chapter 5, dealing with population growth, had to be called 'Demographic Dynamics and Sustainability'. All references to contraception were also removed at the insistence of the Vatican and the Philippines. However, the chapter did support the right of women and men to decide on the number and spacing of their children. It also included the following statement: 'The growth of world population and production combined with unsustainable consumption patterns places increasingly severe stress on the life-supporting capacities of our planet'.

Militarism and international debt proved to be issues that were just too controversial, and were not mentioned at all, despite the obvious fact that both were major problems. They were later tackled at the UN Social Summit in Copenhagen in 1995. The other area of extreme difficulty in the negotiations for Agenda 21 was finance. Maurice Strong's UNCED Secretariat produced an estimate that funding the programmes in Agenda 21 would cost US$600 billion a year, of which about US$125 billion a year should be aid from industrialized countries. That US$125 billion was (coincidentally?) equivalent to the unmet UN target for official development aid of 0.7 per cent of GNP.[6] Western countries were simply not prepared to put forward that kind of money, particularly in a recession, although all of them except the United States had agreed to the aid target in principle. They eventually came up with US$2 billion over three years, directed through the World Bank-controlled Global Environment Facility (GEF) – about 0.5 per cent of the sum asked for. Agenda 21 failed because it was perceived as too expensive, although US$600 billion is only about half what it is estimated that the world spends on environmentally damaging perverse subsidies each year.[7]

The Commission on Sustainable Development

The implementation of Agenda 21 was to be overseen by the Commission on Sustainable Development (CSD), a watered-down version of Strong's Earth Council. The CSD meets annually for three weeks in New York and has a small secretariat. The CSD is officially just one of many subcommittees that report to the UN Committee on Economic and Social Affairs (ECOSOC), notoriously a bureaucratic graveyard. In practice, the CSD is rather more influential than its lowly place in the UN system would suggest. That is because national environment ministers lead the delegations of some important countries. They have far more power in the real world than ECOSOC does.

Nonetheless, the job of coordinating a global transition to sustainable development has rather unsurprisingly proved a somewhat over-ambitious task for a body that meets so little and has so few resources itself.

The South at UNCED

For Southern governments, UNCED was ultimately a failure because the funds and technology transfer they had hoped for from Agenda 21 did not materialize. The thinking behind the South's strategy in the UNCED negotiations was outlined in a policy document from the South Centre, a think tank funded by the G77 group of Southern states:

> Two strategic considerations should guide the South's negotiating position... (a) ensuring that the South has adequate 'environmental space' for its future development, and (b) restructuring global economic relations in such a way that the South obtains the required resources, technology, and access to markets...

> In the UNCED negotiations proper, the South should... insist on tilting the balance towards development and considerations of global economic reform, in order that the South may be offered some hope of being able to follow a path of sustainable development. Issues on which the South should receive firm commitment from the North are: (i) debt relief; (ii) increased ODA [official development aid], (iii).. access to international liquidity; (iv) stabilisation and raising of commodity prices; and (v) access to markets in the North.[8]

The restructuring of global economic relations had been one of the recommendations of the Brundtland report, reflecting Southern concerns. In the 1980s, nearly all countries in the South became trapped in a cycle of debt after the interest rate on apparently cheap loans they had taken out in the 1970s rose dramatically. As a consequence, these countries had to call on the Western-controlled International Monetary Fund (IMF) to avoid complete bankruptcy. The 'structural adjustment' conditions attached to IMF loans were tough. They involved cutting public expenditure (including health and education budgets), privatization of industries, opening markets to imports and increasing exports. Because most Southern countries were dependent on the export of a small number of commodities each, and over 100 countries were increasing their exports in line with IMF instructions, the consequence was that the price of commodities fell on the world market and the Southern countries were no better off. The debt crisis meant that for several years the South was making larger debt repayments that it was receiving in aid and loans. The poorest countries of the world were subsidizing the rich. The cuts in education and health meant that for the people of the South, the 1980s were a 'lost decade' for development. Finally, the pressure for exports to pay the debt encouraged the unsustainable exploitation of the environment.

The crisis that the South had faced for the past decade was at the top of their agenda. They hoped that with the idea of 'environmental space', the limited carrying capacity of the Earth, they had finally found a bargaining chip to get a better deal. Ismail Razali, then Malaysia's UN ambassador, was one of the most important negotiators for the South at UNCED. He told me in frank terms about the strategy pursued:

> We thought here was a chance that we could also blackmail the North into accepting the proposition that the only way you could solve these problems with the global environment was to do something in the South in a very prominent fashion. If the millions of the poor in the South have no chance for development, then a worse environment will result from that. At the end of the day, whether you're a big frog or a small frog, you will die because the pond is contaminated.

The idea was that the North would provide a lot of aid and technology:

> So for a while the industrialized countries were frightened by this prospect. That environmental pollution was transboundary, would go to Europe and the United States. And they would pay money to make sure this didn't happen. But after Rio... very little adjustment was being made in the industrialized world. The onus of change was being placed on the shoulders of the countries of the South. And the promised means of implementation were not there to help phase in sustainable development in the poor countries.

The problem that 'greenmail' has is that essentially Southern countries have to threaten to destroy their own environments with unsustainable development. They will obviously suffer much more from doing that than people in the North, so the threat is not very credible. Razali later seemed to recognize that attempting blackmail over environmental space was not a successful strategy.

The North at UNCED

Northern governments were negotiating from a much stronger position. They had most of the money and most of the power. The money that they did in the end put up for GEF was to fund projects in Southern countries on climate change and biodiversity. It was specifically tied to issues of the *global* environment. It is also worth noting that the three conventions negotiated at UNCED were all dealing with issues that the North was more concerned about than the South. African countries wanted a convention on desertification, but the North was not interested. A Convention on Desertification emerged only in 1994.

However, the UNCED did mark a change in Western attitudes to some extent. The fact that consumption was dealt with at all is really quite remarkable. The non-binding commitment to stabilize carbon dioxide emissions suggested that the West, 20 years after *The Limits to Growth*, was beginning to think about limits to physical growth.

The significance of UNCED

Just before UNCED, the three leading members of the original *Limits to Growth* team published a sequel, *Beyond the Limits*, in which they argued that it was now clear that some important environmental limits had already been passed.[9] They claimed that the hole in the ozone layer had been the first definitive sign that a global limit had been reached. They also pointed to collapsing fisheries around the world and indications of global warming as evidence that further global limits had been passed. On the other hand, they quietly admitted that their earlier predictions about fossil fuel and mineral reserves had been too pessimistic. They also accepted that energy and materials efficiency had increased more than they had expected 20 years earlier. The conclusion they emphasized, though, was that global environmental limits were now in sight in the early 1990s, when in the original computer model they had been expected in the late 21st century.

The Northern interest in the UNCED process was dominated by concern about global environmental issues. Although the Rio Declaration does not reflect it, the feature of UNCED which is most significant was the emergence of *global environment* as a major issue in international politics. Rio was a major political event in a way in which Stockholm had not been. Two national leaders (the prime ministers of Sweden and India) had attended the Stockholm Conference, while over a hundred attended UNCED. Twenty years before, the environment, let alone the global environment, had not been seen as a central political problem. The question which UNCED was unable to settle was how to handle limits to the Earth's environmental space. That is the issue which post-UNCED debates on sustainability centre on, as will be explored in later chapters.

NGOs at UNCED

Despite unprecedented access to the negotiations, NGOs did not have a major influence on the agreements negotiated by the governments at UNCED. Pratap Chatterjee and Matthias Finger, in an overwhelmingly negative account of the UNCED process from a Green perspective, argued that NGOs failed at Rio.[10]

However, they did admit that mutual learning between North and South took place. Martin Khor, president of the Third World Network, wrote:

> The UNCED process forged new and stronger links between Northern and Southern groups, between development and environmental activists. It would now be difficult for environmentalists to stick to wildlife issues or population, without simultaneously addressing international equity and global power structures.[11]

Business Council for Sustainable Development

At the time, another important outcome of UNCED was widely seen as the formation of the Business Council for Sustainable Development (BCSD). It was founded at the initiative of the Swiss billionaire Stephen Schmidheiny who had been appointed as special adviser to Maurice Strong. Schmidheiny persuaded 48 other international business leaders to join his group. Schmidheiny published a book, *Changing Course*, as the BCSD's manifesto.[12] Schmidheiny drew on the theory of Total Quality Management (TQM) to argue for a revision of the business approach to the environment. TQM focuses on the customer and the idea of looking at the overall production process from a product's conception until it ends up at the customer. The TQM approach holds that low quality is a sign of organizational inefficiency. Schmidheiny argued that pollution, like low quality, is a sign of inefficiency and waste. Environmental efficiency, like quality, should be built into the production process from the start. Schmidheiny accepted that the environment cannot complain in the same way as a dissatisfied customer. Preferably, business should regulate itself to avoid government intervention which would ultimately be more rigid and less efficient. When governments got involved, Schmidheiny favoured economic instruments, like ecotaxes, over more rigid regulation. In urgent cases, Schmidheiny thought regulation might be justified.

But in the end, the World Business Council for Sustainable Development, as it was later renamed, proved to be something of a damp squib. It did not lead to significant changes in the business practices of its members.

After Rio: Environment off the agenda

In the day-to-day world of global politics, the environment and sustainable development soon sank down the international agenda after UNCED. In the summer of 1997 'Earth Summit II' met in New York to review progress towards the commitments made in Rio. It had to be admitted that not much had been achieved in practical terms. Agenda 21 had not been funded and very little of it had been implemented. Despite their commitment in the Framework Convention on Climate Change to stabilize greenhouse gas emissions, most Western countries were still increasing theirs.

The South did have some success in controlling the agenda for the UN Conference on Social Development held in Copenhagen in March 1995, called the Social Summit. It dealt with the issues of poverty, unemployment and social exclusion. The South used the Summit as a sounding board for its concerns about the debt burden and unfair trade relations. Without much interest from Northern governments, however, the Social Summit was doomed to be ineffective at bringing about change.

The long-running General Agreement on Tariffs and Trade (GATT) negotiations finally led in 1994 to an agreement by Western countries to lower some of their barriers to Southern imports, in exchange for a lowering of barriers to imported goods in Southern countries and the introduction of strict standards for the protection of intellectual property – most controversially, restricting their access to cheap generic drugs. This development was considered by economists at the time to be good news for many countries in Asia and Latin America, but bad news for the poorest countries, mostly in Africa, which had received protected access to Northern markets under the Lomé Convention. In the event, although Southern countries lowered their trade barriers, Western countries managed to avoid fulfilling their side of the bargain.

The negotiations also led to the creation of an important new international body, the World Trade Organization (WTO), a younger sister to the World Bank and the IMF. For many environmentalists, the creation of the WTO and the move towards free trade was extremely worrying. There is a widespread fear that international free trade tends to encourage a lowering of environmental standards for short term competitive advantage. Proponents of free trade counter-argue that protected industries are often very bad environmentally. Free trade also exposes poor countries to international competition which can prevent them from developing their own industries and which drives small producers to the wall. International trade also means greater movement of goods and therefore greater environmental impacts from transport.

Free trade is justified on the basis of Adam Smith's theory of comparative advantage, which states that countries will always benefit from specializing in what they are best at. But that theory depends crucially on the assumption that capital is not internationally mobile. If it is mobile, as in the modern world, then under free trade capital will concentrate in the countries that are most competitive in each industry and some countries will be impoverished because they are not globally competitive in any field.[13]

What worried environmentalists most was that the WTO Dispute Settlement Body was to decide if regulations were acting as barriers to trade, succeeding the GATT Panel which had already ruled that US sanctions against tuna caught without following safeguards to protect dolphins was an unfair barrier to trade. The strong concern was that the WTO, with much more sweeping powers than the GATT Panel, would be biased towards putting trade before the environment, a worry that was borne out by subsequent events.

WTO rules state that countries cannot discriminate against imported products on the basis of the way in which they were produced. This means that countries cannot restrict imports because of environmental or social concerns. In a replay of GATT's decision about tuna, the WTO ruled that the United States could not ban shrimp caught with nets that trap turtles.

The WTO went even further, though. They ruled that American air pollution standards were an unfair trade barrier to Venezuelan oil products. When the European Union attempted to ban synthetic hormones in beef because of evidence that it could cause cancer and other health problems, the WTO ruled in favour of the United States and the makers of the hormone, Monsanto. The Americans later threatened to take the Europeans to the WTO if they tried to ban genetically modified (GM) crops.

A famous WTO ruling was the one in favour of the United States against the European Union's quota that allowed bananas from small scale farmers in the Caribbean a place in a market that would otherwise be totally dominated by Latin American bananas produced on huge plantations by US corporations. Several small Caribbean countries were dependent on bananas as their primary source of income and faced ruin as a consequence. The European Union accepted the ruling, but tried to buy time for these countries to adjust. That was not good enough for the Americans, who with WTO approval imposed economic sanctions against certain imports from the European Union. Eventually, the European Union gave in.

The WTO is widely regarded as biased because it made an unbroken series of judgements against the environment, public health and social welfare in favour of maximizing trade. It only deviated from this track record in 2001, ruling that France was entitled to ban asbestos, despite the objections of Canada.

The move towards free trade received a substantial setback when the WTO meeting in Seattle at the end of 1999 broke up without any agreement on the next round of negotiations. The collapse was widely celebrated because the United States had hoped to use the negotiations to force the rest of world to accept GM crops and privatize public services. However, the failure of the negotiations also meant that although there was no further liberalization and ceding of power to the WTO, there was also no progress on the issue of reforming the WTO and the international trade regime. The United States and the European Union had gone into the negotiations intending to agree worldwide minimum environmental and labour standards, but Southern countries resisted that, seeing them as disguised trade barriers. On the other hand, the United States and the European Union resisted opening their markets to imports from Southern countries, which still face high tariffs on many of their products, and ending agricultural subsidies. The result was deadlock.

World trade negotiations were revived two years later in Doha. The European Union put forward an environmental agenda to be included in the new round, but were largely over-ruled by other countries. The European Union had pressed for acceptance of the precautionary principle, but the agreement specified that any national action to protect human health and the environment should be in accordance with WTO rules. It was agreed that there would be negotiations on the relationship between WTO rules and international environmental agreements with a view to 'enhancing the mutual supportiveness of trade and environment', but it was specified that this should not prejudice the rights of any WTO member that is not party to a particular environmental agreement, creating a loophole that made the concession almost meaningless. WTO members agreed to launch new negotiations on liberalizing services, including environmental services such as waste management and wastewater treatment markets, opening the door to removal of national control and future WTO weakening of environmental standards in these areas.

It was agreed that agricultural subsidies should be phased out and fishing subsidies should be reduced, but there was no explicit recognition of environmental issues in these areas beyond a pledge that 'non-trade concerns will be taken into account'[14] during the negotiations, although concerns about food security in Southern countries were explicitly mentioned.

It was agreed that Southern countries could produce cheap generic drugs in the event of a public health emergency and that the European Union could favour imports from certain African and Caribbean countries under the Lomé Convention. NGOs campaigning for the environment and development felt that although a few concessions had been made to their concerns, the terms for negotiation were likely to lead to agreements with very negative consequences.

It was initially thought that some progress was made in 2002 at the Monterrey conference on financing international development when the United States agreed to increase its contribution to international aid, but that was soon undercut when George W. Bush signed a farm bill increasing American agricultural subsidies by 70 per cent, at the expense of unsubsidized farmers in Southern countries. American hypocrisy on free trade was also exposed when President Bush unilaterally imposed tariffs on steel imports.

The American influence

A major problem for the environmental agenda has been the influence of the United States, and particularly the Republican Party. After the election of the presidential ticket of Bill Clinton and Al Gore in 1992, environmentalists initially had high hopes. Al Gore, the new Vice-President, had strongly criticized former President Bush's attitude at UNCED and even published a widely praised book supporting action to protect the global environment.[15] President Clinton signed the Biodiversity Convention soon after he took office, but it was never ratified by the US Senate.

At the 1994 World Population Conference in Cairo, the US administration pledged to put in its share towards a fund for women's health and access to contraception. The World Population Conference itself was a considerable success. The idea that access to contraception is a human right proved capable of uniting all states except the Vatican, Sudan, Saudi Arabia, Iraq and Nicaragua. At the 1984 World Population Conference in Mexico, the Vatican had been powerfully supported by the United States, then under the influence of right wing Christian fundamentalists. Meanwhile, since 1984, disputes about whether population growth needed to be stopped had been sidestepped. A large body of research suggested that women across the world wanted fewer children and better access to contraception. The line many developing countries had taken in 1974 and 1984 – that smaller families would have to wait for development – was discredited. A large international programme of aid for family planning measures was agreed, although unfortunately Western donors have subsequently failed to meet the aid commitments they made.

A month after the Cairo conference, the right wing Christian fundamentalists returned to the stage when the Republicans won control of the US Congress. Suddenly, the more constructive line the Clinton administration had taken came to an end. With the Republicans trying to abolish much of America's environmental legislation, the administration was now unwilling to sign up to commitments it could not hope to get past its Congress. At the first Conference of the Parties to the Framework Convention on Climate Change (COP-1), held in Berlin in April 1995, the Americans continued to oppose binding targets or timetables. They were backed up in their opposition by Japan, Switzerland, Canada, Australia, Norway and New Zealand. The group was known collectively as JUSSCANNZ (pronounced 'juice cans'). The Americans argued that they could not be expected to agree to binding targets while emissions from Southern countries were uncontrolled. They were unmoved by the counter-argument that since the per capita emissions of Southern countries were many times less than those of industrialized countries, and particularly the United States itself, it was unfair to concentrate on the South's increasing emissions rather than the predominant emissions of the North.

The Road to Kyoto

The Berlin conference discussed a draft protocol proposed by the Alliance of Small Island States (AOSIS), calling for a 20 per cent reduction in carbon dioxide emissions from industrialized countries by 2005. This target had been suggested by the IPCC scientists as a first step towards a 60 per cent reduction by 2040. The AOSIS Protocol was opposed not just by the United States, but by all the Western countries. Enthusiasm for cutting carbon dioxide emissions was actually much less in Berlin than it had been in Rio. In 1992, several Western countries had committed themselves to ambitious targets of up to 20 per cent reduction in carbon dioxide emissions. However, estimates by the Climate Secretariat in 1995 showed that only two Western countries were not still increasing their emissions. Britain had cut its emissions by closing much of its coal industry and replacing coal with natural gas for electricity generation. This policy had not been pursued for the sake of the climate however, but was an unexpected side effect of the rules for the privatization of the electricity generation industry. Germany was reducing its emissions by counting the old East and West together. Falls in the former East, as inefficient old industry closed, were more than compensating for increases in the former West. Emissions from the other parts of the former Eastern bloc were falling as well for the same reason. In 1992, it had been thought that stabilizing emissions by 2000 would not require much effort. Despite the commitments, little was done and it became apparent that the target was not going to be met.

However, the countries of the European Union, led by the German hosts, wanted the conference to be a success. They were determined to keep the process going, even if the JUSSCANNZ countries would not accept any binding commitments at that stage. Agreement was eventually reached at COP-1 on something called the 'Berlin Mandate'. It instructed the parties to the framework convention to negotiate a protocol or some other legal instrument containing commitments beyond 2000 in time for adoption at COP-3, scheduled to be held in Kyoto at the end of 1997. The objective would be to set targets for the reduction of greenhouse gas emissions by 'Annex 1' (industrialized) countries. At that stage, it was not decided whether any such targets would be binding or non-binding, let alone which gases would be covered, or what dates they would be set for.

The 1995 Second Assessment Report of the IPCC that came out at the end of the year stated that the balance of evidence was that global warming was already taking place. There had been a warming of 0.5°C over the past century, mostly since 1980, and the pattern of warming indicated that it was human-induced rather than natural. They predicted a warming of 1.5–3.5°C over the next century.[16] At the second Conference of the Parties, held in Geneva in July 1996, the Clinton administration accepted these findings and suddenly changed position to accept the principle of binding targets, as did all the other JUSSCANNZ countries except Australia. It was the great turning point in the negotiations, because agreement on legally binding targets would not have been possible without the participation of the United States, the world's largest source of carbon dioxide emissions.

The Kyoto Protocol

The Kyoto Protocol was finally agreed the day after the two-week COP-3 meeting was due to have ended in December 1997. Negotiations had continued feverishly up to the last minute and beyond. The protocol that was finally agreed was an uneasy compromise. It committed the industrialized countries to an overall reduction of 5.2 per cent in their collective annual emissions of the main greenhouse gases in the commitment period of 2008–12 compared with 1990 levels. Different industrialized countries had different targets, though. The United States was to reduce its emissions by 7 per cent from 1990 levels, Japan by 6 per cent, the European Union collectively by 8 per cent, and most of the other industrialized countries by 8 per cent. However, Russia, Ukraine and New Zealand did not need to make any emission cuts from 1990 levels (even though Russia's emissions were about 30 per cent below 1990 levels and Ukraine's were about 50 per cent below). Norway, Iceland and Australia were allowed to increase their emissions (by 1 per cent, 10 per cent and 8 per cent respectively). Norway and Iceland were given the concession because they already get a large proportion of their energy from hydroelectric and geothermal energy respectively. Australia had at the eleventh hour threatened to veto the entire Protocol unless it was given its way. The Kyoto Protocol would enter into force once 55 countries had ratified it, including countries representing 55 per cent of Annex 1 emissions in 1990.

The targets that were agreed were extremely modest compared to the ultimate need to reduce emissions by 60–80 per cent in order to limit global warming. In fact, various efforts were made by the United States, the European Union, AOSIS and Japan to include long term environmental objectives in the Protocol, but nothing came of them because of pressure for negotiating time.

The targets agreed for 2008–2012 were largely a compromise between the European Union (which had become bolder since Berlin) proposing a 15 per cent reduction for industrialized countries (not far short of AOSIS's 20 per cent proposal) and the United States' desire to keep any emissions reductions as small as possible. While the conference was underway, American oil companies funded a disinformation campaign in the United States to mobilize opposition and portraying the negotiations as a devious foreign attempt to undermine the American economy. Their campaign was supported by large elements of the Republican Party. Meanwhile, the European oil companies Shell and BP had left the oil companies' lobby, the Global Climate Coalition, and disassociated themselves from opposition to emissions reduction.

An irony is that since the American way of life is so profligate in its use of fossil fuels it is actually much easier for the United States to make emission reductions than it is for Europe or Japan. However, the US delegation to Kyoto argued most strongly for maximum flexibility in achieving any reduction targets. The Americans wanted emissions trading to enable themselves to buy up unused portions of other industrialized countries' quotas and arrangements where they would pay for emission reductions in Southern countries that could count towards reductions in their emissions. They also wanted to be able to count increases in 'carbon sinks' (such as forests) towards emission reductions. All these ideas were included in the Protocol. The Americans and some other JUSSCANNZ countries even wanted to be able to make up for failure to meet targets laid out in the

Protocol by borrowing emission rights at a penalty rate from future generations. That was too much for Southern countries and the European Union, so was not included in the Protocol.

The European Union wanted some flexibility in meeting targets, but opposed the Americans' continual search to create loopholes. They undermined their own stance, however, by having agreed in advance that there would be 'burden sharing' of the European Union's emission target. It would allow Spain, Portugal, Greece and Ireland to increase their emissions by up to 40 per cent, while other member states would make bigger cuts to compensate within the European Union's 'bubble'. Allowing dramatic increases in emissions by relatively rich countries when the climatic need is to reduce global per capita emissions to about 40 per cent of Portugal's per capita emissions was hardly far sighted, but was the price that had to be paid for internal agreement.

The JUSSCANNZ countries accused the European Union of double standards for proposing a flat rate reduction of 15 per cent for other countries while differentiating responsibility among themselves. They argued that the European Union should use emissions trading rather than make a deal between themselves. The final compromise allowed any group of Annex 1 countries to achieve their targets jointly.

The Kyoto Protocol established three other mechanisms to allow countries to meet their obligations through actions taken outside their territory, although the exact rules for their operation were left to be decided later. These 'Kyoto mechanisms' are joint implementation, the Clean Development Mechanism (CDM) and emissions trading. Joint implementation allows countries to pay for measures to reduce emissions in other Annex 1 countries and count it towards meeting their own emissions target. The European Union, anxious to prevent the Americans simply paying other countries to meet their emissions target for them, insisted that joint implementation should be 'supplemental' to domestic action. After Kyoto, the European Union said that it wanted at least 50 per cent of action to be taken domestically, while the United States opposed a minimum limit for domestic action.

The CDM similarly allows Annex 1 countries to meet part of their targets by funding emissions reductions in Southern countries. Unlike the other mechanisms, reductions in greenhouse gas emissions achieved before 2008 can be counted towards the 2008–12 target. It is the only part of the Protocol that contains an incentive for early action. But since the total savings achieved in the eight years 2000–07 can be counted against emissions in the five target years, it is a potential loophole. And because there are no targets for Southern countries, there is a risk that pollution abating investments that would have been made there anyway by Western companies will be counted towards Annex 1 emissions targets through the CDM.

Emission trading was the most controversial issue. The Americans wanted it to start immediately, but the European Union wanted to have rules laid out first and India argued that there were important equity issues concerning the ownership of emission rights to be considered. Again, the Protocol stated that emission trading should be 'supplemental' to domestic action. Because Russia and the Ukraine had targets far above their likely emissions, there was enormous potential for them to sell their 'hot air' (the unused part of their targets) to the Americans or other JUSSCANNZ countries.

Another area eventually left for later discussion was the rules about carbon sinks. There were two problems underlying the debate about carbon sinks. The first was that there are very high levels of uncertainty about measurements of the sequestration of carbon and about the permanence of such sinks. The second problem was that countries with growing forests might take credit for absorption of carbon that would have happened anyway and not do anything about their emissions. Nobody could come up with a definition of an 'anthropogenic carbon sink' that truly got round that objection. What made matters worse was that these highly technical matters were being negotiated in an extremely time pressured atmosphere by diplomats who lacked the scientific background to understand the issues fully. It was finally agreed that net effects due to afforestation, reforestation and deforestation since 1990 would count towards the emission targets. Negotiation of the rules for 'additional activities' would be left for later.

COP-4 was held in Buenos Aires during November 1998. No real progress was made on the substantive issues of deciding the rules for the Kyoto mechanisms or carbon sinks. Instead, a timetable was agreed for discussions to lead to decisions on these issues by COP-6, to be held at the end of 2000. The nearest to a breakthrough was that the Americans finally signed the Protocol, dispelling doubts that they might never even do that. At COP-5, held in Bonn in November 1999, the European Union promised to ratify the treaty by 2002.

The Hague Conference

COP-6 was held in the Hague in November 2000. It had been timed to be held after the US election so that the identity of the new President would be known. Instead, it took place during the period when, as Bill Clinton put it: 'The American people have spoken, but it's going to take a little while to determine what they said.' In the end, of course, five Republican-appointed justices on the Supreme Court were to order a stop to that process and rule that whatever the American people had said, George W. Bush would be President.

For the climate negotiations, a great deal hung on the outcome of the election. Al Gore had led the US delegation to Kyoto and been the chief advocate of action on global warming within the Clinton administration. George W. Bush, a former Texas oilman, had expressed hostility to the Kyoto Protocol and doubt about whether there really was such a thing as global warming. Clinton's negotiators stuck to the position they had taken before – trying to get the easiest deal they could for the United States.

In the negotiations at the Hague over the Kyoto mechanisms, the European Union argued for financial penalties for failure to meet targets, a quantitative cap on trading (to prevent other countries just buying up Russia and Ukraine's hot air) and a 'positive' list of activities that would be approved for the Clean Development Mechanism prioritizing energy efficiency and renewable energy, and forbidding investment in nuclear power or planting forests. The European Union was opposed by the United States and other countries who wanted to maximize the flexibility of their options.

Negotiations over carbon sinks proved to be the main stumbling block. The European Union wanted to restrict the use of carbon sinks, such as planting forests or attempting to lock up carbon in the soil, in both domestic action and the Kyoto mechanisms because of concerns about uncertainty and impermanence. The uncertainty is that it is very difficult to accurately measure the amount of carbon actually absorbed by forests and soil. More important are concerns about impermanence. A tonne of carbon not emitted from a chimney is not emitted. A tonne of carbon absorbed by a tree will be released when the tree dies, so it just moves the problem into the future. What is more, it is impossible to guarantee that a forest will not burn down or soil will not start releasing carbon in the near future. Worst of all, climate change is likely to lead to die back of forests and the release of carbon from the soil, so that carbon supposedly locked up could be released just as climate change starts to bite.

However, the United States and other members of the Umbrella Group (a new alliance of the JUSSCANNZ countries minus Switzerland, but plus Russia and Ukraine) were keen to exploit a potential loophole in the Kyoto Protocol. Any net absorption of carbon by forests or soil did not count towards the 1990 emissions totals for Annex 1 countries, but according to their reading of the rules, net absorption could be counted in the commitment period of 2008-2012. Because the United States and other countries extensively deforested for agriculture in the past, but then allowed some forests to grow back in the 20th century, there is currently substantial net absorption of carbon dioxide. The idea of the Americans and their allies was to count the absorption of carbon dioxide by forests that had already existed in 1990 as 'additional activities' against increases in emissions afterwards in order to help themselves meet their target. Furthermore, they wanted to count the absorption of carbon dioxide by the soil as 'additional activities' in the same way. If it were all to be counted, the American target would be eased by the equivalent of about 19 per cent of their 1990 emissions, but they only asked for an easing equivalent to 7.5 per cent of their 1990 emissions. The effect would be that instead of a 7 per cent reduction in emissions, they would be allowed a slight increase.

The Europeans were not prepared to accept this kind of challenge to the environmental integrity of the Protocol, but conceded an easing of the target by 0.5 per cent for sinks in order to offer something. The President of the Conference, Dutch environment minister Jan Pronk, put forward a compromise deal that the use of sinks to meet the targets would be limited to 3 per cent of

1990 emissions, failure to meet targets would lead to tighter future targets, countries would 'primarily' engage in domestic action to meet their targets, 'refrain' from funding nuclear power in the CDM and give preferential treatment to small scale projects. The compromise was rejected by both sides.

After two sleepless nights of negotiation, the conference ran over into the morning of the day after it was due to have ended. Early that morning, the British deputy prime minister John Prescott and a delegation of other Europeans appeared to come to an agreement with the Americans. The deal was that there would be a limit of 5 per cent on sinks, no sinks or nuclear power in the CDM (but otherwise no limitations on the kinds of projects allowed), no limits on trading and that failure to meet targets would lead to tighter future targets for countries. But when the deal was taken back to the other Europeans, it was rejected as giving away too much. Prescott stormed out in anger and went home.

To everyone's surprise, the Americans then offered a further concession, coming down to a limit of 3 per cent for sinks, to which the Europeans made a counter-offer of a little over 1 per cent. But the meeting ran out of time because the delegates were forced to leave the conference centre so that it could be prepared for a meeting that the oil industry had rather inconsiderately booked afterwards. There were loud recriminations about responsibility for the failure.

Bush abandons Kyoto

It was decided that there would be a continuation of the Hague conference in Bonn the following May. At the beginning of March 2001, Christine Todd Whitman, Bush's new Director of the Environmental Protection Agency, indicated that the United States would try to reach agreement with the Europeans about the Kyoto Protocol, although they would not be bound by the last-minute offers of Clinton's negotiators. But at the end of March, Bush announced that he was unilaterally withdrawing from the agreement. He was met with protests from around the world. Instead, Bush set up a taskforce on energy policy under Vice President Dick Cheney, another former oilman. They produced a report recommending more oil, coal and nuclear power. The plan implied a 30 per cent increase in US greenhouse gas emissions. The Bush administration asked for time to produce their own proposals for an alternative to the Kyoto Protocol and the Bonn meeting was delayed for two months until July.

In June, the IPCC published their Third Assessment Report.[17] It confirmed the evidence for human-induced climate change, stating that the warming observed was unlikely to be natural, and gave the predicted range of temperature increase over the next century to 1.4–5.8°C. The prediction had increased substantially from the 1995 estimate mainly because it was now believed that emissions of sulphur (which causes short-lived cooling) would in future be lower than expected in 1995.

In order for the Kyoto Protocol to enter in legal force, it is necessary for countries representing 55 per cent of Annex 1 emissions in 1990 to ratify it. After Bush withdrew from the Protocol, Australia announced that it would not support the Protocol without US involvement. Then, shortly before the Bonn meeting, the Japanese prime minister suggested that his country would not be able to support the Protocol without the Americans either. If all three countries refused to ratify, the Kyoto Protocol would not be able to enter into force.

The Bonn Agreement

Despite having obtained a two month delay to develop their own proposals, the Americans did not present any and instead agreed not to obstruct the negotiations in Bonn. Unlike in Kyoto and the Hague, there were no frantic last minute negotiations at the end of the conference. The European Union was desperate to make a deal with the remaining Umbrella Group countries, particularly Japan, and gave ground on many issues. The most difficult issue was compliance. Russia and Japan were strongly opposed to making compliance with the agreement legally binding. In a major concession by the European Union, a decision on that was left until after the Protocol has been ratified and entered into force. However, it was agreed that for every tonne of global warming gases that a nation emitted in excess of its Kyoto target during the first commitment period (2008–12), a non-complier would have to reduce an additional 1.3 tonnes beyond their agreed commitments in the second period (2013–17).

The Bonn Agreement allows for the counting of up to 169 million tonnes of carbon sinks, or 3.4 per cent of 1990 Annex 1 emissions, against the target. That provision alone effectively reduced the overall emissions reduction target from 5.2 per cent to 1.8 per cent. In addition, the European Union lost its battle for quantitative limits on the use of the Kyoto mechanisms. The agreement states rather weakly that they should be 'supplemental' and that domestic action should be a 'significant element' of implementation. The absence of the United States from the agreement will mean that Russian and Ukrainian hot air is in plentiful supply. Its use will further reduce the environmental integrity of the Protocol. Afforestation and reforestation are allowed in the CDM, but nuclear projects are not and CDM funding must be additional to existing aid.

Marrakech

The final rules for the Kyoto Protocol were agreed at COP-7, held in Marrakech in November 2001. The European Union was forced to make significant concessions to demands for more flexibility from Japan and Russia. The conference agreed to double the maximum amount of carbon sinks that Russia can claim from 17 to 33 million tonnes. Japan supported the change and was expected to be a major buyer of the resulting credits. In addition, the conference agreed that for the first commitment period countries would not have to prove their sink accounting was satisfactory to be eligible to use the Kyoto mechanisms. Another difficult issue was whether emission reduction credits could be banked from one commitment period to the next. It was agreed that those from CDM and joint implementation projects would be 'bankable', while those from sinks projects would not.

The concessions decreased the emissions reductions from the Kyoto Protocol still further to an estimated 1.5 per cent. After the amendments in Bonn and Marrakech, the reductions agreed are largely symbolic. However, the Kyoto Protocol still marks the start of a process that may lead to significant cuts in future decades.

Contraction and convergence

A provision in the Bonn Agreement of potential future significance is the statement that emissions should be reduced 'in a manner conducive to narrowing per capita differences between developed and developing country Parties.' It can be read as a hint that the idea of 'contraction and convergence' is under consideration for the future. Contraction and convergence is the proposal that the total amount of emissions produced globally should contract over the next few decades by the IPCC's recommendation of at least a 60 per cent reduction. But each country should have an equal per capita emissions quota. As emissions steadily reduce, the more industrialized countries that would still have higher emissions would have to buy quotas from the countries that emitted less. It is a very radical idea. When it was first proposed in the early 1990s by the environmental activist Aubrey Meyer, it was dismissed as impractical even by many environmentalists. Over time, however, many people have come to the conclusion that it is the only defensible basis for extending emissions targets to every country and the only one that will be accepted. The Americans have always complained that Southern countries do not have targets, but because the United States is so profligate in its use of fossil fuels, contraction and convergence would reduce the American emissions quota to about one tenth of what it is under the Kyoto Protocol. Contraction and convergence has gained the support of the European Parliament, a number of European environment ministers and even the French President Jacques Chirac.

The extreme difficulty in reaching agreement on even very modest reductions, and the current American refusal to accept even that shows that we have a very long way to go to reach agreement on measures that would truly limit climate change.

Outlook for the Global Environment

In many ways, however, there has been much more attention paid to climate change than to some other very important environmental issues. The Biodiversity Convention has been in force since 1993, yet the convention itself is so weak that it has little practical effect. Habitat is being destroyed rapidly, about a quarter of vertebrate species are endangered and it is believed that species are being driven to extinction every day, yet there has been little international action on the issue because of concerns about national sovereignty. Even after ten years, it has been impossible to reach agreement on an international action plan.

UNEP's *Global Environment Outlook 3* shows that nearly all trends are still pointing in the direction of things getting worse, not better.[18] The brightest spots on the global scene are that population growth is levelling off and the ozone layer is predicted to start recovering in the next couple of decades. However, carbon dioxide emissions are continuing to rise, deforestation and biodiversity loss are proceeding as fast as ever, supplies of fresh water are reaching their limits in many parts of the world, and destruction of the coastal and marine environments is intensifying.

The World Summit on Sustainable Development

The World Summit on Sustainable Development took place in Johannesburg in 2002 as a sequel to UNCED, ten years on. It was supposed to be more about development than the environment, as Southern countries had felt that UNCED was more about the environment than development. On both counts, though, it was a disappointment. The United States attempted to block any targets or timetables, but eventually agreed to accept a target to halve the number of people without access to sanitation by 2015. Countries were urged to stop overfishing by 2015 – weaker than previous agreements, but a new commitment was made to establish marine protected areas by 2012. The United States and the oil producing countries succeeded in blocking any target to increase renewable energy. A non-binding aspiration to significantly reduce the rate of loss of biodiversity by 2010 was agreed – also weaker than previous agreements. No new commitments were made to increase aid, relieve debt or tackle the crisis of falling commodity prices. The lack of substantial progress at the World Summit showed that global political efforts to bring about sustainable development had run out of steam, even as the environment continues to deteriorate.

Why is it that sustainability and sustainable development have been such easy ideas to talk about, but so difficult to bring closer to reality? I will address that question in the next part of the book.

Part Two
PRESENT

5

What Does 'Sustainable Development' Mean?

People say that money is not the key to happiness, but I always figured if you have enough money, you can have a key made.

– Joan Rivers

Introduction

The starting point for the concept of sustainable development was the aim to integrate environmental considerations into economic policy. More profoundly, it was conceived as an attempt to bring environmentalist ideas into the central area of policy, which in the modern world is economics. It was to be the ground on which the mainstream was to consider the environmentalist case.

The concept of sustainable development carefully balanced environmental concern with endorsement of economic growth, at least in the South. It was deliberately conceived as being something more palatable than the hardline environmentalist message. Rather than challenge the idea of growth directly, it sought to modify the kind of growth strategies that were pursued.

The result of this aim for balance between environmental and economic concerns was a consensus on a definition that was at the very least rather vague. Some have seen the vagueness as meaninglessness: you can claim anything as part of sustainable development. Another view is that although there is much disagreement at present, with time the meaning will become clearer as people learn a new environmental language. Others have argued that sustainability is like other important political ideas, such as liberty and justice, which are 'contestable concepts'. That people do not agree on the exact meaning does not mean that there is no meaning at all. They argue that sustainable development is a concept that has succeeded in moving the debate forward and towards the environmentalist position.

Underlying the problem is disagreement about what 'development' means. Is it about economic growth and industrialization, as it is commonly seen, or is it about non-material improvement in life? The second part of the chapter will discuss different ideas about how development itself should be seen. It will describe ideas about human development and the apparent paradox that economic development does not seem to make people happier. It will conclude that the whole emphasis on development in terms of economic growth is misplaced.

Defining sustainable development

'Sustainable development' is a meeting point for environmentalists and developers. The environmental scientist Tim O'Riordan argued in his 1988 essay 'The Politics of Sustainability' that the reason for the popularity of the term sustainable development lay in the way that it could be used both by environmentalists, emphasizing the sustainable part, and by developers, emphasizing the development part.[1] The definition of sustainable development given by the Brundtland Commission, 'development which meets the needs of the present without sacrificing the ability of future generations to meet their needs', is often criticized as hopelessly vague or, in the language of experts, non-operationalizable. In his 1988 essay, O'Riordan expressed the concern that the vagueness of the definition would allow people to claim almost anything as part of 'sustainable development', reducing the term to meaninglessness.

Criticism of the vagueness of Brundtland's definition is accepted to some extent by Nitin Desai. When I asked him for his personal definition of sustainable development, he said:

Having been guilty of many, including the ones you see in the Brundtland Report, I hesitate to add yet another. And I would urge at this point, the issue is not defining sustainable development, but understanding it. Take the word 'development' itself. The value of any definition of development is simply the clue that it gives to the moral premises of the person who's giving the definition. So one person will describe development in terms of improving prospects for human beings, human resource development. Someone else will describe it in terms of growth. They are not really very valuable as operational definitions. It's not as if someone decides 'I want development. Now let me find out what it is'. That's never the way things work... Definitions are useful only for the clue that they give you for the premises on which somebody works. If you can't define development adequately, how can you define sustainable development in a simple formulation?

Desai makes an important point. The problem in agreeing on the meaning of sustainable development is not fundamentally about agreeing upon a precise definition, but about agreeing upon the *values* that would underlie any such definition.

Sustainability or sustainable development?

The degree of difference about values becomes apparent when you consider another question: are sustainability and sustainable development the same thing, or are they different? This is a strange question to have to ask. It seems obvious that they must be different because otherwise the word 'development' would be entirely superfluous, but it is politically important for many people to avoid making a distinction. Making a distinction drives a wedge into the consensus that formed the basis of the Brundtland Report and Agenda 21 around the mutual need for environmental protection and development. 'Sustainable development' is the cornerstone of that consensus. In Agenda 21 the terms 'sustainability' and 'sustainable development' were used interchangeably.

Tim O'Riordan drew a distinction between sustainability and sustainable development.[2] He saw sustainable development as a term that ultimately gave priority to development, while the idea of sustainability was primarily about the environment. His analysis is rather borne out by Nitin Desai:

> Maybe I could give you an insight as to how this [concept of sustainable development] appeared in the Brundtland Report... [A]round the time I was brought in there was a feeling that the issue of development was not receiving sufficient attention, that environmental management would stop the very necessary growth which was required in developing countries in order to meet some very basic needs... The notion of sustainable development entered the Brundtland Commission basically as an attempt to find the meeting ground from a perception which saw environmental matters essentially as matters which controlled towards a perception which saw the issue more in terms of *re*directing growth. If you look carefully at that chapter of Brundtland which talks about sustainable development, and look also at the fine print in it, not just the famous definition which everybody comes up with. What were the components of sustainable development which were spoken of there? And you will see that it is an attempt essentially at talking in terms of redirecting development and growth, rather than stopping it. Because it recognises very clearly that you must meet people's needs.

The identification of sustainable development with the growth agenda has made radical environmentalists deeply suspicious of it. The acceptance of the concept of 'sustainable development' by governments and other institutions seen as representing the status quo has fuelled the belief among radical environmentalists (such as Nicholas Hildyard, former editor of *The Ecologist*) that the whole idea is a smokescreen.[3]

Linguistic confusion

Is sustainable development a meaningless concept? Donella Meadows said:

> We're struggling for the language now for a whole set of concepts that are
> urgent in our conversation that hadn't been while the world was unfull...
> We didn't need all this language about limits and sustainability and our
> language is now very much lacking... Sustainability is my word for the
> moment to talk about what I do. Not sustainable development, and lord
> knows not sustainable growth. I mean Herman Daly's very clear, very
> strict definition. You have stable population, you have stable throughput
> and you have that stable throughput for each source and sink below its
> limits. To me that's sustainable society. That's a physical definition...
> Then we have social sustainability, the question of decent human lives and
> justice... Sustainability means meeting those physical requirements; and
> beyond that, meeting those social requirements that have to be met so that
> the system doesn't blow itself apart socially.
>
> I'm very aware that not everybody uses the word in those ways... The
> Eskimos with all their supposed words for snow needed them and pointed
> to this kind of snow – you used this word, and that kind of snow, you used
> that word. Often enough that everyone had a shared experience of snow X
> and snow Y and snow Z. And then they didn't have to go through all the
> rigmarole, but for a while they had to. And that's where we are right
> now... It's a mess. But social transformations are messy.

That last sentence of Donella Meadows' is particularly worth bearing in mind.
There has been disagreement and confusion, but it may not be a permanent state
of affairs.

A 'contestable concept'?

Another view is Michael Jacobs' in his book *The Green Economy*.[4] He argues
that sustainable development is a 'contestable concept' – one that affords a
variety of competing interpretations or conceptions: 'Many political objectives
are of this kind: liberty, social justice and democracy, for example. These
concepts have basic meanings and almost everyone is in favour of them, but deep
conflicts remain about how they should be understood and what they imply for
policy.'[5]

That something is a contestable concept does not mean that it has no
meaning at all. Words have meanings when there is a consensus among a
language community about what they mean. You cannot be like Humpty-Dumpty
in *Alice Through the Looking-Glass*: '"When *I* use a word," said Humpty-

Dumpty in a scornful tone, "it means what I want it to mean, neither more nor less."[6] People do try to distort the use of words for political ends, but there are limits to how far it is possible to succeed in that. Very few people believed that the German Democratic Republic was a democracy.

What kind of definition?

How tightly is it possible to define legitimate use of the term sustainability? Should priority be granted to physical or social criteria? Let me quote the sentences immediately after the Brundtland Commission's famous definition:

> Sustainable development is development that meets the needs of the present without compromising the ability of future generations to meet their own needs. It contains within it two key concepts:
>
> • the concept of 'needs', in particular the essential needs of the world's poor, to which overriding priority should be given; and
>
> • the idea of limitations imposed by the state of technology and social organization on the environment's ability to meet present and future needs.
>
> Thus the goals of economic and social development must be defined in terms of sustainability in all countries – developed or developing, market-oriented or centrally planned. Interpretations will vary, but must share certain general features and must flow from a consensus on the basic concept of sustainable development and on a broad strategic framework for achieving it.
>
> Development involves a progressive transformation of economy and society. A development path that is sustainable in a physical sense could theoretically be pursued even in a rigid social and political setting. But physical sustainability cannot be secured unless development policies pay attention to such considerations as changes in access to resources and the distribution of costs and benefits. Even the narrow notion of physical sustainability implies a concern for social equity between generations, a concern that must logically be extended to equity within each generation.[7]

In this crucial passage, Brundtland seems to be identifying the crucial elements of sustainable development as meeting basic needs, recognizing environmental limits, and the principles of intergenerational and intragenerational equity.

In that sense, sustainable development is not such a vague idea as it is sometimes accused of being. The problem of actually operationalizing sustainable development remains, however. The difficulty in giving an operational definition of sustainable development, or even in reaching agreement on what are the key elements of the idea, lies in the fusion of two concerns that pull in somewhat different directions: the environmental and the social.

The notion of needs leads to Brundtland's concern for intragenerational equity. The notion of limits underlies Brundtland's concern for intergenerational equity. Gandhi is supposed to have said: 'The world has enough for everyone's need, but not enough for everyone's greed.' As David Pearce has pointed out, the biggest obstacle for any attempt to operationalize Brundtland's definition of sustainable development is the seeming impossibility of determining what exactly are 'needs'.[8] It is not necessary to follow the economist's view that no distinction can be made between wants and needs, to accept that the distinction is a difficult one. Is air conditioning a need in very hot and humid climates? Are fresh vegetables in winter a need? They are things that many people have managed without for a very long time and which are environmentally costly, but which people find very beneficial.

Since sustainable development as presently defined seems to be non-operationalizable, is it of any value? I spoke to one initial critic who had been won round to the usefulness of the idea of sustainable development. The Dutch economist Hans Opschoor told me how he had been at a symposium on the Brundtland Report shortly after it came out. He had intended to give a talk criticizing the concept of sustainable development for being vague, non-operationalizable and potentially a cover for all sorts of bad things. Jan Pronk, then a Dutch member of parliament and later Environment Minister, sat next to him at the table waiting for his turn to speak. Pronk looked at Opschoor's notes and told him that if he said what he was planning to, he would be assisting in torpedoing a concept that would have international policy implications. So Opschoor changed his presentation and said that although it was hard to make operational, he was not prepared to reject the concept yet. He told me that he was glad he had done that because it had turned out to be a way to get almost two hundred countries together to discuss the issues and he could not think of another way that would have been as effective.

What does 'development' mean?

A very important aspect of the difficulty in defining sustainable development is that, as Nitin Desai pointed out, people do not agree on what they mean by 'development'. Is it about human development by improving education and health, or about material consumption through economic growth?

The goal of 'development' was first formally enunciated by President Truman in 1949. The objective was generally seen in terms of increasing that newly invented measure, GNP. For the first couple of decades development was pursued through state-directed industrialization. In the newly independent countries, some were more 'socialist' and emphasized state ownership of most of the economy, while others were more 'capitalist' and allowed extensive private ownership. But in both cases an emphasis was placed on the role of the state in promoting industrialization. Another important aspect of that development model was an emphasis on import substitution. Colonialism had made these countries concentrate on exporting commodities, such as cash crops or raw materials. They were almost totally dependent on imports for manufactured goods. The idea was to increase national self-sufficiency by creating an industrial sector so that less had to be imported, and instead goods could be exported. In later versions, the emphasis switched from import substitution to export oriented growth.

The idea was that the available capital (frequently from foreign aid) should be concentrated. The industries created would kick start a wider process of industrialization that would 'take off' and become self-sustaining. The theory also held that the wealth created from growth should be concentrated so that it would be invested in productive activities enabling 'take off', rather than diverted to directly assist the poor. Inequality of incomes would increase for several decades as the society moved from being rural to urban. Only as industrialization became predominant would inequality decrease again. This 'Kuznets curve' (named after the Nobel Prize-winning economist Simon Kuznets) was held to have been the pattern that the developed countries had followed, so it must also be the pattern that developing countries would have to follow.

In the 1960s, doubts about the model began to set in. Although economic growth was taking place, it was not bringing tangible benefits to the poor, and was often even leading to their further impoverishment. Only in countries that took deliberate steps to promote equality through land reform and investment in mass education and health care was the condition of the poor improving. Millions of people from the expanding rural population were migrating to the cities where resources had been concentrated, in a desperate, and usually unsuccessful, search for work. The emphasis on economic growth had overlooked other aspects of social progress. The problem was initially seen as simply lack of jobs, but it was realized by the 1970s that the poor were held back by lack of education, bad health and nutrition, and policies that favoured the elite. A new approach was taken up by the United Nations, based around social inclusion, promoting equity and fulfilling human potential. The 'Basic Needs' approach to development became fashionable in the mid-1970s. It would target meeting the basic needs of the billion people already in absolute poverty. There were basic material needs in terms of food, education, health, housing and sanitation. There were also non-material needs such as fundamental human rights, participation and self-reliance. The approach was taken up by many governments and even by the World Bank for a while. However, the practice tended to concentrate on top-down state provision of basic public services, rather than the non-material aspects to empower the poor themselves.

The Basic Needs approach was quickly swept away by events. The debt crisis that emerged at the beginning of the 1980s created a strong pressure to pay the loans by reducing public expenditure. The IMF and World Bank made such cuts a condition of further loans, as was described in the last chapter. They went on to insist on 'structural adjustment': an economic realignment along free market lines, which involved reducing the role of the state, removing subsidies, liberalizing prices, privatizing industries and opening economies to international trade and finance. The aim of all this was to increase economic growth. It was asserted that the benefits of the growth would eventually 'trickle down' to the poor.

Although the 'Washington consensus' of the IMF and World Bank dictated policy, the basic needs approach continued a kind of semi-underground existence in the 1980s. The Brundtland report put meeting basic needs at the forefront of its definition of sustainable development, although the report simultaneously placed very substantial importance on economic growth (an example of Brundtland's tendency to try to be all things to all people).

Human development

A new alternative development model came to prominence in the 1990s – 'human development'. It had originated with the Indian economist Amartya Sen, who was to win the 1998 economics Nobel Prize for his work, and was taken up by the United Nations Development Programme (UNDP) in its annual *Human Development Report* from 1990. Human development judges a society's standard of living not just according to the average level of income, but according to people's capabilities to lead the lives they value. Commodities are not seen as something to be valued in themselves, but as means of enhancing capabilities such as health, knowledge, self-respect and the ability to participate in society.

The UNDP's Human Development Index (HDI) combines statistics for life expectancy, literacy and income and ranks the countries of the world. Some countries with modest incomes, such as Costa Rica, Cuba and Sri Lanka, have life expectancy and literacy rates that rival those of western countries. The part of the world that is most famous for a high level of human development despite low incomes is Kerala, the homeland of the peoples of the Malayalam nation, on the south western coast of India. In terms of GNP per capita, it is the fourth poorest state in India, yet life expectancy is 73 years (compared with 61 in India as a whole and 76 in Britain and the United States) and adult literacy is 91 per cent (compared with 65 per cent in India as a whole and 99 per cent in most Western countries).

Another impressive statistic is that Kerala has a fertility rate of 1.7 children per family, the same as Britain, rather less than the United States' 2.1 children and much less than the Indian average of 3.1 children. As Sen notes, Kerala has a lower birth rate than China (1.9 children) and achieved its demographic transition in the 1980s both more rapidly than China and without any coercive measures.[9]

Like Costa Rica, Cuba and Sri Lanka, Kerala achieved this by investing much of what little money it had in providing basic health and education services. However, free market critics have argued that this state expenditure prevented private investment in economically productive activities and stalled growth. All these nations experienced rapid human development, but then experienced economic stagnation. In the 1980s, the IMF forced debt-burdened Costa Rica and Sri Lanka to reduce their social expenditure in an attempt to revive their economies. Because of a shortage of money due to poor economic performance, Kerala also reduced its social expenditure in the 1980s, even though it was not under the tutelage of the IMF because it had not borrowed. Kerala later increased expenditure again.

Greens have frequently seen these nations as a model for the rest of the world, achieving much of what growth is supposed to bring in human terms, but without the material consumption and consequent environmental destruction. Sen and followers of the human development approach also see these nations as having experienced 'development' in a more real sense than countries like Brazil which have experienced economic growth, but had disappointing human development. There is a difference between Greens and the followers of the human development approach, however. Human development sees economic growth as a good, but a secondary one, while Greens are doubtful of economic growth at all. Some Greens have argued that Kerala and Sri Lanka are developed enough, even though the people have very little in material terms compared to those in the West. Others seem to have thought that a rather higher level of consumption was optimum, although the extremely high consumption levels of the West are seen as 'overdevelopment'.[10]

The 1996 *Human Development Report*[11] examined the economic growth and human development records of countries. It found that countries that experienced economic growth without human development in one decade did not grow or experience human development in the subsequent decade, while countries that experienced human development with little growth either increased economic growth in the subsequent decade or slipped back into little growth and slow human development. Some of the East Asian tiger economies are the classic example of countries that started with human development and slow growth, but moved into a phase of mutually reinforcing growth and human development in subsequent decades.

The East Asian model

East Asia has widely been seen by non-Green observers as the development model to be followed. For many years the World Bank claimed that its success showed the virtues of the free market approach to economic development. In reality, the East Asian countries had a great deal of state intervention in the economy and had protectionist trade policies to allow their infant industries to develop. In addition, they had invested in education and health and conducted land reform before they started to grow rapidly. Remarkably, because of redistributive measures inequality of wealth did not increase as East Asia grew, (so much for the Kuznets curve). The World Bank only admitted that the East Asian countries had not been so free market in their approach after they ran into economic difficulties in 1997. At the turn of the millennium, the World Bank also admitted that there was more to development than just free market prescriptions.[12] Recent IMF studies have shown that liberalization and removing tariffs barriers has not actually led to growth in poor countries.[13] However, the World Bank and the IMF continue to see growth as the primary objective, and human development as the means, while the UNDP has the opposite perpective.

How easy would it be for other countries to replicate East Asia's economic success? It seems that a crucial factor was early investment in human development and a preparedness to push through land reform. The land reform started rural development and, unlike in many countries, the rural population was not sacrificed to provide cheaper food for the urban population. However, the same sort of policies were also pursued in Costa Rica, Cuba, Sri Lanka and Kerala. The difference is that the East Asian tigers pursued more capitalist policies in other areas. However, Costa Rica and Sri Lanka pursued capitalist policies from the 1980s, but still did not grow rapidly. Sri Lanka was obviously held back by civil war and Costa Rica was hobbled by the crushing debt it had acquired.

Another factor in East Asia's rapid economic growth was its orientation towards exports to the West. Although it pursued protectionist policies, it was allowed access to Western, and particularly American, markets. South Korea and Taiwan in particular were very important US allies who received a great deal of aid and support in the Cold War. Sceptics have also pointed out that Hong Kong and Singapore were city states able to benefit from unusual trade opportunities. However, Malaysia and Indonesia, which grew less and later, did not have such exceptional advantages. Today's WTO rules do not allow countries to build up their infant industries behind protective tariff walls (as every existing rich country except Hong Kong did). But even if that was not so, not every country can export manufactured goods in the way that the Asian tigers have – there simply is not enough demand for such products. If every country did attempt to do that, they would have similar experience to the countries that followed IMF instructions to export more commodities – the additional competition for the market led to a dramatic fall in the prices they could get for their exports.

There is a more fundamental problem with the East Asian model, which is the terrible environmental cost it has carried. Development in East Asia has been accompanied by rampant deforestation, loss of habitat and pollution of the rivers, air and soil. It is sometimes argued that development follows the 'environmental Kuznets curve'. According to this theory, pollution starts out low, then it increases in the early stages of industrialization, before diminishing again as development moves into a less resource-intensive phase of 'post-industrial' growth.[14] It is perfectly true that the early stages of industrialization are particularly resource intensive and polluting, but it is a mistake to believe that the *total* environmental impact of industrialized countries has diminished because the *local* environment is less obviously polluted in Manchester or Pittsburgh today than it was a century ago. The environmental Kuznets curve is frequently asserted, but there is a distinct lack of evidence to support it.[15] Certain kinds of pollution are less prevalent than they were because some processes have become cleaner, but also because the resources used come from further afield (for example, oil and gas from the Middle East rather than coal from Lancashire or Pennsylvania) and the impacts are out of sight, therefore out of mind. It is the case that in recent decades each extra percent of economic growth has not meant an extra percent of energy use, but energy use has only increased less rapidly, not decreased, and consumption of material resources continues to grow along with GNP. New technologies that appear 'clean' to the consumer can involve enormous environmental impacts upstream and downstream. Think of all the toxic chemicals and heavy metals that go into the production of computers and other electronic products. They are not only hazardous for those who handle them in manufacture or after they have been thrown away; those metals have to be mined and refined. It has been estimated that the production of a desktop computer involves the movement of 14 tonnes of solid materials – almost as much as a car does![16] That is not necessarily to say that information and communications technology does not have the potential to increase eco-efficiency, but it is not doing so in its present form.

The development path that the West has followed and that East Asia is following is an environmentally unsustainable one. The deeper philosophical question that the observation leads to is whether the response should be to try to achieve wealth in a more environmentally sustainable manner, or to abandon the pursuit of wealth itself. Many Greens have argued that the affluent consumer society does not truly lead to happiness anyway, and they are backed up by the findings of social scientists.

Does material wealth bring happiness?

Western societies have become much wealthier in material terms, yet studies show that people are no happier than they were 50 years ago. Surveys asking people how happy they are may sound strange, but it has been shown that individuals' assessments of how happy they are match well with the judgements of those around them and with physiological indicators of their level of contentment or stress.

In Japan, incomes increased five-fold from developing country levels to rival those in the United States between 1958 and 1990, yet the people apparently became no happier. Some international comparisons suggest that average levels of happiness in a country do seem to rise as average incomes increase, but that even then this effect wears off once a country reaches a rather modest income level found in countries like Mexico and Malaysia today. However, richer people in each society tend to report slightly greater levels of happiness than poorer people. Societies with more equal distributions of wealth are happier than those with less equal ones. That is because once basic materials needs have been met what makes people happy or unhappy is the comparison with other people around them, rather than the absolute level of their consumption. When hardly anybody else has a mobile phone, possessing one is a status symbol that makes you feel superior. When everyone else has a mobile phone, you feel deprived if you don't have one too. When everybody has a mobile phone, nobody feels happier than anyone did before. Economic growth itself does not seem to bring happiness, except very temporarily. After a short time, people get used to their new standard of living and go back to being as (un)happy as they were before, but at a higher level of consumption.[17]

This argument leads to the conclusion that much of what is conventionally called 'development' is really about joining a rat race of meaningless additional consumption. Unfortunately, the buzz people get from 'retail therapy' is much like the high from cocaine; the pleasure may be short lived, but that doesn't stop it being highly addictive. Indeed, it is the short lived nature of the pleasure that makes it so addictive. And like cocaine, the addiction leads to problems of its own.

Clearly, there are genuine benefits to be had from enabling people to meet their basic material needs and promoting human development. But the conventional development model confuses improving quality of life with achieving an affluent consumer lifestyle. If the development in 'sustainable development' was used to refer to meeting basic needs, as it was in the original Brundtland definition, then it would not be so controversial among environmentalists and Greens. However, 'sustainable development' is very frequently used to refer to old fashioned development through economic growth, while paying lip service to concern about the environment. The emphasis elsewhere in the Brundtland report on economic growth, even in the already affluent West, contributed to that tendency.

Over the ten years since UNCED, 'sustainable development' has become a less and less fashionable expression. The vacuity of the way it is so often used as a euphemism for growth for its own sake has become widely known. Environmentalists never really liked the phrase, but they took advantage of its endorsement by the establishment to themselves start talking more and more about 'sustainability'. Now, even politicians sometimes talk about sustainability. The next chapter will turn from development to examine the concept of sustainability itself.

6

Taking Sustainability into Economics

If economists could manage to get themselves thought of as humble, competent people on a level with dentists, that would be splendid.

– John Maynard Keynes

Introduction

One of the most telling criticisms of conventional economics which environmentalists have been making since the time of *The Limits to Growth* is that in calculating GNP statistics, economists treat the consumption of the Earth's capital as if it were income.

Many economic definitions of 'sustainability' start from this point. The idea has been that a state of sustainability would be achieved if capital was non-declining. It is not so simple, though. There is controversy about whether to consider human-made capital and natural capital together (weak sustainability) or separately (strong sustainability). If they are counted together then increases in human-made capital can compensate for running down natural capital. Is that legitimate? Are the two kinds of capital substitutable in that way?

The question turns largely on the issue of the extent to which technology can compensate for the loss of natural resources. Weak sustainability assumes almost infinite substitutability by technology, an assumption which environmentalists regard with scepticism. Strong sustainability also assumes some substitutability, however. The difficulty is that any assumption about substitutability is ultimately rather arbitrary.

The second part of the chapter turns to a rather different approach to sustainability that has become popular in the last few years. The concept of 'environmental space' attempts to make sustainability more concrete by dealing with the physical components separately. The idea is to look at each component and consider what would be a level of activity that could be supported by ecosystems without irreversible damage. The total amount of activity that could be supported in such a way is referred to as the 'environmental space'.

The environmental space concept is closely linked to the issue of distribution. Starting from the position of a more of less fixed amount of environmental space, the current situation (where it is disproportionately exploited by the industrialized countries) seems unjust. The environmental space concept has been used to argue for a much more equal level of consumption across the world. It is these egalitarian implications that seem to have made it a particularly controversial idea.

In contrast to the natural capital concept, the environmental space concept starts from a more environmental approach to sustainability. It leads quickly to concrete questions about what sort of consumption patterns would be sustainable with present or plausible future technologies and about what sort of lifestyle changes might be needed.

The environmental space concept can be seen as a way of making the goal of sustainability more concrete, but it does not itself imply particular policy mechanisms for implementing the goal. The third part of the chapter discusses ecological tax reform (ETR), a mechanism that has been proposed for the implementation of the environmental space concept. ETR goes beyond the common idea of environmental taxes by aiming to redirect the entire taxation policy away from taxes on labour towards taxes on the use of energy and natural resources. ETR would make energy more expensive, but make labour cheaper. The hope is that the consequence would be to reduce both pollution and unemployment. ETR would ultimately involve restructuring the entire economy and is currently regarded with caution by politicians.

Although the environmental space concept is not directly about limiting economic growth, it tends to suggest that, in order to release enough environmental space for Southern countries to increase their material standard of living, Western consumption patterns should be cut back in some ways. In that way, it leads us back to the debate about limits to economic growth. The final part of the chapter revisits the issue of economic growth and concludes that economic growth may be ultimately sustainable, but not in a form that most people would recognise.

Defining sustainability

The idea of sustainability originally emerged out of 'limits to growth' thinking. The 'sustainable' part of Brundtland's 'sustainable development' is based on 'the idea of limitations imposed by the state of technology and social organization on the environment's ability to meet present and future needs.'

In *Blueprint for a Green Economy*, David Pearce and colleagues defined sustainability in economic terms as 'non-declining capital.'[1] They took capital to mean not just monetary and human capital, as economists conventionally consider capital to be, but 'natural capital', the value to human beings of the Earth itself. The idea of natural capital had already been used in the Brundtland Report. Over the next few pages I will outline the debates both about how to assess sustainability in terms of capital and whether the entire approach is a useful one.

Very simply, the non-declining capital rule can be refined into either 'strong sustainability' or 'weak sustainability.' The strong sustainability rule is 'non-declining natural capital.' The weak sustainability rule is 'non-declining total capital.' Weak sustainability allows human-made capital to substitute for natural capital.[2] Strong sustainability does not. Just how much 'substitutability' of capital is there?

The concepts of weak sustainability and strong sustainability can be refined further. 'Very strong sustainability' assumes no substitutability and would not allow any element of natural capital to be depleted. For example, it would not allow oil to be taken out of the ground. I do not know of anyone who actually belongs to this school of thought. Moderate 'strong sustainability' only allows natural capital to be depleted when it is compensated for in another way. For example, oil can only be taken out of the ground if the revenue is used for the development of solar energy technology. This school of thought includes Herman Daly.

'Very weak sustainability' assumes infinite substitutability and adheres simply to the total capital rule. Moderate 'weak sustainability' conserves 'critical natural capital'. *Blueprint for a Green Economy* explained:

> There are many environmental assets for which there are no substitutes. No one has yet found a way of (feasibly) recreating the ozone layer, for example. The climate-regulating functions of ocean phytoplankton, the watershed protection functions of tropical forests, and the pollution-cleaning and nutrient-trap functions of wetlands are all services provided by natural assets and for which there are no ready substitutes. If man-made and natural capital are not so easily substituted, then we have a basic reason for protecting the natural assets we have.

> Technological advances could of course one day advance the degree of substitution between the two types of capital. *Perhaps*, one day, we will not need the oceans for food or climate regulation, or the nutrient values of the world's coastal margins, but that raises the issue of how to behave if we cannot be certain that such substitution will take place. If we do not know an outcome it is hardly consistent with rational behaviour to act *as if* the outcome was a good one. Most of society is 'risk-averse': we act so as [to] avoid bad consequences. If environmental risks have the potential for large negative payoffs then risk-aversion dictates that we protect natural environments, at the very least until our understanding of how they function in terms of life-support grows.[3]

Some economists have criticized the entire notion of sustainability. They argue that the aim must be to maintain income, rather than capital. The conventional economic goal of 'optimality' already does that, they say.

Why not 'optimality'?

The most forthright attack on the theoretical basis of sustainability has come from Wilfred Beckerman, a former economics professor at Oxford, in his anti-environmentalist polemic *Small is Stupid*.[4] He draws a simple distinction between 'strong sustainability' and 'weak sustainability'. He claims that environmental economists originally favoured 'strong sustainability', but then they realised it would mean no oil, so they switched to weak sustainability. He then goes on to claim that 'weak sustainability' is in practice exactly the same as optimality.

Beckerman does not appear to understand the concept he is criticizing. He seems unaware that even very weak sustainability counts the consumption of natural capital against income. Conventional measures of optimality fail to do this, and count such consumption as income.

Secondly, Beckerman assumes total substitutability of human-made capital for all forms of natural capital, without any apparent awareness that this is in any way a problem.

A much more sophisticated critique of the theory of sustainability than Beckerman's comes from the Cambridge economics professor Partha Dasgupta. At the World Bank's International Conference on Environmentally Sustainable Development held in Washington DC in 1993, he attacked the definition of sustainability in terms of non-declining capital, provoking an illuminating dispute with Andrew Steer, director of the World Bank's Environment Department.

Dasgupta[5] attacked the definition of sustainability as non-declining capital as being far too loose to be of any use. No net accumulation of the overall capital base is recommended. He condemns this as 'foolishly conservative'. If an economy happens to be poor in its resource base today, the formulation condemns it to poverty in perpetuity. Instead, he recommends the theory of 'optimal development'. Dasgupta goes on to say:

> Much attention has been given in recent years to defining sustainable development. One early thought – that whatever else it may imply, it must imply non-negative changes in the stock of natural resources (such as soil and soil quality, ground and surface water and their quality, land biomass, water biomass, and the waste-assimilation capacity of the receiving environments) – is a non-starter – not because it is an undesirable goal, but because it is an impossible goal. However, leaving this aside, there is the weakness that the requirement is imposed as a matter of definition on the determinants of well-being (the means of production of well-being), not on well-being itself. Presumably, the focus of concern should be present and future well-being, and methods of determining how well-being is affected by policy. History, introspection, and experience with analytical models since the early 1960s tell us that reasonable development paths would involve patterns of resource substitution over

time, and also of substitutions among resources and various types of capital stocks, including knowledge and skills.[6]

He goes on to ask the question 'What should be sustained?' He says that sustaining current well-being is not a coherent answer because current well-being is not a given. Many authors have recognised that the starting point should be to consider a just distribution of well-being over time. Dasgupta attacks the idea that this requires the constraint of non-declining natural capital stocks. He accepts that *some* natural capital would have to be conserved for a minimum level of welfare for the future to be guaranteed. But why introduce it as an additional constraint to the maintenance of a minimum level of welfare for future generations? Preservation of an index of natural capital ought to be derived from considering the path of optimal development.

Dasgupta goes on to criticize the lack of ethical argument in formulations of sustainable development. He thinks a better approach would be to look at the total well-being of future generations over different paths of development. Dasgupta uses an approach from Tjalling Koopmans' work on the problem of intergenerational justice, which is to conduct a number of thought experiments about the intergenerational implications of alternative sets of ethical assumptions in plausible worlds. The premise is that no single ethical judgement should be taken as decisive.

Dasgupta uses this approach to show that there is a difference between the consumption discount rates used in cost-benefit analysis and discounting of the well-being of future generations. The consumption discount rate turns out to reflect the assumed rate of productivity of capital. This is a point which he says is often misunderstood in much of the environmental literature that is critical of social cost-benefit analysis. On the other hand, the work of economists on global warming assumes that incomes will grow regardless and discounts its costs to negligible amounts.

Dasgupta sees a problem of market failure in the environment needing the construction of shadow prices to reflect the value of environmental goods. He adds that risk and irreversibility must also be taken into account, so the option value of conserving environmental goods must also be included in calculations.

In the discussion after Dasgupta delivered his paper, Andrew Steer summarised Partha Dasgupta's view as being that while the concept of 'sustainable' development is useful in motivating enthusiasm for the environment, it has no useful meaning in theory – and hence, presumably, none in practice. Dasgupta was taking the economist's stance: if you get the intertemporal optimization right, and use the correct shadow prices, the correct policies will simply fall out of the analysis. This approach was put forward as being much better than assigning 'sustainability' rules, which inevitably will be arbitrary.

Steer commented that when Herman Daly read Dasgupta's paper he was very troubled because he saw a threat to real world policy making from theoretical economics. In the real world, it is not possible to do the careful intertemporal optimization calculations using shadow prices.

Steer said that to be on the safe side, we can choose to make a requirement that the value of natural capital does not decline below today's levels. This would provide a broad assurance that welfare accruing to future generations from the natural capital stock will not be less than to today's generation. Dasgupta would argue that such a constraint is quite arbitrary and might lead to sub-optimal intergenerational welfare. Steer asked if Dasgupta agreed that in the real world we need some arbitrary rules of thumb to give some assurance that future citizens can lead a good life.

Steer went on to say that economists like himself need to know their limits. There are some things you cannot put a money value on. Often, values imputed to the environment by human beings stem from deeply held spiritual and cultural roots. For many environmental assets, these non-measurable values may be the most important of all. The job of the economist is to do as good a job as possible in estimating those values that can be measured, which should be respected as an important input to the decision making process, but not the only one. Decisions need to be informed not only by such calculations but also by the views people express in open discussion and the political process – so sound environmental policy making can operate only in an atmosphere of participation and democracy. In practice, he said, economists tend to condescend to policy makers when decisions are made on 'non-economic' grounds and environmentalists tend to harshly criticize economists whose valuation exercises suggest that, on economic grounds, the costs of protection outweigh the benefits. Steer gave the example of debates over global warming: 'The real reason we should do something about global warming is not that it is going to affect the economics of our lives 200 years from now. Rather, it relates to the much deeper spiritual and moral reasons associated with the fact that you and I do not want to hand on to our children's children a world that is very different from the one we inherited.'[7]

Partha Dasgupta was unimpressed. He said he did not think the notion of sustainability helped to understand matters. Taking as an example the idea that some index of capital ought to be preserved to sustain consumption, he argued that some types of capital, like coal stocks, would probably be reduced, while others, like water quality, might improve. So there would be a changing mix of capital stocks along the chosen sustainable path. 'Thus, to create the index of capital that, by implication, must be preserved, we will need shadow prices, or some surrogate of shadow prices. Where will we get these shadow prices? Plainly, we will need a valuation criterion to obtain them. Thus, we are back to the notion of optimal policies, and the prior question of the distribution of well-being across generations.'[8]

The difference between Steer and Dasgupta is partly over how much weight to place on calculations of shadow prices, and partly over how much weight should be given to the principle of precaution. Their exchange brings out the fact that what underlies the definition of sustainability in terms of capital is a desire to *guarantee* the welfare of future generations. Dasgupta does recognize that risk is an issue, and criticizes economists who do not take account of the downside of risk in their calculations – but his own approach is not very risk-averse. He suggests increasing the well-being discount rate for technological developments by the probability of the extinction of the human race as a consequence!

The moderately weak sustainability advocated by Steer elsewhere[9] still assumes that human-made and natural capital are to a large extent substitutable, although also complementary. The full functioning of the economy is seen to require at least a mixture of the different kinds of capital. Since the boundaries of the critical limits for these kinds of capital are unknown, he says it is sensible to err on the side of caution in depleting natural capital.

Sustainability and survivability

Rules of sustainability based on notions of natural capital are generally justified in terms of keeping options open for future generations. Here, it is helpful to take up John Pezzey's distinction between *sustainability* and *survivability*.[10] He defined sustainability as a path of development that would not lead to declines in average levels of well-being in the future. Survivability was a path of development that would not lead to declines in well-being below a certain minimum necessary for human life. Both sustainability and survivability, according to Pezzey's definitions, are examples of what are called *maximin* rules – rules which seek the best worst option, or to maximize the minimum. They are much more cautious and risk-averse than the utilitarian approach economists have traditionally used since the invention of welfare economics in the late 19th century. Pezzey's approach to survivability would avoid paths of development that risk disaster. Dasgupta's approach to optimal development would discount the value of such paths in proportion to the probability of such a disaster. What underlies notions of sustainability is not a failure to understand economics, but a more risk-averse approach to life than Dasgupta's. Sustainability is related to the *precautionary principle*, which states that 'when there are threats of serious or irreversible damage, lack of full scientific certainty should not be used as a reason for postponing measures to prevent environmental degradation'.[11]

Taking this argument further, it becomes evident that the degree of substitutability of different kinds of capital is crucial. The most cautious approach would be that of very strong sustainability, but it would make human life as we know it impossible. Strong sustainability assumes that natural capital can be substituted for by human-made capital, such as when it allows increases in solar energy technology to compensate for the consumption of oil reserves. Its point is that running down any kind of natural capital must be specifically compensated for by an equivalent increase in another kind of capital. For example, loss of forest in one area should be replaced by new forest of a similar type elsewhere, and receipts from depleting oil reserves should be invested in renewable energy technology.

Instead, someone like Andrew Steer, who calls weak sustainability 'sensible sustainability',[12] would maintain total levels of capital intact, but allow depletion of natural capital as long as 'critical' levels of natural capital were kept. An example would be investing receipts from oil depletion in education.

Herman Daly and John Cobb argue that substitutability is much more limited because labour and capital are used to make things, they are not used up in the way that resources are. While there may be significant substitutability between the two funds, labour and capital, or among various resource flows, there is very little substitutability between funds and flows:

> You can build the same house with fewer carpenters and more power saws, but no amount of carpenters and power saws will allow you to reduce very much the amount of lumber and nails. Of course one can use brick rather than wood, but that is the substitution of one resource flow for another rather than the substitution of a fund for a flow. Funds and flows, efficient and material causes, are complements, not substitutes...

> Let us suppose, now, that capital can be accumulated faster as renewable natural resources are exploited unsustainably. Will the extra accumulation of humanly created capital be sufficient to offset the extra loss of natural capital? We believe it will be far easier to accumulate enough capital with sustainable use of resources to enable such use to continue than to accumulate enough capital with unsustainable use of resources to meet human needs in the resulting wasteland.[13]

Andrew Steer sees the problem of natural capital in more specific terms:

> In my judgement, we environmentally aware people like to *broaden* things. We like to say 'that's related to that, and that's related to that'... When you come to sustainability, what one wants to do is focus on critical limits which can be fairly specific. So for example people say, 'We can't keep on using as much energy as we're using.' It's just not true. We could use ten times as much energy. But we can't use this *kind* of energy. What's the issue? Where are the real critical ones? Ozone. We crossed the limit... Global warming is clearly another very clear limit... Forests I think are an issue. One of the things that frustrates me about biologists and ecologists is that they're not willing to make statements about thresholds at all. At one level ecologists like to talk all the time about thresholds, but when you actually say 'OK, are we *close* to the threshold in tropical moist forests? We've been losing them at 0.8 per cent a year. We can't keep on doing that forever. How close are we? What's the real situation?' I would think that 20 years from now, if tropical forests in particular are declining

by more than, oh, a fifth of a percent a year, we may be in very deep waters. The plain fact of the matter, though, is it's a specific issue.

Steer's remarks raise an important point. For a supporter of weak sustainability, what is important is to conserve a *critical minimum* of, say, forest. For a supporter of strong sustainability, it would be important to conserve the present amount of forest. For moderately weak sustainability, natural capital can be turned into human-made capital as far as it is deemed ecologically possible. For moderately strong sustainability, natural capital should be preserved unless there is a substitute that can be invested in with the proceeds. Herman Daly's four principles of sustainability reflect that:

1. Limit the human scale (throughput) to that which is within the Earth's carrying capacity.

2. Ensure that technological progress is efficiency-increasing, rather than throughput-increasing.

3. For renewable resources harvesting rates should not exceed regeneration rates (sustained yield); waste emissions should not exceed the assimilative capacities of the receiving environment.

4. Non-renewable resources should be exploited no faster than the rate of creation of renewable substitutes.[14]

I think it is useful to distinguish between two different kinds of natural capital which are usually conflated in the natural capital literature. I will call them *non-ecospheric natural capital* and *ecospheric natural capital*. The former consists essentially of mineral reserves and the latter consists of the ecosphere. What is the difference between 'ecospheric natural capital' and critical natural capital? Ecospheric natural capital would be defined more widely. Critical natural capital includes only those aspects of the ecosphere known to be vital for the maintenance of the Earth's life support systems. Ecospheric natural capital would incorporate every aspect of the ecosphere, including those parts whose practical value to humans (if any) remains unknown.

I want to distinguish between the kinds of natural capital that are of value solely as resources (mineral reserves) and those kinds that may have other values attached. Of course, in reality any extraction of mineral reserves involves some 'collateral damage' to the ecosphere, but disregard that for now.

Generally (although they don't directly state it) supporters of strong sustainability seem happy to deplete non-ecospheric natural capital, as long as there is investment in future substitutes. They are much less relaxed about depletion of ecospheric natural capital, believing that you can't create a substitute for the natural world.

Strong sustainability is criticized by opponents for its allegedly arbitrary insistence on the maintenance of present levels of natural capital. Supporters of weak sustainability often argue that human-made capital will substitute for natural capital, so we can run down natural capital stocks as long as we remain above a certain minimum. But there are a number of problems with this idea. Firstly, there is the question of how sensible it is to run down our stocks of non-renewable resources without explicitly investing in the development of substitutes. Secondly, how do we know what would be an ecologically 'safe' level of ecospheric natural capital? Thirdly, weak sustainability might support the depletion or destruction of some kind of natural capital that could later turn out to be vital in some as yet unknown way. Fourthly, the rule of the maintenance of total capital implies that it is valid to do calculations of shadow prices comparing the net present value of say a wetland with the net present value of a shopping mall to be built upon it. Weak sustainability, like optimality, is based on such calculations and in practice is not so very different. It is vulnerable to exactly the same criticisms that Andrew Steer made of Partha Dasgupta. I will examine further the philosophical problems with these attempts to 'put a price on the planet' in the next chapter.

Environmental space

Although strong sustainability seems a much better rule than weak sustainability, it is not so useful a guide to practical action as is often imagined. Consider an attempt to draw up national accounts for natural capital (this has actually been done in some countries). Suppose that the country in question is rich, even though it has few natural resources of its own, and the country is noted for its high environmental standards. The nation's natural capital accounts show that its forests are growing, its rivers are clean and there are few primary extractive industries to deplete its non-renewable resources. But there is another side not revealed in the country's natural capital accounts. It is the world's largest consumer of rainforest timber, the world's largest importer of oil, and its corporations' factories abroad are notorious for their lax environmental standards. Critics accuse the country of 'exporting unsustainability'. The point is that sustainability is global. There can be no such thing as 'sustainability in one country'.

An approach that has become popular among environmentalists in recent years is to use the concept of environmental utilization space (usually shortened to 'environmental space'). The idea first appeared in a 1982 paper on the economics of global life support systems by Horst Siebert, a German economist.[15] His paper considered environmental constraints on the economy. He took ecological phenomena like resource regeneration functions and pollution absorption functions as a constraint on economic activity, and called the limits to environmental impact they set the 'environmental utilization space.' In 1987, the idea was taken up and popularized by the Dutch economist Hans Opschoor. He decided that environmental space might be a practicably applicable tool, and started research on the question of what the size of the environmental space actually is. Opschoor told me why he had liked the idea:

I saw a couple of advantages in it. In the first place, it sort of reflects this notion of scarcity or limitedness that I think the environment entails. In the second place, and as an economist it made a lot of sense to me, once you are doing that in the sense of space and so forth, people start asking 'How is this space distributed?', which you don't easily get with similar concepts such as carrying capacity because that seems to be expressed in numbers of people or animals, rather than the *potential* of the environment.

Opschoor was chairman of the Dutch government's Advisory Council for Research on Nature and the Environment from 1990 to 1995. In a report published in 1994, he wrote:

This study starts from the general notion that sustainable development implies that the environmental impacts of human activities stay well within limits of how much environmental space the biosphere can take. We shall refer to this notion as 'environmental space'.

Environmental utilisation space (or environmental space) is a concept which reflects that at any given point in time, there are limits to the amount of pressure that the earth's ecosystems can handle without irreversible damage to these systems or to the life support processes that they enable. This suggests to search for the appropriate threshold levels beyond which actual environmental systems might become damaged in the sense indicated above, and to regard this set of deductively determined critical values as the operational boundaries of the environmental space...

Although some authors tend to argue in favour of a single overall indicator of the environmental space, we feel that at least three different dimensions should be represented:

a. pollution of natural systems with xenobiotic substance or natural substances in unnatural concentrations;

b. depletion of natural resources: renewable, non-renewable (and semi-renewable);

c. loss of naturalness (integrity, diversity, absence of disturbance).[16]

There is a rather similar concept, the *ecological footprint*, which looks at the area of land a particular lifestyle uses, but its weakness is that is unidimensional, considering only that area of land used. Although it is a reasonable way of looking at topics like the food or paper consumption of countries like the Netherlands or Britain and the extent to which they import resources, it is not good at dealing with other issues like global warming. For that reason, the environmental space concept is better.

Environmental space was taken up by the Dutch ministries of Development Cooperation and of the Environment. *Caring for Tomorrow*, a 1988 report from the National Institute for Public Health and Environmental Protection concluded that the Netherlands would have to reduce its resource and energy consumption and its production of wastes to a fifth of the level at that time by 2010.[17]

Environmental space was also taken up by Milieudefensie, Friends of the Earth Netherlands. In 1992, just before UNCED, they published a report translated into English the following year as *Action Plan Sustainable Netherlands*, which explicitly linked sustainable development to environmental space.[18] The Milieudefensie report claimed that as soon as the present overuse of environmental space is recognized, the question that immediately rises is about distribution. The rich countries, with one quarter of the world's population, use three quarters of the raw materials and energy traded in the world, and are responsible for most of the pollution in the world. Milieudefensie argued:

> In order to deal effectively with environmental problems such as the greenhouse effect and the destruction of the ozone layer, the participation of Third World countries is essential. It is no surprise that the representatives of these countries have little interest in introducing a severe environmental policy, since the rich countries keep consuming the largest piece of the cake. A more equitable distribution of the access to natural resources is therefore a tough political condition for the realisation of sustainable development. The West will have to severely limit its unrelenting consumption of resources and simultaneously help the Third World countries to increase their standard of living...

> To decide whether a certain country's way of production and consumption meshes with sustainable development, the use of resources and the pollution of that country can be compared with the environmental space belonging to that country. That particular part of environmental space involves the 'world environmental space' divided by the world population and multiplied by the number of inhabitants the country has. Such an exercise shows in a stark manner how far the rich countries live beyond their means.[19]

Action Plan Sustainable Netherlands went on to outline how far the Netherlands was living beyond what Milieudefensie regarded as the environmental means of the Earth. They started their calculations from the assumption that the aim was to prevent further environmental degradation, while enabling the entire world population to live at roughly the same level. They calculated that resource consumption and pollution in the Netherlands would have to be reduced by 80–90 per cent for most activities. The good news was that although life would become much more conservation-minded, involving extensive recycling and the loss of many throwaway items, most of the material comforts of present day Dutch life would still be possible with the use of technologies already available, or that could be expected by 2010. The big exceptions were air travel, use of cars and meat consumption. All these would have to be reduced very significantly from present Dutch levels and even so carbon dioxide emissions would remain well above a sustainable level. The Milieudefensie calculations were rather 'back of the envelope', but are impressive nonetheless because they suggest that it could be theoretically possible for a population of several billion people to live in an environmentally sustainable manner with a broadly Western standard of living.

When I spoke to Maria Buitenkamp, the chief editor of the report, I asked her about whether people in the West would be prepared to accept the sort of lifestyle changes proposed. She told me that was a common criticism. People had told her that aeroplanes, cars and high meat consumption are important, not marginal, parts of modern Western life. The report had said that what was being suggested was not a return to the 1930s, but she admitted that for those aspects of life, the changes would be a return to the early 1960s for Dutch people.

Friends of the Earth Europe took up the concept of environmental space for a continent-wide campaign. The FoE group in each country did similar calculations, this time looking forward to 2040. In the report for Britain, the calculations now showed no need to reduce meat consumption. The need to drastically increase the fuel efficiency of cars and drive less was briefly touched on in the book, but no mention was made of air travel except in a diagram that included the text: 'Road transport and air travel are the fastest growing sources of CO_2 emissions.'[20]

Environmental space is a powerful idea because it expresses the idea of sustainability in a concrete way. Mathematically, the environmental utilization space is a set of steady state conditions that are all by definition sustainable: steady state combinations of extraction from the environment, pollution, and the capacities of the biosphere to buffer against those things. Every point on the surface of the space is a sustainable state. The surface of the space is a set of all possible sustainable ways of using the environment at various levels.

Hans Opschoor said:

What level of sustainable exploitation does a society want? It normally wants to be able to at least carry on the way it is at the moment... Sustainable development is a pattern of economic development and activities that can be continued over time. What this means in terms of environmental constraints is defined by the environmental utilization space. So they might be mirroring concepts in a way. Environmental space is more explicit, isn't it? It suggests the need to operationalize, to quantify how much space, and so on. Space where? Space for whom? That sort of thing... You still have to say how much nature you wish to protect, and that defines how much acid you allow to fall on any hectare of land, for instance. You're back at the question of making estimates of things that are very imprecisely known. And then if they are, how to relate to the uncertainty? Do we make safe estimates, or do we make unsafe estimates? If you accept the bare minimum structural approach to the environmental utilization space, you're not very far away from weak sustainability. So it's a suggestion of precision and accuracy which is there, and which I like to hang on to. And it's also the implicit notion which antagonizes a lot of people that you have to dematerialize also, at least in the North. It's much more provocative in debates than sustainable development.

The Dutch and Norwegian governments were the first in the industrialized world to show any interest in environmental space. In 1994, the Norwegian government hosted a symposium on 'sustainable consumption'. The keynote address was made by Gro Harlem Brundtland. She said:

An average person in North America consumes almost 20 times as much as a person in India or China, and 60 to 70 times more than a person in Bangladesh. It is simply impossible for the world as a whole to sustain a Western level of consumption for all. In fact, if 7 billion people were to consume as much energy and resources as we do in the West today we would need 10 worlds, not one, to satisfy our needs.[21]

She went on to say that traditional economic growth has meant producing more and more goods using more and more natural resources, placing an increasing strain on the environment. She said that perpetuating that kind of economic growth was neither necessary for employment nor environmentally possible and talked optimistically about decoupling economic growth from the consumption of resources.

Criticisms of the environmental space concept

Only one of the speakers at the symposium was critical of the idea of 'sustainable consumption'. That was David Pearce, Professor of Environmental Economics at University College London and a former adviser to the British government. In a paper later reprinted in the book *Blueprint 4*, he claimed that the references to sustainable consumption in Agenda 21 are confused. In particular, he wanted to distinguish between consumption in the sense of use of goods and services and the consumption of materials, energy and the assimilative capacity of the environment. He was implicitly criticizing many of the other papers presented at the symposium, which dealt with strategies to tackle consumerism in the West. Pearce said that reducing consumption could only come about by either raising the fraction of income that was saved for investment, or by reducing incomes generally. Governments can increase the rate of saving by changing the tax system or interest rates. But '[c]ontrol of the overall rate of change of income in the economy ('economic growth') is not by and large under the control of governments, although there is undoubted scope for lowering economic growth over the short term through sheer mismanagement.'[22]

Pearce said that, if savings were increased, some of the increase could be diverted to foreign aid, a transfer of income from North to South. But reducing incomes in the North would do nothing for the South, and would be very likely to make it worse off. That was because the lost income in the North would not magically reappear in the South. Because some of the consumption in the North spills over into demand for products from the South, the South would be worse off, since it would lose a market. Sacrificing economic growth in the North would make both North and South worse off.

Reducing resource consumption would not automatically improve the well-being of the South. If the North reduces its ratio of energy use to consumption, this conserves energy reserves, but a ton of oil not consumed in the North does not become a ton of oil consumed in the South, Pearce said. The power to consume a resource only comes about through the generation of income. He went on:

> Of course, if the North's resource consumption falls significantly, resource prices could fall. This would benefit the South if the South imports the resources in question. But it will make the South worse off if they export the resource. Ironically, those who call for reductions in the North's consumption are invariably those who complain about low commodity prices on world markets. The two goals may well be inconsistent. The only exception is if we believe that the future growth prospects of the South are going to be constrained by lack of resources. This is possible, but not very likely, at least as far as the supply of materials and energy is concerned.[23]

Pearce agreed that there was a legitimate sense in which conservation of resources by the North could help the South. The really scarce resources are not materials and energy, he said, but the assimilative capacities of the environment. They are damaged through the use of materials and energy. Since they are shared globally, damage is shared by everyone, both North and South. Pearce added that there was evidence the South suffered disproportionately more from some types of global environmental damage. Reducing resource consumption would also reduce environmental impacts on the North itself, so it would also make sense for the North to do it out of self-interest.

In Pearce's opinion, the thing to do was to move consumption patterns away from resource intensive products towards less resource intensive products. Pearce concluded that it was not desirable to reduce overall consumption or the overall increase of consumption in the North. That would only lead to unemployment and social unrest. The answer was to drive a 'policy wedge' between the consumption of goods and services and the consumption of materials and energy. Pearce would do that by using economic instruments, particularly ecotaxes.

There was a gap in David Pearce's argument. He explained why a reduction in Northern demand for material and energy resources from the South would damage Southern economies. In this way, his argument revealed a flaw in Milieudefensie's claim that Northern countries must reduce their consumption of resources to enable Southern countries to afford those resources. But he did not explain any way of avoiding similar economic problems for the South if his own policy prescriptions were followed.

There is another flaw in Pearce's logic. He says that he is unable to see why reduced growth in the North could benefit the South. He sees the entire issue as being about altering the ratios of resource consumption to GNP. It seems obvious, however, that *both* the ratio of resource consumption to GNP and the absolute size of GNP influence the amount of environmental impact a country has.

Dematerialization

From the oil shocks of the 1970s until the early 1990s, Western economies gradually became more energy efficient, but economic growth more than swallowed up all the efficiency gains made, so that energy use and carbon dioxide emissions are significantly higher now than in 1973. Yet it is well known that there is still an enormous untapped potential to 'dematerialize' economies by making energy and resource use much more efficient even with existing technologies and at no cost or even negative cost.

In the 1970s, it was Amory Lovins who first drew attention to the enormous potential for energy efficiency at negative or zero cost to solve the 'energy crisis', rather than the nuclear option that was then favoured by policy makers.[24] Over the next two decades, his ideas about reducing bills to consumers by encouraging investment in energy saving rather than expensive new capacity became a major influence on the regulators of America's electric utilities. In 1996, with Ernst-Ulrich von Weizsäcker and Hunter Lovins, Amory Lovins published *Factor Four*, arguing that energy and resources efficiency could be quadrupled with the widespread adoption of existing efficient technologies that could already pay for themselves through lower consumption of energy.[25]

Much Green literature following in the tradition of Fritz Schumacher's *Small is Beautiful* has called for the abandonment of high technology and the adoption of a utopian programme of village socialism. The authors of *Factor Four* comment on the irony that in the 1970s, early Greens were pessimistic about the capacity of new technologies to solve the problems of population, development and the environment. The anti-environmentalists argued that expansive technologies like nuclear power and giant irrigation projects were the way forward. What actually happened was that new resource-efficient technologies emerged over the next 20 years. Now the environmentalists call for the adoption of new technologies while the anti-environmentalists argue that they would be too difficult or costly or unreliable to introduce. The roles have been reversed.

Ideas about environmental space and factor four mark a new direction that Green thinking took in the 1990s. Many Greens no longer see the problem in terms of a need to end global economic growth almost immediately and reduce the environmental impact of Western lifestyles through a programme of Gandhian voluntary simplicity. The potential for an efficiency revolution reduces the degree of social and cultural revolution that is regarded as necessary.

Factor Four starts off with 50 examples from around the world of such techniques for reducing energy and materials intensity. It then turns to address the market failures (many of which Lovins had identified 20 years before) that prevent the implementation of energy and materials efficiency. There are an enormous number of hidden subsidies, information deficits and perverse incentives that counter environmental efficiency. Worldwide, subsidies for energy use alone total several hundred billion US dollars per annum. People don't realize how much energy they are wasting with things like inefficient light bulbs, poorly insulated homes and badly designed cars. Technological innovations that save energy go unexploited because manufacturers often have no incentive to make changes to increase the energy efficiency of their products.

The authors of *Factor Four* ridicule free-market economists like Professor William Nordhaus, who notoriously calculated in 1990 that attempts to reduce American carbon dioxide emissions by 20 per cent would cost around US$200 billion per annum.[26] Nordhaus had simply assumed that more efficient use of energy could not be cost-effective at present prices, because if it were, it would already be in use. This is an example of the free-market economist's belief that the economy is already optimal because it is according to the assumptions of the theory. There is a joke satirizing this kind of thinking: An economist is walking down the street with his daughter when she sees a $20 bill lying in the gutter. When she reaches to pick it up, he tells her 'Don't bother, if a $20 bill really was there someone would have picked it up already.'

Nordhaus had gone on to assume that in order to reduce energy demand, it would be necessary to increase taxes to discourage energy consumption. He then calculated how much energy taxes would have to be raised in order to depress energy use by 20 per cent, and how much that level of taxation would decrease total economic activity. The basic fallacy underlying Nordhaus' thinking was claiming that everything is optimal already, because his theoretical approach assumed it, just like Voltaire's Candide claimed that 'all is for the best in this best of all possible worlds', whatever disaster befell him. If the market is already optimal, then any policy intervention can only make things worse.

There's no such thing as a free lunch

One of Amory Lovins' favourite sayings is that not only is there such a thing as a free lunch, as Milton Friedman so famously denied, but that energy conservation is a lunch that you get paid for eating. That is because the cost of many energy savings is much less than the cost of the energy saved.

But there is a problem. Since so many energy savings do more than pay for themselves, people who save energy end up with more money left to spend on other things which use energy. The trouble with a lunch you're paid to eat is that you can end up spending the money on a second lunch and make yourself excessively fat. For example, the British government's programme for reducing national carbon dioxide emissions is based heavily on negative-cost energy efficiency measures and takes no account of the tendency for the savings to be spent on extra energy consumption in other ways. Lovins recognizes this danger and supports ecological tax reform to counter the tendency.

Ecotaxation

Many environmental economists, not as Panglossian as Nordhaus, support the introduction of economic instruments such as taxes and tradable permits to encourage environmental efficiency. They recognized that energy prices often do not incorporate the 'external costs' to society of the pollution caused by energy use.

In the 1970s and for much of the 1980s many environmentalists were ideologically opposed to the use of economic instruments and favoured regulation, arguing that economic instruments allowed the rich to pay to pollute. Gradually, however, the environmental movement became more pragmatic and today only a few ultra-leftists still oppose economic instruments. The main opposition comes from sectors of industry which see ecotaxes as a threat to their future – particularly the oil, chemicals and car industries.

A steady shift in the tax burden from labour to energy and raw materials has come in recent years to be seen as the way to combine the political and economic imperative of growth with the ecological imperative of decreasing environmental impact.

The first attempts to introduce carbon taxes were by the European Commission and the Clinton Administration in the early 1990s, but they failed. In 1991 modest carbon taxes were introduced in Sweden and Norway, but then reduced because of opposition from business. The Netherlands introduced a carbon tax on households and small businesses in 1996, dealing with concerns about the effects on the heating bills of the poor by offering a tax-free allowance for modest consumption.[27]

Ecological tax reform

The green goal of 'ecological tax reform' or ETR is much more ambitious. Ernst-Ulrich von Weizsäcker, the foremost proponent of ETR, argued that the lack of success of early schemes for carbon taxes was because they were misconceived.[28] They were formulated as a means of raising revenue with a green gloss, not truly as part of a reform programme. People and businesses will always resist extra taxes. Von Weizsäcker's ETR instead reduces labour taxes to compensate for the new energy taxes. Secondly, because von Weizsäcker is not interested in short-term revenue raising, but in transforming society, he proposed introducing the taxes at very low levels and ratcheting them up at 5 per cent a year. This avoids the economic shock of sudden price increases. Because of the power of exponential growth, an increase in real terms of 5 per cent a year would, over 40 years, make energy prices rise nearly eight-fold. By that point, renewable energy sources, which would be exempt from the tax, would easily be cheaper for most uses. Long before that point, ETR would promote a dramatic shift in technological innovation. Currently, as since the beginning of the Industrial Revolution, much technological innovation in production processes is aimed primarily at increasing labour productivity. What that means is that fewer worker-hours are required per unit of output. This 'labour-saving bias' has always existed because employers want to save on labour costs. In today's Western societies, workers are both highly paid and highly taxed. Meanwhile, a major problem in these societies is that mass unemployment has become a structural feature. Yet most forms of energy and raw materials are much more lightly taxed than labour. There is a clear bias in the tax system, effectively promoting unemployment and pollution. Put in those terms, the case for ETR sounds unanswerable. The appeal of ETR is only partly in terms of green credibility. A major appeal is that it should help to reduce unemployment and make industry more internationally competitive. That is because it stops taxing labour out of the market. It instead taxes energy and raw materials inputs, which do not vote, and plays to the strength of Western economies – technological innovation, rather than their weakness – high labour costs.

ETR is an extremely important idea in the intellectual and political development of the green movement. ETR, unlike 'no growth' economic strategies or the redistribution of environmental space, is not simply a message of enforced self-sacrifice to the populations of Western countries. It actually offers quite an attractive carrot: reduced unemployment, as well as less pollution.

Putting ecological tax reform into practice

Green parties quickly took up ETR. The German Greens soon made it their central policy plank. It was extremely attractive to them precisely because it combined the environmental imperative with a policy to do something about reducing Germany's extremely high rate of unemployment. The German Social Democrats were initially wary, being closely tied to trade unions heavily committed to some very energy intensive industries.

Aside from the usual unpopularity of new taxes, a particular difficulty with ETR is that in industrialized societies energy taxes proportionately fall most heavily on the poorest in society and least on the richest. When the former Conservative government put value added tax (VAT) on domestic fuel, the Labour Party and the Liberal Democrats had opposed it on the grounds that it would make it harder for poor and elderly people to heat their homes adequately. When Labour came to power they reduced the rate of VAT on domestic fuel from the standard rate of 17.5 per cent to 5 per cent – the lowest rate allowed under the EU tax regime. ETR can take the problem into account, by increasing other taxes on the richest and redistributing them to the poorest in compensation, but the alternative doesn't seem to have been considered.

In 1998, a Social Democrat-Green coalition government was formed in Germany. The principal policy demand of the Greens was the introduction of ETR. After negotiations, agreement was reached between the coalition partners on what may turn out to be the start of a long-term programme of ETR. Taxes were to be raised on petrol, heating oil, electricity and gas in three steps over four years. About €18 billion (US$18 billion) was to be raised over the four years through the tax increases, helping to finance an eventual 5.7 per cent cut in payroll taxes. Initially, there was to be a complete exemption for energy intensive industries. After intense lobbying, it was announced that all industries would pay only 25 per cent of the main tax rates to be payable by commercial and domestic energy users. The electricity tax would apply to all sources, including renewable ones, although the funds raised from renewable electricity were to be refunded to the industry. For reasons of social justice, it was eventually decided that housing that already had night storage heaters would only pay half the standard rate of tax. Chancellor Gerhard Schröder said that Germany could not develop ETR any further than planned for the first four years without an EU-wide approach. Environmental groups condemned the measures as too timid and warned that they would not be enough to enable Germany to reduce its carbon dioxide emissions. Industry remained implacably opposed to even these small steps, although they were eventually passed into law.

In 1999, the British government announced the Climate Change Levy, a tax on industrial and commercial energy raising £1.8 billion (US$2.7 billion) per annum from 2001, with the revenues to be recycled in reduced national insurance contributions for employers. Later, after intense lobbying, exemptions and reduced rates were offered to energy intensive industries, reducing the tax to £1 billion (US$1.5 billion) per annum. However, the reductions were to be tied to companies agreeing to make other energy efficiency measures, so it was claimed that the environmental benefits would be even greater than with the original policy.

The most ambitious attempt at ETR has been in Denmark. The tax on households and on industrial heating is 600 DKK per tonne (about US$75). But the rate for light industrial processes is only 90 DKK per tonne and the rate for energy intensive processes a mere 25 DKK per tonne.

Despite the seeming attractiveness of ETR, it has not yet been properly adopted anywhere. Why is that? There are a number of reasons. The first is that industry is overwhelmingly opposed. ETR is fiscally neutral overall, but it involves winners and losers. The overall winners are the less energy intensive parts of the economy and the overall losers are the most energy intensive. It is a well known political rule that the people who will gain from any policy change usually won't thank you, while the losers won't forgive you.

A second problem is that public opinion is sensitive about large increases in the price of domestic fuel or petrol. When in 1997 the German Greens proposed tripling the price of petrol over ten years (equivalent to an increase of 12 per cent a year) their support in the opinion polls fell from about 12 per cent to about 6 per cent overnight and did not recover when they abandoned the policy. However, when the Conservative government in Britain started increasing the tax on petrol (which accounts for 80 per cent of its price) by 5 per cent a year from 1993, there were complaints from motoring organizations, but no public outcry. In 1997, the annual increase was upped to 6 per cent by the incoming Labour government. However, by 1999 serious opposition to the policy had emerged from road hauliers and, rather opportunistically, the Conservative Party. As the price of petrol started to rise significantly above the level in other European countries, the media and the public began to become aware of the 'escalator' and critical of it. At the end of 1999, the policy was abandoned. It was promised that any future increases in petrol taxes would be recycled into road building(!) and public transport. But when the market price of oil continued to rise in 2000, protests spilled onto the streets in many European countries, and particularly Britain. The tax on petrol was cut in response.

ETR is revenue-neutral, unlike those taxes, but research I have recently conducted with colleagues in five European countries has found that most members of the public who had actually experienced ETR in Germany and Denmark did not know that the higher energy taxes they were aware of had been compensated by lower taxes on employment. Some did not believe that it was true even when they were told about it. People in all the countries also did not understand the rationale for such a tax shift and were sceptical even when it was explained to them. However, if the funds from the taxes would instead be put into promoting energy efficiency and other environmental measures then there would be much more understanding and support.[29]

A third difficulty for ETR is concerns about international competitiveness. If a country raises its energy prices, then its manufactured goods and some of its services will become more expensive on the international market than those of its competitors. Meanwhile, foreign firms will be able to undercut domestic companies in their home market. The solution would be to increase tariffs on such foreign goods enough to compensate – but you can't do that if you are in a free trade area. That is why European countries that have introduced energy taxes have been so wary. The savings from energy efficiency measures and lower taxes in other parts of the economy would compensate for some of this effect, but high energy taxes could lead to a loss of jobs in energy intensive sectors and a corresponding transfer of production to untaxed industries abroad.

There is a related problem. Suppose that the European Union decided to introduce ETR and imposed compensatory tariffs based on the energy contents of foreign goods and services. The WTO would certainly rule any such tariff to be discriminatory and illegal. The European Union could only go down the line of ETR if it was prepared to break with the WTO. However, unlike a single country, the European Union is so big and economically powerful that it could take on the challenge and hope to get away with it. The alternative would be to get WTO rules changed.

Finally, there are concerns about whether the energy prices that ETR would lead to would be just too high. Many economists agree that energy is undertaxed nearly everywhere in the world. But that is not to say that they would support von Weizsäcker's ETR. They worry that the kind of drastic increases in energy prices that the ecological tax reformers talk about would introduce economic distortions of their own. Increasing energy prices eight-fold would mean a tax on energy amounting to about 90 per cent of the total price, which is very high. The World Bank's Andrew Steer is a fervent proponent of increasing energy prices. He argues that one of the main things that destroyed the economy of the Soviet Union was low energy prices, which prevented technological innovation. He thinks energy prices in most countries are too low. But he told me he didn't think that energy prices in Italy needed to be raised any more to take account of global externalities.

As von Weizsäcker often points out, Japan overtook the United States and Italy overtook Britain in terms of GNP per capita with the highest energy prices in the world. By contrast, the economy of the Soviet Union collapsed under some of the lowest energy prices in the world. Low energy prices discourage investment in new technology and modern equipment. They also effectively subsidize pollution and wasteful use of resources. But it is obvious that it must be possible to have energy prices that are too high. Where is that point?

Evolving beyond the optimum

From the point of view of a neoclassical environmental economist, what you should do is calculate the 'optimum' price of energy. The aim is to internalize all the external costs to the rest of the economy in terms of pollution and the like. This approach was pioneered by Pigou back in the 1920s. Once all the external costs have been internalized, you have the optimum price.

However, doing just that takes no account of technology. Once you have internalized all the costs, you will, in terms of neoclassical theory, push the economy to a new equilibrium some distance away from the state it is now in. But technology will also adapt. New technologies will be developed which save energy more cheaply than would have been the case without the policy intervention. That will create a new optimum price which is even higher. So you can raise the price of energy again, promoting the development of new technologies, raising the optimum price further. There is a law of diminishing returns at work, but this effect means that over time it is possible to raise prices of energy (or materials) substantially higher than the neoclassical optimum figure. The economic approach which deals with technology in this way is *evolutionary economics*.[30] The long-term effect of ETR would be to restructure the entire economy. A different course of economic and technological development would follow because of it. Such a thoroughly different path does not lend itself to neoclassical optimum price calculations. How can you calculate what the outcome of the future path of technological development will be?

An interesting objection to ETR is that it might become a victim of its own success. If governments end up dependent on revenues from taxes on energy and materials, they may be tempted to *encourage* their use in other ways. This is similar to the way in which governments are often half-hearted about anti-smoking efforts because they make so much money from taxing cigarettes. A related danger is that rapid technological innovation could lead to sudden declines in income from ecological taxes, forcing other taxes to rise rapidly. The answer von Weizsäcker gives to this objection is that ecological taxes should not become too dominant a source of government income, so that governments do not come to be dependent on large revenues.

Many economists do not believe that a shift in taxes from labour to energy would reduce unemployment. They argue that a reduction in labour taxes may increase the demand for labour in the short term, but in the long run the increased demand for labour will raise wages, causing employment to fall again. This argument depends on the assumption of neoclassical economic theory that there is an equilibrium unemployment rate. These economists view the supply of labour as almost fixed. They believe that the problem of unemployment is that the unemployed are not prepared to work for the wages on offer. Few people except economists believe this. If that assumption is indeed untrue, then a shift in taxes from labour to energy can lead to long-term reductions in unemployment.[31] Furthermore, because ETR involves a steadily increasing tax burden on energy and away from employment, any tendency for the increasing demand for labour to be eventually eaten up in higher wages would be countered as the goalposts keep shifting.

Is there an alternative?

If we are to make the sort of radical cuts in greenhouse gas emissions that would be required in order to bring emissions down to a level that will not keep increasing the concentrations of these gases in the atmosphere, it is hard to see a better option than ETR. If global agreement could be reached, tradable emission permits for nation states would theoretically be the most economically efficient way of distributing global limits on emissions. But setting up a market in tradable emission permits for carbon dioxide within each state would be an extraordinarily elaborate approach to take except for energy-intensive industries and other large users. A carbon tax is obviously much simpler. If we want to make significant reductions in emissions over the longer term without sudden economic upheavals, then the path of smoothly increasing energy prices advocated by ETR seems the best option.

Ecological tax reform and environmental space

The thinking about environmental space from Friends of the Earth and von Weizsäcker's thinking about ETR are not inconsistent. Indeed, the Wuppertal Institute, which von Weizsäcker directed, was given responsibility for research for Friends of the Earth's *Sustainable Europe* report. ETR is a politically attractive device to free up environmental space. The rationale von Weizsäcker gives for the imperative of ETR is based around the argument that there is not enough environmental space in the world for the South to ever be able to live as people currently do in the West. He claims that if the entire world immediately adopted the present Western way of life, the resource demands would cause environmental collapse in five or ten years.

ETR is a measure that would attempt to exploit market forces to counter the tendency of existing market forces to squander resources. But it would not stop economic growth. If the world economy grows at 3 per cent per annum, it will quadruple in size in about 45 years. The power of exponential economic growth could quickly wipe out even impressive improvements in resource efficiency. ETR is really a device to buy time in which to bring about the much more fundamental changes in values which its advocates believe to be necessary in the long term.

Beyond the call for 'factor four' is a call for 'factor ten'. The rationale for factor ten is that the present use of environmental space is at least twice what is sustainable, while resource use per head in industrialized countries is about 5 times the global average and the world population will increase substantially over the next decades. The conclusion that can be drawn is that the environmental impact of the industrialized countries needs to be reduced by at least a factor of ten.

Achieving a factor of ten over 45 years would require a reduction in materials intensity of over 5 per cent per annum. However, if Western economies grow at 2.5 per cent per annum over the next 45 years then they would triple in size. Maintaining the environmental impact of the West at its present level while continuing to grow at that rate would require a reduction in materials intensity of the same 2.5 per cent per annum. Halving the West's total environmental impact over 45 years at the same time would require a reduction in materials intensity of 4 per cent per annum. Reducing the environmental impact by a factor of ten while tripling the size of the economy would require a reduction in materials intensity of over 7.5 per cent per annum.

Clearly, economic growth makes already challenging targets even more difficult to achieve. And if the richest countries keep growing, the poorer countries will always be left behind. UNDP calculated that the ratio between the incomes of the countries with the richest 20 per cent of the world population and the incomes of the countries with the poorest 20 per cent of the world population increased from 30:1 in 1960 to 80:1 in 1995.[32] The Brundtland Commission had argued that richer countries have to keep growing in order to provide capital and markets to enable poorer countries to grow. Yet according to the UNDP's statistics, the poorest countries actually got poorer in absolute terms between 1960 and 1995. Far from there being a trickle down of wealth, there has been a trickle up.

But how would you run an industrialized economy without growth for any time and avoid unemployment, under-investment and all the other ills of an economic recession? In 1977, Herman Daly wrote that comparing a failed growth economy to his proposed 'steady-state economy' was like comparing an aircraft falling out of the sky to a helicopter: 'The fact an airplane falls to the ground if it tries to remain stationary in the air simply reflects the fact that airplanes are designed for forward motion. It certainly does not imply that a helicopter cannot remain stationary.'[33]

That was just a rhetorical statement, however. Daly has still not directly explained how to avoid the problems found in non-growing capitalist economies. The most immediate problem is rising unemployment if the economy is growing more slowly than labour productivity. What primarily drives rising labour productivity in the long run is labour-saving technological innovation. Unfortunately, as Daly has often pointed out, much of the labour-saving of the past century or two has come at the price of increasing energy and resource consumption: What is more, statistics show that the environmentally-burdening activities like industry and agriculture which provide about 25 per cent of employment, generate about 65 per cent of the increase in national income.[34] Daly argues that the increase in the income of service professions like barbers in

Northern countries over the past century is due to the income from increases in environmentally burdening activities, rather than improvements in the productivity of barbers.[35]

Although ETR or tradable permits would redirect technological innovation towards resource-saving, it is hard to picture labour-saving innovation itself coming to an end – particularly in the age of information technology. Because ETR is intended as a transitional measure with exponentially rising energy prices, it is not intended for the management of a no-growth economy, where taxes would be kept more or less constant. Daly's suggestion of tradable permits, with specific limits for each kind of resource input in order to maintain what he calls a 'Plimsoll line' for material flows through the economy, might be appropriate for a no-growth economy.

Taxes or tradable permits would prevent material flows from growing, but if technological innovation continued to allow labour productivity to grow even slowly, unemployment would steadily increase. Daly does not directly address this issue in his writings, but he does propose a policy that would seem to address it: the minimum income scheme.[36] It would pay every citizen a guaranteed minimum income regardless of whether or not they worked. Any income from employment would be added on top. The intention of the minimum income scheme is to diminish the need for people to engage in full time employment in order to support themselves. The idea is that it would encourage people to work part time, become self-employed, or take part in alternative economic arrangements like Local Economic Trading Systems (LETS) to supplement their incomes. People, so the thinking goes, would become more interested in increasing their leisure time and people would work shorter hours, allowing work to be spread more thinly among the population. The minimum income scheme would also move away from the stigma associated with current systems of unemployment benefit, which usually require the recipient to actively seek paid employment. The aim is to move away from a society where paid employment is a requirement for acceptance as a full member of society. The minimum income scheme would also act as a redistributive measure to counteract the regressive effects of raising the price of energy and materials.

The minimum income scheme has been strongly criticized on the grounds that it would allow a lazy minority to do no work if they wanted and live off the rest of society. The Green socialist Martin Ryle has argued that such a scheme is politically unviable because the people in the formal economy would object to subsidizing other people's leisure.[37] Ryle also argued that the minimum income scheme depends on the formal economy to finance it, so it is not such a transformative idea as its advocates think, being more of a self-limiting reform.

Do we need economic growth?

The successful introduction of a minimum income scheme would depend on people developing a different attitude towards work from that prevalent in industrialized societies today. But if a minimum income scheme would require a transformation of social values, it is nothing compared to what would be required to bring about the acceptance of an economic strategy not based on ever-growing GNP.

A great deal of Green literature is devoted to attacks on the status of GNP as a measure of welfare. It is pointed out that GNP is just a measure of economic activity. It indiscriminately counts all sorts of economic activity towards its total. Notoriously, the *Exxon Valdez* disaster temporarily increased the GNP of Alaska because of all the expenditure on cleaning up the damaged shoreline. It cannot be pretended that GNP is a reliable measure of human welfare. As previously mentioned, GNP also takes no account of the sustainability of economic activity, counting the depletion of natural capital as income. Green economists have developed alternative indicators, the best known being Herman Daly's Index of Sustainable Economic Welfare (ISEW).[38] Calculations of ISEW include adjustments for depletion of natural capital, the costs of pollution and social issues like increasing unemployment and inequality. Both Daly's calculations for the United States[39] and calculations by Tim Jackson and Nick Marks for Britain[40] have shown the measure of ISEW increasing until the 1970s or early 1980s and then declining. These calculations are put forward as evidence that although GNP growth may have been associated with increasing welfare in the past, it is no longer doing that. Any calculation of ISEW is of course based on subjective assessments of the emphasis placed on different issues and Friends of the Earth UK offers a website where you can construct your own ISEW by giving different weightings to different issues.[41] Such work is valuable in encouraging people to question the status of GNP as a measure of 'progress' and to think about what economic welfare really means. But there are reasons for the continuing influence of GNP that calculations of alternative indicators do not address.

When I interviewed David Pearce, he gave me two reasons for opposing an end to Northern economic growth. Pearce argued that ending economic growth is politically impractical and that there is a confusion between growth in the use of resources and economic growth.

Pearce's first allegation was that ending economic growth was *politically impractical*:

> ...I am totally at a loss to know who the people out there are who'll vote against economic growth. It really amounts to saying 'I don't want a television. I don't want a car. I don't want an extra fiver in my pay packet at the end of the week.' I don't know who these people are. I've never seen them in my lifetime. What you describe is a fanciful world. It's a world that arises from people who spend too long in armchairs talking in

academic circles.... It doesn't have anything to do with the real world of ordinary people. The world in which I was born and have never escaped from is a world in which people desire to be richer in a very conventional sense.

By contrast, Herman Daly had told me:

...there are two kinds of impossibility. There's a political impossibility and a biophysical impossibility, and right now it's like the horns of a dilemma. I prefer to be impaled on the politically impossible horn because that's not as fundamentally impossible. Things which are presumably politically impossible frequently do change. The Berlin Wall fell. That was politically impossible. A few other things have happened that were politically impossible. But I don't think we're going to change the dimensions of the earth or reverse the laws of thermodynamics, those kind of things, which are the fundamental limits.

David Pearce's second point was that there is a *confusion between growth in the use of resources and economic growth*:

....if you look at Daly's work, it changes its nature quite neatly after the early 1970s when he writes his anti-economic growth arguments. What he is challenging is economic growth, the concept of additional wealth. When he's challenged that to oppose economic growth is to oppose the aspirations of ordinary people, the man on the Clapham omnibus or the guy in the village in Nigeria, when he realized that in a sense he had been attacking the wrong thing, he changed it to say that what he was in favour of was economic development, and what he was against was the consumption of materials and energy. What *he* defines economic growth as is the increased consumption of energy and materials. *Nowhere* in economics literature can you find economic growth defined in that way. Nowhere. It's perfectly possible to have economic growth, value added, without increasing the consumption of materials and energy.

How fair is David Pearce being to Herman Daly? Daly does in fact make a distinction between economic growth (growth in the value of goods and services) and what he calls throughput growth. But it is also true that his famous book *Steady-State Economics*[42] is an argument not just against growth in the throughput of energy and materials, but also against growth in the value of goods and services in the economy. Daly called, back in 1977, for the need to maximize resource efficiency. He wrote:

no doubt it is true that at 'some finite cost' we could live on renewable resources, as mankind essentially did before the industrial revolution. But the finite cost is going to include a reduction in population or per capita consumption levels or, at the very least, a cessation of further growth.[43]

He ridiculed the idea that improving materials and energy efficiency could be combined with economic growth:

> The idea of economic growth overcoming physical limits by angelizing GNP is equivalent to overcoming physical limits to population growth by reducing the throughput intensity or metabolism of human beings. First pygmies, then Tom Thumbs, then big molecules, then pure spirits. Indeed, it would be necessary for us to become angels in order to subsist on angelized GNP.[44]

But it is true that Daly is more circumspect about the possibilities for improving resource efficiency in what he says and writes nowadays. When I interviewed Daly and asked him about his ideas for controlling Northern consumption, he said:

> I'm talking about a reduction in matter-energy throughput in the North. To the extent we're able to increase productivity of that matter-energy flow and satisfy our needs to a greater and greater extent with the same, then it isn't going to cost us very much. And to the people who are technological optimists, I would say 'I hope you're right. If you are right, it'll be easier to deal with.' I tend to think it'll not be quite so easy. We should certainly go as far in the direction of technological improvement as we can, but that remains to be seen.

Both Daly's arguments against growth and Pearce's arguments for a continuation of growth depend on the empirical question of the extent to which it is possible to 'angelize' the economy.

Is a no-growth economy inevitable? Imagine that the industrialized economies have undergone ETR and managed to reduce their material and energy intensity by a factor of five or ten from the levels of today. Suppose that technological progress is continuing and is leading to an increase in labour productivity of say 2.5 per cent. In order to prevent the throughput from rising again while maintaining employment, it would be necessary to reduce resource intensity by at least 2.5 per cent per annum. In other words, for each unit of economic activity, the use of energy and materials would have to reduce by 2.5 per cent per annum. That process cannot continue for ever, because there is a fundamental minimum amount of energy required to do a certain amount of work. It will always take 4.2 joules to heat a gram of water by 1° Celsius. As Daly said, we cannot endlessly 'angelize' the economy.

If the resource intensity of the economy diminished by 2.5 per cent per annum, it would become ten times more efficient in a little less than a century.

However, if we imagine ourselves starting from a position of being five or ten times more efficient than at present, we are talking about ending up 50 or 100 times more efficient than at present. At that level, we really would be running into fundamental thermodynamic limits.[45] Of course, there is no guarantee we could ever become anything like so efficient. But if we allow 50 years for ETR and another 100 years to reach fundamental thermodynamic limits, we are looking at maybe 150 years before economic growth on Earth would have to come to a halt. A technological optimist might say that by then we would be able to get round the limits to growth on Earth by expanding into space and continue to grow there (although exponential growth would soon require us to expand to new solar systems faster than light).

Let's be a bit more cautious and suppose that we would actually run into practical limits to increasing efficiency long before we reached the theoretical thermodynamic limits on Earth and before it would possible to make a seamless transition to an interplanetary growth economy (not unreasonable suppositions to make). Let's suppose that at 5, 10 or 20 times as efficient as we are now, we will run into practical limits. What could we do then?

One answer is that emphasis could be placed on increasing the quality, rather than the quantity of production. Unfortunately, increasing quality usually implies greater embedded energy in a product.

Unless innovation was forbidden and any kind of economic development halted, there would still be some trend towards increasing labour productivity. As in present Western economies which are moving away from manufacturing, the labour freed up could be absorbed in an increasing emphasis on services. Much discussion about services is confused, because it lumps together all non-extractive and non-manufacturing sectors of the economy. Clearly, an economy that is not growing physically could not have increasing numbers of travel agents and shop assistants, as their work depends indirectly on energy and materials intensive activities. But there seems to be no reason why increasing proportions of the population could not be trained and employed in service occupations that would be difficult to automate such as educators, psychotherapists, carers, masseurs and entertainers. This response implies that measured GNP could indeed increase, even without increasing consumption of resources or technical improvements in resource efficiency, as services such as these became increasingly prevalent in response to increasing labour productivity in other areas due to continuing technological progress. However, it is important to understand that this growth would simply be an increase in personal services and money flowing around the economy. It would not be much like growth as we have experienced it in the last couple of centuries, because it would not be about an increasing material standard of living. This relates back to Daly's point about why barbers' incomes have risen in the past century.

The ecological economist Paul Ekins told me that the problem is that 'what people want are Ferraris, not personal services.' In other words, he thinks that the sort of growth people want is the more environmentally burdensome kind, rather than the angelic kind. Clearly, a steady-state economy would require a different set of cultural values that would be difficult to bring about. People in industrialized societies expect their material standard of living to increase in the long term and would not find it easy to adjust.

Capitalism, notoriously, depends on the creation of new desires and new markets for its dynamic. But it would be simplistic to suppose that a socialist economic system would be immune to the craving for growth. People in Eastern Europe yearned for Western consumer products even if they had never been exposed to advertising and marketing hype for them.

An economic system based ultimately on the power of greed and self-interest has proved to be very good at bringing about growing material standards of living. However, it does not appear to be the sort of economic system that would be appropriate for a steady-state economy. As a consequence, Greens have always tended towards a degree of socialism.

Greens and socialism

The vision of a Green economy is usually one based around workers' cooperatives as the predominant model of organization. Historically, Greens liked the idea of cooperatives and a kind of market socialist economy as a third way between Western capitalism and Soviet state socialism. Some more left wing Greens have thought that the cooperatives should operate in a kind of locally planned economy, rather like the vision of the early 19th century utopian socialists.[46] The main problem with a locally planned economy is ensuring that there is a sufficient variety of products available. A centrally planned economy allows the flow of goods across a large geographical area, and is bad enough for lack of choice, but a locally planned economy is likely to be extremely simple, not to say spartan, in what it can provide.

Other Greens thought that there should instead be a market socialist economy. Interestingly, most of the objections to a market socialist economy are much less troubling if you are uninterested in economic growth. It is perhaps telling that over a century earlier John Stuart Mill had advocated a 'stationary state' economy based around workers' cooperatives.

Market socialism has a number of attractive features. Unlike in state socialism, there is no need for central planning – the cooperatives function in a market rather like private firms under capitalism. If there is competition between cooperatives, there are incentives for efficient use of resources and decent customer service. However, because the workers are also the owners, there is much less potential for exploitation by management than under capitalism. Because the workers direct the cooperative, it is potentially much more democratic than either capitalism or state socialism. Even nationalized industries in democratic countries are inherently top-down. One of the great appeals of market socialism is that it is a system of self-management. Cooperatives are also usually fairly small and decentralized, even if they often belong to larger cooperative federations. The decentralization and democracy of cooperatives is in keeping with Green ideology.

However, there are a number of problems with market socialism. From a Green perspective, markets encourage self-interest and attempts to cut corners. If it is no longer possible to exploit the workers under market socialism, it is still possible to exploit the environment, so there would still be a need for regulation.

State socialists pointed out that since the system would involve markets and competition, it would lead to winners and losers. Some cooperatives might become rich while others could go bankrupt. A cooperative going bankrupt is even more serious than a capitalist firm going bankrupt because the workers have their own capital invested in the cooperative and have more at stake than their jobs. An economy based around cooperatives would need a high level of state intervention to protect members of unsuccessful cooperatives.

Another problem is the question of where workers' stakes in the capital of their cooperative comes from. If workers have to pay for their share in the capital of the cooperative, then there are all sorts of potential problems with access to employment – everyone has to become a capitalist. Often, the worker borrows the money upon joining and pays for it out of subsequent wages. But if the cooperative later goes bankrupt or just gets into trouble, the worker will effectively lose a large part of their savings. If workers don't have to pay for their share of the capital, then there is the problem of where the capital comes from in the first place. In Britain, the John Lewis Partnership belongs to its workers, but it came to them as a gift from the founder when he died. Further problems can arise if a cooperative wants to expand or needs to contract. Employing extra workers dilutes the stake of existing members of the cooperative and makes it unusual for workers' cooperatives to grow to any size. Shedding members in bad times can be very difficult.

Advocates of market socialism point to the Mondragon network of cooperatives in the Basque Country, which has shown that cooperatives can have higher productivity than capitalist companies. Mondragon grew rapidly from one cooperative of 24 people in 1956 to a network with thousands of members within 20 years and to over 30,000 members today. The secret of its success was that it combined a group of industrial worker cooperatives with a consumer cooperative bank to provide capital. Its size enabled Mondragon to form its own social protection system for its members as an alternative to the state.

However, Spain's entry into the European Community forced Mondragon into fierce competition with foreign multinationals. Mondragon had previously faced relatively little competition in Spain's protected market. In order to survive, Mondragon abandoned some cooperative principles. It opened non-cooperative joint ventures with capitalist firms and moved production to non-cooperative factories in low wage economies in order to compete. The cooperators became capitalists of a sort.[47]

It is hard to avoid the conclusion that a market socialist economy would not be as dynamic (or exploitative) as a capitalist one. For a steady-state economy, that would not matter so much. The dynamism and initiative of capitalism is something that would no longer be needed. The priority would be egalitarianism because in a steady-state economy it would not be possible to justify inequality on the grounds that it leads to growth from which all benefit in the end. Instead, the lack of growth dynamic in a market socialist economy can be seen as a point in its favour from a Green perspective.

An alternative approach that has been favoured by some more moderate Greens is the social democratic one, where there are very high rates of taxation on the rich. In the long run, these taxes would break up concentrations of wealth and create a 'property owning democracy'. Such policies were pursued for some time in Scandinavia and even briefly in Britain in the 1970s, but fell out of favour because it was felt that they discouraged enterprise. In other words, greater equality was seen to cost growth.

Much of the contemporary debate between economists and environmentalists is about exactly this trade-off between growth and equality as well as their better known dispute over growth versus environmental protection. In recent years, environmentalists have increasingly taken up the former role of the left, arguing for equality. However, there is an interesting twist to these debates, because the environmental space argument allows environmentalists to put forward the view that one price of inequality is environmental destruction.

7

'Putting a Price on the Planet'

What is a cynic? A man who knows the price of everything and the value of nothing.

– Oscar Wilde

Introduction

The mainstream economist's approach to environmental decision making is based on cost-benefit analysis. It involves attempting to calculate what a set of environmental goods is worth to people in monetary terms; crudely, finding out what people would pay to preserve a feature of the environment as it is. The figure derived is compared with the monetary value of economic exploitation. Whichever alternative of preservation or exploitation that raises the greatest sum is held to have won the cost-benefit analysis.

Since environmental goods are not normally traded in the marketplace, traditional cost-benefit analyses tended to ignore the loss of the values derived from aspects of the environment when economic development takes place. In recent years, economists have put much more effort into attempting to identify the economic values associated with preservation. This has involved the construction of 'shadow prices' based on surveys of what people would be prepared to pay for the preservation of an environmental good.

The economist's approach is controversial, though. Many environmentalists assert that nature has an intrinsic value beyond the value that people attach to it. Cost-benefit analysis also turns out to place value on the interests of different people in proportion to the wealth that they command. It assigns greater value to the interests of the rich than those of the poor. The use of money as a common measuring rod for expressing people's values through cost-benefit analysis and the entire approach of 'welfare economics' does not appear to be compatible with the concerns about equity that are so important to the concept of sustainable development. The actual practice of cost-benefit analysis is not even philosophically coherent in itself.

Welfare economics is based on an individualist utilitarian framework with no room for considerations of intragenerational or intergenerational equity. Bringing these concerns into cost-benefit analysis would involve not only a revision of its techniques, but of the moral assumptions behind mainstream economic theory.

Putting a price on the planet

David Pearce told me that he was annoyed to be so reviled by environmentalists. He was associated with the idea of 'putting a price on the planet', but complained that 'people would say "this man is out to put a price on everything." I've never said that. It's a bit too much.' Pearce went on to tell me that, however:

> The idea that you *cannot* put a value on global warming damage is self-evidently wrong because it's been done. People may want to argue with the results, but it's been done... *[W]hy* can't you put a value on global warming? I don't understand why not. If I look at it very simply, if I have global warming and I have sea level rise, then the relationship between warming and sea level rise is a scientific issue. It has nothing to do with economics. The fact that the land has a number of economic sectors on it permits me to go on and say what would happen if those economic sectors were lost. So there's absolutely no reason why you shouldn't try to value these things.

> If somebody says that the estimate that you get is uncertain, then I would agree of course.... The idea that any of this should be definite within 99 per cent confidence limits is laughable. If people are saying you can't value global warming, I think I would have to say that the ball is in their court to say why not.

In *For the Common Good*, Herman Daly and John Cobb had argued that global warming was an example of the sort of pervasive externality that cannot be costed.[1] They wrote that, even if you assumed predictable physical changes from global warming, the economic losses would be subject to wide disagreement and uncertainty. Should costs be based on how much people would be willing to pay to avoid the change? Or on how much it would cost to put things back the way they were? They pointed out that since these kind of changes are not the kind of things that can be purchased piecemeal on markets, people would have to express their valuations in terms of answers to hypothetical questions. Are such answers meaningful? Even assuming that problem could be solved, they outlined the difficulty of tracing through all the consequences and costs of global warming, including all the relocation costs, disruption of food supplies, loss of species, and so on:

> We submit that, while perhaps barely conceivable to a Laplacian demon, such a calculation involves so many guesstimates, uncertainties, and arbitrary assumptions that it is a will o' the wisp, an ignus fatuus, a red herring. The change is too nonmarginal, too systemic and pervasive for prices to mean anything. Yet that is what the logic of internalization demands. Is there not a more operational and less arbitrary procedure for

approximating the Pigovian ideal of full cost prices, and for recognizing at the same time that a change like the greenhouse effect is not something to be paid for, but something to be avoided?[2]

David Pearce can say that he has done these calculations, so it is not impossible. The question, however, is not whether such a calculation can be done at all, but whether the answer derived is meaningful. Pearce led a team of economists whose chapter on the social costs of climate change for the second report of the IPCC was rejected by governments at an IPCC meeting held in Montreal at the end of 1995.

The equity question

The chapter on social costs was rejected because a number of Southern countries, including India, supported a critique of the assumptions it was based on that had been published by a small London-based lobby group, the Global Commons Institute (GCI). The economists had calculated that following a 'business as usual' scenario, global warming would cost 1.5–2 per cent of Gross World Product annually by the second half of the next century. They had calculated that action to limit global warming would itself lead to losses of 2 per cent of Gross World Product annually. GCI argued that these calculations were based on flawed, indeed immoral, assumptions.

GCI contested several assumptions, but the crucial charges were that the economists had ignored scientific uncertainties in their calculations, and that they had used an approach to calculating costs that generally underestimated them and in particular discriminated against the South.[3]

The economists had made their calculations based on the assumption of 2.5°C warming, in the middle of the IPCC range of 1–3.5°C. However, this range was itself based on climate models which in fact contained much larger uncertainties (incidentally, more recent estimates tend to be higher). Their assessments of damage costs were also based on uncertain calculations. Most significantly, the damage costs calculated were extremely sensitive to the surmised death rate, which was predicted largely on the basis of a single study into the effects of a 4°C rise on the inhabitants of 15 US cities, and a series of extrapolations. The economists had only considered deaths due to heat stress and storms, not due to disease or malnutrition.

A problem with the economists' calculations that GCI did not touch on was that they had started from the same assumptions as those of Nordhaus, discussed in the last chapter, that there are no zero- or negative-cost emissions reductions to be made, and that a carbon tax would not be recycled to reduce distortionary taxes. What is more, it is estimated that there are currently environmentally damaging perverse subsidies of at least US$1.1 trillion per annum worldwide.

About US$650 billion per annum, 2 per cent of Gross World Product, takes the form of perverse subsidies for road transport and fossil fuels.[4]

GCI's fundamental challenge to the economists was over the calculations of differential value between rich and poor countries. They valued the loss of land in Southern countries at one tenth the rate of land in Western countries. Based on an assessment of 'willingness to pay', the IPCC economists had valued the cost of a lost life in Western countries at US$1.5 million for their calculations. They had valued a life at US$100,000 for the rest of the world. Aubrey Meyer of GCI called this 'the economics of genocide'. Meyer was born in South Africa and said that the kind of thinking behind such a differential valuation of life reminded him of apartheid. GCI also pointed out that 'willingness to pay' is used normally in cost-benefit analysis to assess benefits. To assess costs, it is normal to use 'willingness to accept compensation', which gives higher figures.

David Pearce said that the critics did not understand the methodology: 'The report simply says that people value risks differently. That valuation is affected by the level of their incomes.'[5] The alternative proposed – to value everyone's life equally – would increase the amount spent on disaster aversion and foreign aid: 'We would end up allocating all our national income to life-saving.'

What the IPCC economists were doing was making explicit the fact that we live in a world where the rich count for much more than the poor. If we valued the lives of people in the South equally to those in the West, we would do something about fact that millions of children die of malnutrition each year. But when Pearce told *New Scientist*, 'this is a matter of scientific correctness versus political correctness',[6] he was attempting to use the status of science to justify what was actually a political judgement.

Two of the IPCC economists, Samuel Fankhauser and Richard Tol,[7] responded to GCI, claiming that the issue of differential valuation was a red herring. They said they had no problems with using a global average value of life to assess world damages. But it would be an average value, not the Western value. Using such an average value would not change the overall results of their work. They also claimed that the difference between 'willingness to pay' and 'willingness to accept compensation' was irrelevant to the question of regionally different value estimates. 'Willingness to accept compensation' estimates might be higher, but they would still differ between regions. They added that the concept of uniform values at Western levels, as GCI had proposed, was flawed because the whole purpose of the regional damage analysis they had done was to capture the regional diversity and assess the differences in vulnerability.

The summary for policy makers on social costs[8] did not use the economists' figures, because of GCI's lobbying, but it emphasized that, while estimates for the damage to industrialized countries due to global warming were only one to a few percent of their GNP, estimates of damage to agricultural Southern countries were several times higher. The irony is that the responsibility for global warming lies with the industrialized countries which have been responsible for the vast majority of greenhouse gas emissions. Global warming is an excellent example of an issue that involves questions of both intergenerational and international equity.

What really made the economists' work so controversial was that their analysis did not take account of the inequity of the situation. It is in the nature of cost-benefit analysis that it ignores questions of equity. Instead, it values the luxuries of the rich more highly than the necessities of the poor, because by definition the poor cannot pay as much for necessities as the rich can pay for luxuries. This problem had been explored a few years earlier by Kerry Turner.[9] Cost-benefit analysis assumes that the losers will be compensated by the gainers. In this case, that would mean that the families of each Bangladeshi drowned because of rising sea levels would be compensated to the tune of US$100,000. But in practice, as Turner noted, those who gain in a cost-benefit analysis never have to compensate the losers.

Reliance on pricing discounts the welfare of people who are poor or not yet born. An irony is that David Pearce was one of the people who in the late 1980s showed that environmental degradation tends to hurt the poor, who cannot afford to protect themselves, more than the rich. Florida and the Netherlands can afford to protect their inhabitants from rising sea levels and storm damage in a way that Bangladesh cannot. Morally, it is impossible to justify the idea that Americans are worth 15 times more than Bangladeshis. The reality of the world we live in is that the lives of Americans do count for much more than the lives of Bangladeshis. Should our assessment of the cost of climate change be based on morality or current economic reality?

If we are talking about *Realpolitik*, the lives of people in the South count for almost nothing. The cost of ending hunger in the world would be a few billion dollars annually. Yet the rich choose instead to spend far more than that on countless luxuries for themselves.

An assessment of global warming damage based on 'willingness to pay' values is utterly pragmatic. But it is a political decision itself. Aubrey Meyer said:

This is another way of saying that people do not have an equal right to be here in the first place; your rights are proportional to your income. In terms of achieving sustainable development globally, this is nonsense. For practical as well as ethical purposes, each human being is – and must be recognized as – the fundamentally equal unit for measuring sustainability and this is the irreducible level of decision-taking.

At sub-global levels of 'economic' debate, this kind of wrangle is of familiar vintage. It is the substance of the traditional left/right arguments where those without money make 'equity-for-equity's sake' (principle) arguments, whilst those with the money make 'efficiency-for-efficiency's sake' (practicality) arguments. Whatever the rights and wrongs of this approach, equity and efficiency are seen as being traded off against each other between the left and the right. Much of the history of our political economy is a story about this false dichotomy.

At a global level this kind of economic discrimination is simply suicidal. It is discriminatory on a greater scale than before. But it is also dangerous and different in a manner which is without precedent... [T]here is nowhere else to go. There isn't a global carpet under which the waste, the pollution and the 'poor' can be swept and then ignored....[10]

Meyer's argument is rather like the 'greenmail' approach that the South attempted at UNCED. The problem that 'greenmail' has is that essentially Southern countries have to threaten to destroy their own environments. They obviously suffer much more from doing this than people in the North will. In the case of the global commons, like carbon dioxide emissions, the North itself is already acting in an unsustainable fashion. And, again, the South is much more vulnerable to the negative consequences than the North is. This makes the North feel that 'greenmail' is an implausible threat.

In a sense, it is irrelevant to Northern governments how much the people of Southern countries will suffer from global warming. The power to avert global warming lies with the North. All that the South can do is threaten to aggravate it. According to cynical *Realpolitik*, Northern countries will only take serious action against global warming if they believe that their countries will lose more if they do nothing to prevent it than if they take action. Actually, as Klaus Meyer-Abich has pointed out,[11] because political decisions are almost invariably taken on the basis of short-term rather than long-term considerations, drastic action on climate change will very likely only be taken if there is a short-term threat, such as from migration.

This all sounds rather depressing for anyone who cares about the poor or the future. The experience of sanctions against the apartheid regime in South Africa is worth bearing in mind, though. It took decades, but eventually the strength of the moral argument for solidarity with black South Africans came to predominate over arguments of economic self-interest and disingenuous arguments about protecting the welfare of the black population. Similarly, the strength of moral arguments eventually made the West intervene forcefully to stop ethnic cleansing in Bosnia and Kosovo. What these examples show is that morality doesn't really count for nothing in the world of international politics; but it only counts in rather exceptional circumstances when moral pressure has built up to a point where the short-term political pressures for action are greater than the short-term political pressures against such action. The Kyoto Protocol was a sign that the balance of such pressures had shifted in the direction of taking at least some action.

Discounting

Unfortunately, conventional economics reinforces this tendency in society towards short-term thinking. The practice of discounting future costs and benefits at the current rate of interest may make sense for individuals seeking to maximize their investments, but it encourages unsustainability. If US$1000 is discounted at a typical rate of 7 per cent per annum over 100 years, it is worth less than US$1 (0.1 per cent) at the end of the century. If a development will cause an environmental catastrophe costing US$1 trillion in 100 years' time, it is only worth taking action to prevent the disaster now if it will cost less than US$1 billion. If not, it is considered economically rational to go ahead and accept the future catastrophe.

There are essentially two rationales for discounting. The first is that people prefer the present to the future because of impatience, the risk of death and uncertainty about the future – 'a bird in the hand is worth two in the bush' is the saying frequently quoted. The second rationale is that we should discount the future at the current rate of return on investment. The idea here is that if I can expect to earn say 7 per cent per annum by investing my money now, it would be foolish of me to tie it up in something that would be worth less at the end of the term.

Economists often argue that discounting doesn't necessarily discriminate against future generations. Money invested today in economically productive activities will be worth more in the future. Additionally, given economic growth, people in the future will have higher incomes than people today. Because they will be richer, costs which seem huge to us will be more affordable. However, as environmentalists have frequently pointed out, this line of argument is based on a fallacy: more money doesn't mean more environment. Indeed, as economic growth degrades the environment, it is actually making environmental goods scarcer and therefore more valuable. Environmentalists accuse economists of being mistaken in their implicit assumption that the environment behaves like and can be compared to a sum of money.

The value of natural resources

The fundamental difference between economists and environmentalists is about what they value. The way that the depletion of 'natural capital' has been counted as income in national accounts symbolizes the way economists historically have treated the environment as valueless. Natural resources have been regarded by economists as free gifts. As late as the 1990s, Wilfred Beckerman tried to defend this practice. He argued that, although for some small developing countries dependent on a limited natural resource base, it might be a worthwhile exercise to adjust GNP for changes in natural capital, for large industrial countries or the whole world, it is 'a waste of time'.[12] For Beckerman, nature only has value so long as it can be turned into something economically valuable. Technology can turn many things which were once economically useless into valuable resources. He gives the example of unused land which can be made valuable by clearing it, or of bauxite that only became useful once techniques to turn it into aluminium were developed. He writes that 'if we were to adjust GNP estimates to allow for new discoveries as well as for resources used up, the result might be an upward adjustment, not a downward adjustment as is claimed by the environmentalists who clamour for more money to be spent on making estimates of 'sustainable' GNP.'[13]

The belief that underlies this view is that 'natural resources' are infinite or infinitely substitutable. Labour and capital are scarce, so valuable. Resources are not scarce, so they have no value beyond the cost of the labour and capital needed to obtain them. Beckerman claims that if we run out of anything, we will always be able to find a substitute because of technical progress. To what extent can we rely on technical progress? It depends on what it is for. Technical progress allows us to substitute for copper wire rather well. When Paul and Anne Ehrlich say that aluminium is an inferior substitute for copper as a conductor of electricity,[14] they sound rather desperate. Fibre optic cable is a superior substitute for copper wire as a carrier of information. The trouble is that there are many natural assets for which there are no feasible substitutes, the things like the ozone layer, rainforests and wetlands which David Pearce called 'critical natural capital'. Beckerman does not directly address the idea of 'critical natural capital'. His discussion of the idea of natural capital, as mentioned earlier, ignores such subtleties.

Money as a measuring rod

David Pearce argued in *Blueprint for a Green Economy* that the best way to protect natural capital is by assigning it an economic value. Environmental services, in particular, are often not bought and sold in the marketplace. If the market is left alone, environmental services will be treated as free goods and overused. Pearce proposed that the answer is to assign prices to these services based on what people would be willing to pay for them:

> Very simply, given limited resources, the rational thing to do is to choose between our preferences in an effort to get the most satisfaction – or 'welfare', to use the economist's term – we can. If we apply economics to environmental issues, then, we should expect to obtain some insights into the desirability of improving the environment further, taking the social objective of increasing people's overall satisfaction (or welfare) as given. This assumption about the social objective used to derive measures of gains and losses is important.

To be clear, what is being said is that an improvement in environmental quality is also an economic improvement if it increases social satisfaction or welfare.[15]

Pearce admitted that there are a number of questions and problems about the approach. What if we can improve the welfare of the present generation only at the expense of future generations? Should we look generations, centuries or millennia into the future? Is it legitimate to only consider human welfare, and not the welfare of other living beings? He wrote that social objectives must be chosen so that short-term gains in welfare do not lead to policies which are ultimately inconsistent with human existence or some minimum quality of life.

Pearce went on to defend using money to measure the preferences that people have. He wrote that money was a good measuring rod because it expressed the strength of preferences well. What does it mean to put a money value on the Californian condor or the African rhinoceros? People could object that these animals were 'beyond price'. Pearce wrote that nothing could really have infinite value. Even human life has a finite value, because we are not prepared to spend infinite sums of money to save lives.

Pearce's work shows quite well the way in which the application of cost-benefit analysis to global environmental issues works against the principles of intergenerational equity and intragenerational equity that lay at the core of the Brundtland Commission's definition of sustainable development. Because decisions are based on ability to pay, less weight is given to the interests of the poor and the future. Between people living at the same time and with similar incomes, money is a good indicator of strength of preferences. It is hard to see how it is a good measuring rod when comparing the preferences of Americans and Bangladeshis, or people today and people a hundred years from now.

My point is that there are two quite different ideas of what morality is. One view of morality is David Hume's – mutual cooperation for common benefit. The other view of morality is Immanuel Kant's – the equal consideration of interests. The first view means that more weight is given to the more powerful. The second view means that everybody's interests are regarded as equal.

Welfare economics

Welfare economics originally attempted to square this circle. The theory of marginal utility states that an additional unit of consumption (say, a dollar) is worth less in terms of welfare to a rich person than to a poor person. This means that, in determining which course of action leads to the greatest total welfare, it is important to consider not just what leads to the largest total wealth for society, but also the distribution of that wealth. It would seem like an impossibly difficult task to work out what that distribution would be.

According to orthodox economic theory, competitive markets will arrive at a *Pareto optimum distribution*, the largest total amount of wealth. Since it is the largest total, it is impossible to have a different distribution that would make one person better off without making another worse off. When economists refer to *optimality*, it is this situation they normally mean. Since very few projects will produce only gainers and no losers, in cost-benefit analysis, the *potential Pareto optimum* is instead used. The potential Pareto is the distribution where the losers from the proposed project are compensated for their losses by the gainers. Since a project is only deemed worthy by cost-benefit analysis if the economic benefits outweigh the economic costs, there will still be some money left over for the gainers to keep. However, in practice losers are not compensated. The entire logic behind cost-benefit analysis is lost.

Another problem is that even if a potential Pareto distribution was achieved (by gainers compensating losers), if the original distribution did not optimize welfare (rather than total wealth), the new distribution will not either, except by fortuitous accident. That is because the redistribution does not solve the problem of the suboptimality of the earlier distribution. It only compensates the losers from the new distribution for the change.

Cost-benefit analysis is central to neoclassical welfare economics. Welfare economics, taking account of marginal utility theory, regards the best distribution as the most egalitarian one that still maximizes the total income. Redistribution distorts the market and reduces total income, so neoclassical economists oppose it. However, a certain amount of redistribution would actually *increase* total welfare even when *reducing* total income, because it is redirecting income to those for whom the marginal utility of an additional dollar is greater. In principle, it is possible to try to adjust the results of cost-benefit analysis by weighting the effects on poorer groups more than on wealthier groups, but that is rarely done. Instead, welfare economists decided in the 1930s that interpersonal comparisons of utility were 'ethical' and so 'unscientific'. From now on, they would value everything in terms of money, not utility, rather detaching welfare economics from its philosophical foundations.[16]

Contingent valuation

Cost-benefit analysis of nature preservation relies on *contingent valuation* surveys. In these surveys, ordinary people are asked how much they personally would be prepared to pay for some environmental benefit or to prevent some piece of environmental destruction. Based on the average amount of money people say they would be prepared to pay, economists calculate the total monetary value members of society place on that aspect of the environment. If the economic benefits of a development would exceed that sum, it is deemed to be of net benefit.

Many people have been doubtful about the validity of the conclusions of contingent valuation surveys as they make assumptions that can be challenged. Contingent valuation assumes that people perceive their environment as a set of discrete objects that could be bought and sold. It also assumes that value is essentially derived just from individual self-interest. Certainly, these are assumptions that are taken as correct by nearly all economists. But do ordinary citizens think that way? And do they feel the questions they are asked are meaningful?

It has been known for a long time that many people surveyed for contingent valuation refuse to answer the questions. But what do the people who do participate think? People who had taken part in a contingent valuation exercise were asked what they thought about it by a separate team of researchers. It turned out that the people valued nature as a common good, not in terms of money. Many told the researchers that they felt they had been misled by the economists, who had not told them how their answers would be used. They thought that decisions about conservation should be based on open democratic debate, rather than the results of secret questionnaires.[17] These findings cast very serious doubt on the validity of contingent valuation surveys.

Contingent valuation surveys were originally introduced as a way of attempting to reform cost-benefit analysis so as to account for environmental values. Traditional cost-benefit analysis ignores environmental values entirely, and effectively gives them zero weight. Even when separate environmental impact assessments are made as well, such as for road building schemes in Britain, planners have tended to pay them very little attention.[18]

Cost-benefit analysis attempts to use money as a common measuring rod to express people's values. When resources are scarce, we have to make decisions about how much to prioritize different choices. It is commonly said that human life is 'priceless', but in reality we are not prepared to spend all our income on life saving. Michael Jacobs asserts that no one actually thinks a life is 'worth' a certain amount of money.[19] Human lives are not saleable commodities. The use of money values for human lives reflect that decisions must be taken between alternative states of affairs, and one must be regarded as more valuable than another. His point is that 'value' in this context is simply a relative term expressing a ranking between alternative states of affairs. It does not require any connection with money or any other external scale of measurement. Jacobs argues that irreversible environmental losses (like the extinction of a species) are regarded by people in a similar way. He does not think it is meaningful to say that the preservation of a particular species, say, is 'worth' less than a million dollars a year. It must be compared with the alternatives. People might think that it was less valuable than spending a million dollars to prevent a famine, but more valuable than spending a million dollars on nuclear weapons.

Cost-benefit analysis and sustainability

The fundamental weakness with cost-benefit analysis from the viewpoint of sustainability is that it is not really able to deal with the concept. In *Blueprint for a Green Economy*, David Pearce proposed that in addition to cost-benefit analysis, a sustainability constraint should exist as an additional criterion for decision making. To simply forbid any project which depleted natural capital would be stultifying, but part of the proceeds from any proposed project that depleted natural capital should be put into compensatory projects to maintain natural capital, such as reforestation schemes.

Kerry Turner identified four levels of environmentalism in terms of their attitude to cost-benefit analysis.[20] Conventional cost-benefit analysis has an 'exploitationist' world view. It is based on a particular kind of individualist utilitarian framework which has no interest in considerations of equity. It views nature solely as a collection of goods and services of instrumental value to human beings. The future value of the environment is discounted and justified by the assumption that economic growth will allow human-made capital to substitute for natural capital.

The modified cost-benefit analysis proposed by environmental economists has a 'conservationist' world view. It requires maintaining a constant stock of natural assets out of concern for future generations. Turner claims that this is incompatible with utilitarianism, as it involves conferring 'rights' on members of future generations who do not yet exist. It implies a contractarian moral philosophy, perhaps based on the theories of John Rawls. A 'conservationist' world view protects nature only on the grounds that human beings can benefit from its existence. The interests of non-humans are not directly considered, although the conservation of natural capital would tend to conserve the habitats of non-human life forms.

The radically modified cost-benefit analysis proposed by many environmentalists puts environmental considerations before economic ones. Economic analysis would be used only to indicate the most cost-effective ways of achieving environmental goals. This 'moderate preservationist' world view would allow for some exploitation of ecosystems as long as they remained 'healthy' and biologically diverse. Turner links it to Aldo Leopold's 'land ethic'.[21] Essentially, it gives value to biological diversity, but not to individuals.

According to Turner, deep ecologists abandon cost-benefit analysis in favour of granting intrinsic value to nature. Intrinsic value is independent of any usefulness to human beings. The aim becomes to maximize the sum of intrinsic and instrumental values, or some variant of this rule. One possibility would be to place intrinsic value above instrumental value so that human society has to use the minimum of resources in order not to deplete intrinsic value more than absolutely necessary. Turner claims that such an approach might involve sacrificing basic human values, including 'fundamental rights to exist at an acceptable standard of living.'[22] Turner argues that the incidental effect of maintaining constant natural capital is to protect the values that are of concern to believers in the intrinsic value of nature.

Conventional cost-benefit analysis appears unable to deal with the implications of thinking about sustainable development. A concern for intergenerational equity would at the very least require an additional sustainability constraint to safeguard the interests of future generations, as David Pearce proposed in 1989. In addition, the current practice of cost-benefit analysis takes an approach to questions of intragenerational distribution which is internally inconsistent.

The problems with cost-benefit analysis go beyond that, though. Basing ethical decisions on economic value seems by its nature to skew decisions so as to favour the interests of wealthy people in the present day. The interests of the poor, future generations and other species are all discounted by the approach. The problem lies not simply in the practice of cost-benefit analysis, but is really a result of the utilitarian ethical framework of mainstream economics. The next chapter will argue that a reform of mainstream economic theory to incorporate the concerns of sustainability and sustainable development would involve replacing its rather strange version of utilitarianism with a different ethical and political framework.

8

The Ethics of Sustainability

The true measure of a man is how he treats someone who can do him absolutely no good.

– Samuel Johnson

Introduction

The ethical framework of economic utilitarianism may be unable to cope with the concerns of sustainability, but what should be put in its place? The issue is about what we regard as ethically acceptable in terms of the distribution of well-being, sacrifice and risks between rich and poor, the present and the future, and humans and non-humans. That is an enormous field of moral philosophy to consider. Fortunately for our purposes, much of the recent debate has centred around the influence of one work, John Rawls' *A Theory of Justice.*[1] Rawls concentrated on the issue of equity within generations in his work, putting forward a strong critique of the utilitarian approach. It is not always appreciated how well his approach can be extended to consider the issue of equity between generations. This chapter outlines Rawls' ethical framework for relations within and between generations, and goes on to suggest implications for a Rawlsian approach to the ethics of sustainability. Finally, the chapter considers the tensions between sustainability and liberalism, concluding that sustainability is more compatible with ethical socialism.

Utility or fairness?

There are basically two approaches to moral philosophy which have been popular in the West since the 19th century. One has been utilitarianism, the other has been contractarianism. The whole idea of equity as a fundamental principle is alien to utilitarianism, which seeks primarily to maximize the total amount of happiness (utility). The very idea of intergenerational equity is therefore contrary to utilitarianism, which largely explains why mainstream economists have had such difficulty in coming to terms with it.

Contractarian moral philosophies, like Rousseau's and Kant's, had an enormous influence in the 18th century Enlightenment and continued to be highly influential in continental Europe. But in English-speaking countries, the utilitarian philosophies developed by Bentham, Mill and Sidgwick for a time became extremely influential among the intellectual elites. What is more, because of the interest the utilitarian philosophers had in economics, their moral assumptions were adopted by economists throughout the capitalist world as the only rational approach.

The aim of classical utilitarianism is to maximize total utility. Jeremy Bentham put it as 'the greatest good for the greatest number.' The idea utilitarians had was that it was possible to create a 'calculus of utility', working out what would be the gains and losses in happiness over time resulting from any particular action. The morally correct action would be the one that would lead to the greatest increase in total happiness.

One well known objection to classical utilitarianism was that it seemed to call for an increase in population until the point where the increase in total happiness (marginal utility) of each additional person was only slightly greater than zero. What that would mean was a world with an enormous, but overcrowded and impoverished, population. Surely, critics said, there was something wrong here? One utilitarian who agreed was John Stuart Mill. He put forward an alternative conception of utilitarianism, where the aim was the greatest *average*, not total, utility.

Most philosophers, and many other people, continued to find utilitarianism morally obnoxious. Acts which, on balance, lead to an increase in average utility are regarded as moral, regardless of the suffering they may cause to innocent individuals. The dignity of the individual counts for nothing in utilitarianism. This was brilliantly satirized by Aldous Huxley in *Brave New World*.[2]

The weakness of the utilitarians' opponents was that, although they had good arguments against utilitarian morality, they could not put forward a similarly broad social theory, or one that did not seem to rely on highly subjective judgements. John Rawls countered utilitarianism by reviving Kant's tradition of contractarian moral theory in a modern form. He started by considering what kind of social arrangements free and rational people would agree to in an original position of equality. This hypothetical situation would take place behind a 'veil of ignorance'. They would not know their place in society, their class, their natural abilities, the society's level of economic development or what generation they lived in. They would not even know what their personal conception of the good life would be. The veil of ignorance would prevent individuals or groups from being able to engineer the structure of society on the basis of particular interests. A society based on principles that would be agreed in this original position could be seen as 'fair' for all.

Rawls argued that people in his original position would choose a society based on two principles. The first would be of the most extensive basic liberties for each person consistent with a similar liberty for others. The second would be that social and economic inequalities of outcome, such as inequalities of wealth and authority, are just only if they result in compensating benefits for everyone, and in particular for the worst off. The principles rule out justifying institutions on the grounds that hardships for some are offset by greater good for others. Rawls claimed that it is unjust for some people to have less so that other people can be better off, but it is not unjust for some people to be better off than others provided that the situation of the less fortunate is improved by the inequality. The idea was that since everybody's well-being depends on cooperation, without which nobody could have a satisfactory life, the division of advantages should be of a kind that everyone, including the worst off, could accept. Greater natural ability or being born into a better social position are not deserved, he said, and inequality of outcome can only be justified to the worse off if they benefit in absolute terms from it.

Rawls' second principle is a maximin rule. He drew from game theory to support his claim that his original position is one where the rational strategy is maximin. A maximin strategy is best in situations of uncertainty where probabilities are difficult to predict, when it is not worthwhile to take a risk of a poor outcome for a particularly good one, or when some potential outcomes are particularly poor. All three conditions apply to the original position.

Rawls pointed to a paradox in utilitarianism: 'when society is conceived as a system of cooperation designed to advance the good of its members, it seems quite incredible that some citizens should be expected, on the basis of political principles, to accept lower prospects of life for the sake of others.'[3] Rawls argued that utilitarianism requires self-sacrifice by the most disadvantaged members of society for the benefit of the more fortunate. Would anyone who might actually find themselves in this situation be prepared to agree to it?

Rawls claimed that the fundamental problem with utilitarianism is that it does not take seriously the distinction between individuals. The principle of rational choice for one person – to maximize happiness – is taken as the principle of social choice as well. Utilitarianism sums all individuals into an infinitely sympathetic and impartial spectator. The spectator is one self who includes all desires and satisfactions within one experience while imaginatively identifying with all the members of society. Only a perfect altruist would be capable of doing this. To choose to live in a utilitarian society, you would have to be a perfect altruist. Utilitarianism may be the choice of an outside observer, but actual human beings would be incapable of living that way.

Although the publication of *A Theory of Justice* created a philosophical sensation upon its publication in 1971, it has subsequently drawn a great deal of criticism. Although Rawls' theory at first appears extremely systematic and thorough, careful reading reveals numerous contradictory details.

Most importantly, Rawls' claim that the difference principle is the most rational choice from behind the veil of ignorance has been widely criticized by many philosophers. The difference principle is the most inequality-averse choice of a range of distribution schemes that could be chosen. A utilitarian distribution would be the least inequality-averse choice. There are an infinite number of distributions in between offering different trade-offs between average welfare and the well-being of the least fortunate. Conversely, Rawls' difference principle depends on the assumption that people are not envious. They would not object to inequality *per se*, provided that everyone was better off in terms of social goods as a consequence. This assumption has been criticized as unrealistic about human nature. Rawls, however, argued that envy is not a *just* emotion.

Equity between generations

So much for Rawls' discussion of equity between individuals, but what about equity between generations? He saw this as being a particularly difficult problem for any ethical system. His discussion of intergenerational equity preceded currents concerns about the global environment, and was mostly concerned with the rate of savings. Even so, Rawls' ideas about intergenerational equity are still quite interesting to examine.

Rawls' aim was to maximize the long-term prospects of the least favoured over future generations. Each generation should not only preserve the benefits of culture and civilization it inherited, but also set something aside for capital accumulation. Rawls argued that, although it might seem that the least favoured first generation would have no obligation to save for later generations, actually justice between generations should not follow his difference principle in the same way as for justice within a generation. That was because there is no way for later generations to help or harm earlier generations: 'We can do something for posterity, but it can do nothing for us. This situation is unalterable, and so the question of justice does not arise.'[4]

He looked at the problem of the savings rate between generations from the standpoint of the original position: 'The parties do not know to which generation they belong, or what comes to the same thing, the stage of civilization of their society.'[5] People in the original position would ask themselves what they would think would be a fair savings rate at each stage of civilization, without knowing what stage they would live in. Rawls thought that at times when people were poor and savings difficult, a low rate would be required. In a wealthier society, the real burden of a higher rate of saving would be lower. Once the society had become wealthy and developed enough to have acquired all the institutions of Rawlsian justice, the savings rate would fall to zero. He did not see the goal of society as great wealth, but liberty and justice for all. He felt that beyond a certain level wealth would become a distraction or even a temptation to indulgence.

Each generation would save in order to enable the next generation to enjoy a better life, because they care about their descendents. Each generation, except the first, would benefit from previous capital accumulation. So the people in the original position, who might find themselves at any stage of civilization, would consider what would be a fair savings rate at any point in history. They could then apply the appropriate rate for their generation.

Writing 20 years later, Rawls modified his theory to contain the stipulation that the people in the original position must agree to a savings principle subject to the further condition that they would have wanted all previous generations to have followed it.[6]

It seems to me that the biggest problem with Rawls' approach to intergenerational equity is the conceptual difficulty people have with it. John Pezzey said to me:

> I've heard *endless* arguments about the philosophy of intergenerational equity and they all come back to some sense that if you were forced to choose between where you are now and some future generation then might you think differently? Might that not be cause to consider what would be a fair thing to do? And the answer that I always come out with is that is *such* a hypothetical consideration that it would be meaningless to most people... I have this fairly naive reaction that at least it is in some sense physically possible to *conceive* of taking you from your current economic and social position and swapping you with some bum on the streets or queen in her palace... It would violate all sort of human rights, but we could physically conceive of it happening... Time travel doesn't exist. You *cannot* switch yourself with someone a hundred years ago or a hundred years in the future... You're being asked to hypothesize something that's *completely* infeasible. There is not going to be any kind of intergenerational contract. This notion of getting different generations to meet behind a veil of ignorance, it's *so* bizarre that I can't attach any great significance to it.

Pezzey is right in suggesting that trying to apply contract theory to intergenerational equity seems bizarre. The Kantian imperative to do to others as you would be done by them makes some practical sense when others are in a position to retaliate. But there is no way to enforce any kind of intergenerational contract. Even so, Pezzey has written that it is very hard to give a reason for caring about potential people in future centuries other than by appealing to basic intuitive notions of fairness.

In fact, there is a difference between Rawls' treatment of justice within generations and justice between generations. For justice within a generation Rawls' theory of 'justice as fairness' is to imagine a *procedurally* fair way for a group of people who did not care for each other's welfare to agree on a structure for society that defended everyone's interests. But Rawls' thought experiment could never be conducted in real life because the participants would know what their actual personal attributes were and would be influenced by that knowledge.

The difference in the case of justice between generations is not so much the impossibility of a meeting between generations, but the impossibility of enforcement of any intergenerational contract. Without a time machine, later generations are absolutely powerless to retaliate against a non-cooperative earlier generation. Rawls himself saw this fact preventing the inclusion of members of different generations in the original position. However, one of his students, David

Richard, did not accept this view.[7] He argued that a person's generational position is a morally arbitrary fact in the same way as their sex or race. It is a question of whether justice is a matter of mutual advantage or a matter of equal consideration.

There are difficulties in extending the original position to a meeting between generations, but it is interesting to consider the idea. As Brian Barry[8] pointed out, Rawls' treatment of justice between generations assumes that if each generation cares for its children, all will be well. Rawls did not consider the possibility of doing things that might not have negative effects for several generations. But Barry does not work through the implications of this comment. Rawls had rejected the idea of applying the difference principle to justice between generations on the grounds that the poorest first generation would not save to allow later generations to become more prosperous.

But the issue of justice between generations is much more complicated than Rawls allows. There is no reason to suppose that the first generation is necessarily going to be the worst off one. Wilfred Beckerman claims that the strict application of Rawlsian principles to justice between generations would either lead to all generations sharing the poverty of the first, or 'if we can rely on technical progress without savings and capital accumulation, earlier generations would be justified in running down their initial endowment of natural capital.'[9] But Beckerman is assuming that 'technical progress' can occur without any investment, and that natural capital can be expended without negative effects on future generations. The first assumption is impossible, the second merely extremely improbable, depending on a very high rate of technical progress capable of solving all problems indefinitely.

When you think about what Rawlsian principles would mean intergenerationally, it becomes clear that the choices of each generation influence which future generations, if any, exist. It is perfectly reasonable to rely on Rawls' idea that the people in the original position do not know which generation they belong to. Not knowing which generation they belong to, it is their job to draw up the principles they would be prepared to live by if all other generations lived by them too. However, we have to consider not only the generations which will actually exist, but all the *potential* generations which might exist. Beckerman objects that temporally different generations cannot be represented because the choice in the original position will determine how many generations exist. That is a literal-minded misunderstanding that even some philosophers have also fallen into when discussing Rawls. The whole point of the original position is as a device to force the reader to consider what kind of structures they would agree to live under if they did not know where in those structures they would actually end up.

Rawls' idea was that the savings rate should start out very low in a poor society, rise as incomes rose, and then fall away to zero when a prosperous society had emerged. Rawls saw no value in an extremely affluent society, as it implied an emphasis on materialist and consumerist values. If you imagine yourself in the original position, not knowing which generation you would belong to, this slight deviation from the difference principle is not so unreasonable, because very large economic benefits accrue to later generations for the sake of a small sacrifice from the earliest generations, thanks to the power of exponential increase.

When you consider environmental risks, which Rawls ignored, the difference principle re-emerges as a sensible strategy under situations of uncertainty where the actual risks are unknown. In this case, it is the difference principle not between members of the same generation or between different generations. It is the difference principle between potential worlds. In other words, it seems to me that you would want your predecessors to have chosen the path of development with the best worst-case outcome for your generation. The first rule to fall out of this would be the precautionary principle. The second rule would be strong sustainability. Anything less than strong sustainability does not guarantee future generations the ability to maintain their welfare in a worst-case outcome.

Genes for the future?

An alternative approach to sustainability, pioneered by John Pezzey,[10] is by appealing to genetically-based motivations. Human beings generally show a great deal of concern for their children's futures. Dennis Meadows told me: 'They *do* care about their children. They don't care about anybody else's children.' This is a common sceptical response to the claim that people care about the future. The general point was dealt with by Herman Daly and John Cobb. They pointed out that your great-great grandchild will also be the great-great grandchild of 15 other people in the current generation, and presumably your great-great grandchild's wellbeing will depend as much on the other 15 as on you. The further in the future you look, the greater the number of people in the present generation who will be their ancestors, and consequently the more of a public good is any provision made for the distant future.

Daly and Cobb argue that the consequence of sexual reproduction is towards community concern and away from individualism. John Pezzey instead makes the rather different point that it is sexual reproduction which makes concern for the future a public good, rather than something to be left to individuals.[11] He speculated that we discount the future to reflect the dilution of our genes over the generations. Pezzey developed a mathematical model which shows that the 'mating externalities' of sexual reproduction would tend to lead individuals to reduce their bequests to their children below the 'socially optimal' rate that would be calculated in traditional economic models which assume asexual reproduction. Pezzey showed that even when considering the welfare of the next generation or two, sexual reproduction introduces externalities that can lead to the future being treated in a suboptimal (let alone unsustainable) way. Sexual reproduction makes sustainability and the welfare of your descendants a public good. The nature of the situation means that individuals' concern for their children is not enough; sustainability is a public good which requires public policies to influence behaviour.

It seems that the genetic dilution caused by sexual reproduction may make it a rational strategy for individuals to discount the welfare of future generations in personal decisions, but also makes it rational for individuals who care about the long-term success of their genes to support the collective welfare of the group their descendants will breed within. Such arguments have been used by evolutionary psychologists to explain the evolution of morality.

The distinction between private and public choices, between situations where free riding is easy and where it is hard, is the difference between being a consumer and being a citizen. Michael Jacobs has argued that while it is rational to discount the future as a consumer, it is not rational to do so as a citizen.[12]

The idea of genetic dilution makes things more complicated, though. When people think about the situation of their descendants, they tend to think of people in a similar relative social position to themselves. But in industrialized societies, class structures are not so rigid between generations. New Right thinkers like Hayek have used this point to support the idea that large inequalities of wealth reflect differences in individual effort and ability, rather than social oppression. So they call for us to leave the distribution of wealth to the invisible hand of the market, as classical utilitarianism does. However, the New Right elevates the freedom of bequest to the status of a basic human right, which undermines economic efficiency (and social justice) by creating a class system. The choice of rich people who want genetic success would be a rigid class system. People at the bottom of the social scale would want a socialist revolution tomorrow to increase their immediate genetic success. The bulk of people between the two extremes would want a social minimum to protect their less fortunate descendants. But they would perhaps not want such an inequality-averse society as the Rawlsian one, as that would not serve the interests of their more fortunate descendants.

In a society with reasonably open breeding patterns, the long-term genetic interests of the individual converge over several generations with the interests of the entire future society. It would be highly irrational to favour any policy which might conceivably threaten the long-term survival of the genetic group, still less the species. In fact, the rational strategy to support would be a maximin one which chose the approach to the economy and the environment where the best of the worst conceivable outcomes was chosen. Mainstream economists, such as Partha Dasgupta, would consider this strategy highly 'risk averse', but that is only because, just as economic utilitarianism fails to take seriously the difference between the individual and society, it fails to take seriously the difference between the individual and the species.

No matter how seriously you take arguments from genetic self-interest, it should be clear that there is something very irrational about risking the extinction of our species for potential economic advantage. When Partha Dasgupta suggested discounting the benefit of economic developments by the percentage of the risk of their making the human race extinct, he unwittingly showed how unreal mainstream economics is. Such a view comes from the economic approach of summing all possible futures from any set of policies and then looking to see which set of policies gives the highest average income across different futures. The extinction of the human race counts as an outcome leading to zero income.

It might be objected that taking such extreme risks is not unknown. We took the risk of extinction in the Cold War nuclear arms race. It was a strategy satirized as saying 'better dead than red.' It wasn't a situation that was freely chosen, though. It arose by historical accident. The approach mainstream economics takes to environmental issues is to *choose* the risk of extinction rather than give up the possibility of a higher income. It seems to miss the point that the extinction of the human race is quite a serious thing to risk for the possibility of greater economic gain: 'better dead than green' could be the motto.

A similar argument can be applied against the claim of economists like Nordhaus that it is economically irrational to forego more income by limiting increases in greenhouse gas concentrations than it is expected to cost.[13] Assuming for a moment that the estimate of the costs of global warming is not mistaken, the question that has to be asked is how confident you can be that global warming will turn out exactly as the economist expects. Wilfred Beckerman likened the precautionary principle to buying an expensive padlock for a cheap bicycle that was very unlikely to be stolen.[14] The difference, of course, is that you can always go out and buy another cheap bicycle if yours is stolen, but it is difficult to go out and buy a new planet if the one you live on is environmentally devastated. The situation is rather more comparable with taking out fire insurance on your home. The insurance company has calculated how likely it is that your home will burn down and calculates the rates so that it makes a profit. Only an idiot (or perhaps an economist) would not take out fire insurance on the grounds that the expected loss from fire was somewhat less than the expected loss from the insurance premium. If your house burns down and you have no insurance, then your life will be ruined. An insurance premium is affordable protection against such a disaster. Beckerman argued that because the precautionary principle is preventative, it is more like a smoke detector than fire insurance. But it is extremely difficult to understand his view that prevention is worse than compensation.

It is sometimes claimed that the precautionary principle demands absolute proof of safety and will accept no risk, which are of course impossible demands to make in the real world. But in reality the precautionary principle just shifts the burden of proof from those who want to avoid risks to those who want to take risks, much as the burden of proof lies with the prosecution in criminal trials or with the hypothesis in statistical tests. The prosecution does not have to prove beyond *any* doubt that the defendant is guilty, only that the evidence puts their guilt beyond *reasonable* doubt. The reason for that is because it is held that condemning an innocent person is significantly worse than allowing a guilty person to go free. For a new scientific hypothesis to be accepted by the scientific community, there has to be evidence showing that it is much more likely than the alternatives. This is because science tries to avoid accepting new hypotheses too readily.

Development brings risks as well as benefits, so it is not unreasonable to demand solid evidence of safety. This demand is already made before the introduction of new medicines. In the United States and some other countries, evidence of safety is demanded before the introduction of new pesticides. But in areas such as nuclear power, ozone depletion, global warming and genetic modification, it has instead been the case that in most countries the burden of proof has been placed on those who sought to minimize risk. In other words, they have had to show that it is much more likely that it is dangerous than that it is safe. It is worth noting in this context that the nuclear and biotechnology industries have been unable to obtain liability insurance on the commercial market, but have instead persuaded governments to indemnify them against liability.

The preceding discussions have revealed something important: that although sustainability may be compatible with Rawlsian liberalism, it does not seem to be consistent with utilitarian liberalism. That is not to say that sustainability is necessarily incompatible with a collectivist form of right wing politics, such as some kind of conservatism. But it is inconsistent with utilitarianism's disregard for risk and with economic liberalism more generally, which cannot allow the workings of the market to become subservient to collective concerns. As Anthony Giddens has pointed out, the anti-capitalist traditional conservatism of the landed gentry is more or less extinct today. Contemporary conservatives are in fact economic liberals.[15]

Liberalism and sustainability

The ecocentric green Robyn Eckersley has claimed that a sustainable society could only be socialist and not be liberal because of the necessarily expansionist and individualist nature of capitalism.[16] Her challenge has been addressed by Marcel Wissenburg in his attempt to at least partially reconcile the green agenda with liberalism.[17] Wissenburg admits that there is a serious problem with the Lockean justification of private property which has traditionally underpinned liberalism, because it is based on the assumption that natural resources are abundant, so that a property right to a resource presumes that enough is left for others; modern variants (such as Robert Nozick's[18]) assume that there can be infinite compensation for stock reductions, requiring infinite recycling (which is of course thermodynamically impossible). Wissenburg believes that there are limits to growth. However, Wissenburg supports Nozick's view that the absence of a justification for private ownership does not automatically justify collective ownership, so any attempt to defend collective ownership would be met with the same problems. This is a *non sequitur* because it begs a number of questions.

From an ecocentric perspective, it can be asked why we should assume that human beings do have right to own the natural world, so there is no need for a forced choice between private and collective ownership. But even if that was granted, unequal private ownership of resources means that some people will be left without enough, if resources are scarce rather than abundant, in a way that is not the case with collective ownership. Finally, there could be strictly equal private ownership. Nonetheless, Wissenburg goes on without discussion to assume the legitimacy of unequally distributed private property, despite having notably failed to give any argument for doing so.

Wissenburg also holds that the individual owns themselves, including the products of their natural endowments and talents. Here, he takes issue with Rawls' argument that the distribution of talents and handicaps among people is morally arbitrary, requiring compensation of some kind. Wissenburg supports the argument that just because somebody does not deserve their natural endowments does not mean that society does. Wissenburg adheres to the view that Rawls is more a social democrat than a liberal, as he does not entirely support the tenet of the individual's self-ownership because Rawls sees society as a system of cooperation. Wissenburg's idea that an individual is entitled to the marginal market value of their economic activities is based not only on the idea that distribution of rewards on the basis of natural talents is just, but also on assumptions about the legitimacy of private property and the 'naturalness' of the values assigned by the market.

However, Wissenburg does not believe in completely unrestricted private ownership. Attempting to green liberalism, he proposes the 'restraint principle', which states that:

> No goods shall be destroyed unless that is unavoidable and unless they are replaced by perfectly identical goods; if that is physically impossible, they should be replaced by equivalent goods resembling the original as closely as possible; and if that is impossible, a proper compensation should be provided.[19]

Wissenburg's justification of the restraint principle starts from Rawls' reformulation of his savings principle. The new savings principle states that parties in the original condition would be mutually disinterested, but 'agree to a savings principle subject to the condition that they would have wanted all previous generations to have followed it'.[20] Additionally, society is conceived as 'a system of cooperation between generations over time'.[21] Wissenburg claims that Rawls is seeing generations as existing next to each other, rather than one after another, thereby doing away with the need to assume concern for the next generation. Wissenburg argues that although a generation could defect on the requirement to save, they would lose the social bond and with it the benefits of social cooperation, so it would be irrational for them to do so. Therefore, people in the original condition would be bound to choose the revised savings principle.

Wissenburg goes on to argue that individuals in *any* liberal theory of society would follow Rawls' revised savings principle because it would simply be rational for goal-maximizing individuals to seek the mutual benefit of a savings principle. Wissenburg asserts that the intergenerational savings principle should take the form of his 'restraint principle'. However, the restraint principle is like very weak sustainability because it allows for 'proper compensation' in monetary terms for the use of resources that cannot be substituted, with no recognition of critical natural capital.

There prove to be significant conflicts between sustainability and liberalism. The crucial idea for Wissenburg, as a liberal, is that individuals should be allowed to live according to their individual views of the good life. He examines the issue of population, considering a dozen arguments for restricting people's freedom to have as many children as they want in order to prevent overpopulation. Wissenburg is only prepared to accept controls on procreation for the sake of *survival*, not *sustainability*:

> ...we would have to do something our stringent interpretation of liberal democracy will not allow us to do: discuss and if necessary dismiss people's ideas of the good life: that is, violate the liberty of life. In particular, it would lead us to question... the relative benefits of having children and of preventing a reduction of natural capital, a deterioration of the natural environment or however it be expressed. In other words, we would be forced to say that a plan of life that requires the depletion of our natural resources is not reasonable, hence that individuals' reasons for procreating should be open to public scrutiny and judgement... [I]t is a special case of a more general problem: the procedural view of justice inherent in our moral standard is incompatible with the substantive standards that any theorist and proponent of the sustainable or green or Green society would have to set.[22]

Turning to consumption issues, Wissenburg concludes similarly that people's desires for things that they themselves consider necessary for a tolerable life cannot be interfered with: 'people's needs – for company, children, food, technology, travel and trinkets – are private affairs; control, if possible at all, is impermissible.'[23]

Another liberal, Mark Sagoff, has argued that liberalism and environmentalism are not incompatible because environmentalism deals with public matters, such as the flow of pollution into rivers, while liberalism is concerned with protecting freedom in the private sphere, such as the bedroom.[24] But unfortunately Wissenburg's view that issues of personal consumption also fall into what liberalism considers to be the private sphere appears to be shared by most liberals, including Sagoff.

Wissenburg's book painfully reveals the limits of liberalism. Faced with unlimited individual wants and limited resources, the liberal prefers the tragedy of the commons to state intervention. Far from answering Eckersley, Wissenburg seems to confirm her criticism that 'liberal ideas were born in and depend upon a frontier setting and an expanding stock of wealth, with claims for distributive justice being appeased by the 'trickle down' effect (which maintains relative inequalities in wealth and power).'[25]

The liberal conception of freedom is about 'freedom from' acts of coercion by others (negative liberty). It is not about 'freedom to' actually be able to do something (positive liberty). If some people's personal consumption fills up the atmosphere with greenhouse gases that leads to climate change which drowns the homes and livelihoods of people in Bangladesh or the Maldives, the right to freedom from state intervention in the first group's private affairs must outweigh the latter group's freedom to live in their homes. Luke Martell has argued that liberal theories are so obsessed with the threat of state coercion that they open up the way for other forms of compulsion – through natural necessity or market forces – which are rather perversely not considered to be limitations on freedom.[26]

It is a familiar objection to liberalism. What is new is that it is today used as an argument about the role of environmental limits. Liberals generally defend themselves against criticism of negative liberty by citing Isiah Berlin's famous essay 'Two Concepts of Liberty'.[27] Berlin argued that although the two conceptions of liberty were not originally so different, the concept of positive liberty had lent itself to the notion of being the 'master of oneself.' From there it was a short step to the idea that certain desires and passions should be restrained; that there is a 'true' freedom to be found through the mastery of history by a class, a state or a nation. The freedom of individuals to do what they actually want is subsumed to this ideology.

It is interesting to note that Berlin's objection to positive liberty was not anything in the concept of positive liberty itself, but its Jacobin and Leninist perversions. Berlin's critics also pointed out that negative liberty could easily be used as a justification for a different kind of oppression. Berlin later admitted that this was true:

It is doubtless well to remember that belief in negative freedom is compatible with, and (so far as ideas influence conduct) has played its part in, great and lasting social evils. My point is that it was much less often defended or disguised by the kind of specious arguments and sleights-of-hand habitually used by the champions of 'positive' freedom in its more sinister forms. Advocacy of non-interference (like 'social Darwinism') was, of course, used to support politically and socially destructive policies which armed the strong, the brutal, and the unscrupulous against humane and the weak, the able and the ruthless against the less gifted and the less fortunate. Freedom for the wolves has often meant death to the sheep.[28]

Berlin also admitted that in the absence of the minimum conditions to exercise a freedom it is meaningless: 'what are rights without the power to implement them?'[29] Perhaps rather disingenuously, he claimed that the case for social legislation, planning, the welfare state and socialism could be constructed in terms of negative liberty as much as positive liberty. He gave the explanation for the liberal emphasis on negative liberty as being because the evil it was directed against was not *laissez-faire*, but despotism. Writing in 1969, he went on to say: 'Each concept seems liable to perversion into the very vice which it was created to resist. But whereas liberal ultra-individualism could scarcely be said to be a rising force at present, the rhetoric of 'positive' liberty, at least in its distorted form, is in far greater evidence, and continues to play its historic role (in both capitalist and anti-capitalist societies) as a cloak for despotism in the name of wider freedom.'[30] Today, the situation is rather different.

Sustainability is implicitly based on the concept of positive liberty. The conservation of natural capital is a limitation of negative liberty in the present in order to allow future generations greater positive liberty by leaving them more choices. A critic could argue that sustainability involves restricting liberty for the sake of a supposedly 'higher' freedom – rather like Communism did. That is what a liberal like Wissenburg might say. I think that the objection would only have real strength if sustainability was implemented undemocratically, by means of terror, like Jacobinism and Communism. They can be criticized for failing to live up to their own promise of increasing positive liberty and in that perversion of their own stated objective they contradicted themselves. There is no movement for the authoritarian imposition of sustainability precisely because the experience of Communism has shown that you cannot impose a better society on an unwilling population by force or terror.

Nonetheless, sustainability is not like, say, a policy of redistributing the land to peasants, which clearly increases positive liberty now. Sustainability is really about increasing positive liberty in the future. It relies on the goodwill of people in the present towards people in the future – not an easy thing to rely on and an issue which I will return to in the next chapter. But if the majority of people would sign up to the objective, would they be violating the human rights of the minority, as Wissenburg implies?

I think it is quite clear that the idea of limiting each individual's material consumption violates human rights only if you accept the Lockean justification for private property rights – that my expropriation of natural resources does you no harm as there is enough for you. If we live in a world with material and environmental limits, then that argument does not hold. Resources have to be shared so that there is enough for everybody, both now and in the future.

Socialism and sustainability

Sustainability is a philosophy that has a lot in common with socialism. Sustainability, like both liberalism and socialism, derives its moral force from the Enlightenment concept of equal consideration. While liberalism is based on a conception of legal equality (equal rights and formal equality of opportunity), socialism and social democracy go further and look for real equality of opportunity and a degree of equality of outcomes.

Sustainability is based on the ethical position that which particular generation a person was born into is a morally arbitrary fact, like which sex, ethnic group or class they were born into. Sustainability is not very compatible with conservatism, because for a true conservative such morally arbitrary characteristics can be allowed to determine a person's life chances, because they have done so traditionally.

Sustainability is concerned with the positive freedom of people in future generations to be able to meet their needs. The concern is not that there are laws forbidding them to do that, but that the present generation is preventing them from having the material means to do it. Sustainability starts from the view that there are physical and environmental limits to the resources of the Earth, while the liberal justification for private property starts from the assumption that there are no such limits. If natural limits exist, then the liberal justification for private ownership of resources collapses.

The Brundtland Commission argued that '[e]ven the narrow notion of physical sustainability implies a concern for social equity between generations, a concern that must logically be extended to equity within each generation.'[31] They also recognized that this implied a more equal sharing of the resources of the planet, although they were limited in how far they could take this line of thinking by the need for consensus among the members of the commission. Nonetheless, '[s]ustainable global development requires that those who are more affluent adopt life-styles within the planet's ecological means – in their use of energy, for example.'[32]

The Brundtland report took a broadly social democratic view of the implications of the limits to the Earth's resources. They saw the case for equality, but argued on pragmatic grounds that growth in the North had to continue even as the South attempted to catch up. A radical reshaping of the global economy along dark green or socialist lines was not on their agenda. Nonetheless, Brundtland was a social democratic document, belonging to a time when social democracy was still seen as a viable political option.

In an irony of history, the rhetoric of sustainability was adopted onto the political agenda in the 1990s at precisely the same time that the classical political philosophies that could support its concerns (democratic socialism and social democracy) were being abandoned by politicians on the centre left as they moved towards neoliberal free market ideology. The gap between the rhetoric of sustainability and the reality of free markets was more or less successfully brushed under the carpet until the debacle of the world trade summit in Seattle at the end of 1999.

Although sustainability has a lot in common with socialism, that of course does not mean that sustainability is the same as socialism. Socialism as an ideology does not really say anything about obligations to future generations. Socialists have always pursued growth policies and historically showed little or no concern for environmental issues. Marxism was a powerful influence on most strands of socialist thought for over a century, including social democrats and democratic socialists as well as those who identified themselves as Marxists. Marx's denial of natural limits and identification of freedom with the domination of nature had disastrous environmental consequences. In fact, by denying natural limits, Marx undermined the ethical argument for socialism and replaced it with an ultimately false notion of an inevitable historical process. The identification of socialism with nationalized ownership (another of Marx's ideas), which ended up as ownership by politicians and bureaucrats, was also deeply mistaken. In retrospect, Marx did socialism a terrible disservice by lumbering it with these notions. It is not surprising that socialism as it was practiced became discredited. The trouble is that the failure of the practice of socialism has come to be seen as meaning that 'there is no alternative' to the workings of the free market.

We can try to be sustainable or we can pursue the free market, but we can't do both. Unfortunately, the failure of socialism has not only been seen to discredit its original ethical principles, but it has also revealed just how difficult it is to consciously take hold of the direction of human history or even to successfully manage society. The final chapter will examine the implications of the end of socialism for any attempt to bring about sustainability.

Part Three
Future

9

The End of Sustainability?

Prediction is very difficult, especially about the future.

– Niels Bohr

Introduction

The driving force of modernity was faith in Progress. Just as reason was applied to the material world by science and technology, the political left believed in the application of reason to the social world. The connection of these two ideas found its apotheosis in the writings of Karl Marx. The left came to believe that there was a historical inevitability to its advance, and for a long time that seemed to be borne out by events. The left's faith survived all sorts of disasters, but finally died at the end of the 20th century.

The implications of the collapse of Communism have been widely debated. Do they mark the end of socialism and show that we now live in a world where economic planning is impossible? Do they mark the final triumph of liberal democratic capitalism and the end of History, in the sense of a debate about the best political and economic system? Or do they mark the end of Progress, by revealing the limits to control of both nature and society?

The widespread realization in recent years of the unavoidable reflexivity of the world is the common factor underlying both disillusionment with socialism and the rise of the environmental movement. Any attempt to control nature or the direction of society leads to unintended and undesired consequences which frequently serve to frustrate the goals of the intervention.

The paradox is that sustainability is a philosophy firmly based on the notion that attempts to transform nature are likely to be self-defeating, but is itself committed to attempting to transform society and control its future direction. The Green movement attempts to get round this problem by advocating radical decentralization of decision making, so that sustainability can be implemented from the grassroots upwards. One difficulty with that answer is that sustainability is a global problem requiring global coordination of action. Leaving all decisions to local communities is not very different from the neoliberal solution of leaving everything to the market to decide; there is every possibility for free riding and the tragedy of the commons. These supposed solutions are popular because of the failures of planning, but they do not in truth provide real answers to the problem of having to make extremely difficult decisions.

Sustainability is trapped between the reflexivity of the world (which is how we got into this mess) and the need to be able to transform and control the direction of human society, which reflexivity implies is impossible. There does not appear to be a satisfactory answer to the conundrum.

The Modern Age

The success of the use of scientific reason from the 17th century onwards led to the idea that reason could be applied in the social sphere as well to create a better world. The French Revolution of 1789 was the first attempt to create a self-consciously rational political order. Feudalism and absolute monarchy were abolished, replaced by the doctrines of the rights of man and democratic government. But the outcome of the French Revolution showed that even the best-intentioned attempts to better humanity could backfire. In a foreshadow of many 20th century revolutions, fanatics took power and seized the opportunity to persecute their rivals. The Jacobin Terror consumed most of the original leaders of the revolution. They were despatched by a scientifically designed means of execution, the guillotine.

Despite its terrible outcome, the French Revolution inspired the idea of a progressive politics towards the goals of liberty, equality and fraternity. Its horrors also supported the argument of conservatives such as Edmund Burke[1] that attempts to make things better would tend to make things worse. Revolutionaries believed in the perfectibility of mankind: that the bad in people, as Rousseau had claimed, came from society rather than human nature. Reason, they thought, was a force for good that would drive out the irrational bad in people. The conservatives still accepted the Christian doctrine that man had been cursed with Original Sin after the expulsion from the Garden of Eden and was therefore imperfectible.

The French Revolution was followed by another with still more momentous consequences – the Industrial Revolution. More than the French Revolution, this was the application of reason to change the world. The Industrial Revolution broke the emergent political Left into two camps. Liberals supported the changes because they were breaking the power of feudalism. Romantics and socialists worried that the oppression of feudalism was being replaced by the oppression of capitalism and the factory system. Early socialists hoped that people could be educated to see that it was more rational to produce for the common good than for private profit.

Karl Marx and Friedrich Engels ridiculed these 'utopian socialists', and put forward their own doctrine of 'scientific socialism'. They saw capitalism as part of the progress of human history. It would be brought down, not by appeals to morality, but by its own internal contradictions. In many ways, Marx became the leading prophet of modernity even for non-socialists. He saw capitalism as a progressive force through its subjugation of nature to the human race:

The bourgeoisie, during its rule of scarce one hundred years, has created more massive and more colossal productive forces than have all preceding generations together. Subjection of Nature's forces to man, machinery, application of chemistry to industry and agriculture, steam-navigation, railways, electric telegraphs, clearing of whole continents for cultivation, canalization of rivers, whole populations conjured out of the ground – what earlier century had even a presentiment that such productive forces slumbered in the lap of social labour?[2]

Marx also identified the central feature of modernity: the way that the new continuously replaces the old:

Constant revolutionizing of production, uninterrupted disturbance of all social conditions, everlasting uncertainty and agitation distinguish the bourgeois epoch from all earlier ones. All fixed, fast-frozen relations, with their train of ancient and venerable prejudices and opinions are swept away, all new-formed ones become antiquated before they can ossify. All that is solid melts into air, all that is holy is profaned, and man is at last compelled to face with sober senses, his real conditions of life, and his relations with his kind.[3]

As everyone knows, Marx believed that there were some features of capitalism which would not change and which would ensure its downfall. He thought that capitalism's tendency towards periodic and successively worse slumps, towards the immiseration of the working classes and towards monopoly (bringing former capitalists into the proletariat) would lead to its overthrow. It would be replaced with a socialist system of production based on rational planning, rather than the anarchy of the market.

In the end, of course, things didn't turn out the way Marx had predicted. Capitalism proved capable of reforming itself when faced with the prospect of self-destruction at the time of the Great Depression. Elements of economic planning were introduced to counteract the boom-and-bust cycle of capitalism. During the 20th century, Western capitalist countries introduced universal education, progressive income tax and restricted inheritance. For a time, they nationalized central banks, communications, railways and many other industries. In short, they enacted most of what was called for in *The Communist Manifesto*. What they failed to do was abolish capitalism entirely. As J.K. Galbraith wrote, Marx's mistake was to believe that capitalists were infinitely cunning except in the matter of ensuring their own ultimate survival.[4]

The darker side of modernity was apparent from the beginning. The guillotine was one example, and the factory system was another. Adam Smith extolled the division of labour in a pin factory as the model of economic rationality. The horrors of life in the dark satanic mills of the early 19th century inspired Marx to become a socialist. But it was the confident belief of both liberals and socialists in their different ways that the modern age would work through its defects and ultimately allow people to achieve freedom.

Another part of the concept of Progress was the idea that scientific and technological advance would not only make life better, but that people in more advanced societies would become more rational and civilized – better people. This theory was sometimes used by liberals as a justification for colonialism, despite the fact that colonialism actually often involved the slaughter or even the extermination of native peoples. At the turn of the last century, western Europeans were confident that they had become enlightened and civilized. Two frequently quoted examples of this complacency are found in the 1911 edition of the *Encyclopædia Britannica*. The article on TORTURE said that 'the whole subject is of only historical interest as far as Europe is concerned.'[5] The article on WAR, discussing the immunities of civilians under the Hague Convention, noted 'This has all been done with the object of making the operations of war systematic, and enabling the private citizen to estimate his risks and take the necessary precautions to avoid capture, and of restricting acts of war to the purpose of bringing it to a speedy conclusion.'[6] The historian Eric Hobsbawm[7] comments on how Russian pogroms of Jews at that time shocked European opinion, although the casualties were by our standards tiny – a few dozen. He also refers to the way that Friedrich Engels had been horrified when Irish Republicans planted a bomb in Westminster Hall – he thought that the division between combatants and non-combatants should be honoured.

The first blow to Europeans' belief in inevitable progress was the slaughter of the First World War. A belief in social progress was able to survive because so much of the horror could be blamed on the stupidity and callousness of the traditional ruling classes. The First World War destroyed their legitimacy and much of their power. It was widely seen to strengthen the case for democracy and socialism.

A generation later, the Holocaust made people doubt that *any* kind of moral progress had been made in the past few centuries. How could supposedly civilized Germany have committed such a dreadful crime? Nazism rejected the values of the Enlightenment and hankered back to pagan Germanic myths. Yet it had been very effective in the use of the rationality of 20th century science and bureaucratic organization. It appeared that pre-modern prejudices could go hand in hand with mastery of modern techniques.[8]

The Holocaust was not seen as unique because it involved genocide. The crime of genocide had not been uncommon in history, or even after the Enlightenment. The British had completely exterminated the aboriginal people of Tasmania in the middle of the 19th century. White Americans had been responsible for the deaths of millions of Native Americans. Europeans had reduced the indigenous population of Argentina to a few hundred. The Belgians under King Leopold had killed millions in the Congo. The Germans themselves had killed 80 per cent of the inhabitants of South West Africa in the 1890s and 1900s. Genocide on a massive scale had taken place earlier in the 20th century, when the Turks rounded up and killed over a million Armenians in 1915. What was perhaps unique about the Holocaust was the industrialization of the process.

Hitler rejected the values of the Enlightenment, even though he was prepared to use tools that it had given him. More damagingly for the cause of the Enlightenment, Stalin committed equally terrible crimes in the name of socialism and progress. To bring about his *reductio ad absurdum* of the Enlightenment vision of a rationally ordered society, he had tens of millions of people shot, deliberately starved or sent to their death in the gulags. It was the Jacobin Terror all over again, but on an infinitely larger scale.

Then nuclear weapons gave human beings the capacity to destroy the modern civilization that had enabled their creation. The Cold War's 'balance of terror' was based on mutual threats by the United States and the Soviet Union to exterminate the populations of each other's countries, the doctrine of Mutually Assured Destruction. This time, however, the political leaders of both countries pulled back at the brink in confrontations over Berlin, Cuba and the Middle East rather than fight a nuclear war.

The death of socialism

The final blow to faith in a rationally planned society came with the disillusionment in socialism worldwide after the economic disintegration of the Soviet system.[9] Everybody knew for a long time that the system was unfree and undemocratic. But from the 1920s to the 1960s, the Soviet Union was economically catching up with the United States. When Khrushchev told the Americans 'We will bury you,' he meant that his economy would one day surpass theirs, and many in the West believed him. In the 1970s, it became increasingly apparent that the Soviet Union and Eastern Europe were falling further and further behind the West. But nobody expected it all to collapse.

The Communist system failed in its own terms – as an economic system that would prove its superiority to capitalism. When the economic failure became blindingly obvious even to the rulers, they lost faith in it themselves and in many cases abandoned power with little or no struggle.[10]

Eric Hobsbawm describes how after the 1960s, when the era of crash industrialization came to an end, the socialist economies found themselves increasingly unable to keep up with Western technological innovation.[11] When inventions were made, there was little incentive to exploit them (unless they were militarily useful). The consumer sector of the economy never matured and the products were of depressingly low quality. There was no proper system of prices and no feedback about what consumers wanted. Additionally, the use of energy and natural resources was extremely inefficient. Possibly because of Marx's scepticism about the idea of 'natural limits', environmental considerations were not regarded as a priority, and so pollution was very severe. The use of human resources was extremely inefficient as well. There was a social contract based on the principle 'we pretend to work and they pretend to pay us.'[12]

These facts were all well known for a long time, and apparent to almost anyone who had the opportunity to compare Eastern and Western Europe. Socialists in the West had for a long time had little but criticism for the Soviet model, but its eventual collapse damaged the credibility of socialist ideas in general. Eric Hobsbawm argues that central planning, which had been invented to industrialize a backward agricultural country, was extremely crude and incapable of running a sophisticated modern economy. He claims that it would be possible to have a socialist economy with decentralized planning and market pricing.[13] However, the failure of the Yugoslav socialist economy suggests that the economic problem was deeper than over-centralization. In Yugoslavia, cooperatives were supposed to compete in a socialist market. In reality, though, cooperatives were not allowed to fail and the state would bail out loss makers, so some firms accumulated huge losses. Workers generally treated their cooperatives as belonging to the state, rather than themselves, and tended to consume any profits rather than reinvest them. The eventual result was an economic crisis.[14]

If the experience of nationalization and state planning in democratic countries had been successful, the failure of Eastern European socialism would probably have been seen to be due to the lack of democratic feedback and personal freedom needed for a dynamic modern society. However, the failure of the Soviet system was an extreme version of the problems with nationalized industries and economic planning that had been experienced in democratic countries. The response in the latter had been a shift in policy towards privatization and markets. By the end of the 1980s, social democracy had lost its zeal.[15] However, the recent bankruptcies of Enron in the United States and of Railtrack in Britain have shown that deregulation and privatization can themselves be disastrous.

The end of something

It is widely agreed that the collapse of Communism marked the end of something much broader than the Leninist tradition itself. But it is less clear quite what has ended. It has been described variously as the end of socialism, the end of Progress or (famously) the end of History. What connects all these claims together is the notion that the central political debates of the two centuries from 1789 to 1989 have been largely superseded. Is that because liberalism is the final form of human society, as Francis Fukuyama suggested in *The End of History and the Last Man*? Is it because the old arguments between left and right have become irrelevant and we have entered into a new kind of modernity, as Anthony Giddens claims in *Beyond Left and Right*? Or is it because modernity itself is coming to an end, as Richard Norgaard argues in *Development Betrayed*? Each of these thinkers acts as a spokesperson for a different ideological position: liberal capitalist, post-socialist and Green respectively.

The End of History

Francis Fukuyama made himself famous with his article 'The End of History?', published just a few months before the fall of the Berlin Wall.[16] He argued that Marxism's ideological implosion was seeing off the last rival ideology to democratic capitalism that had the potential to appeal to people around the world. Fukuyama took the phrase 'end of history' from Hegel. It was Hegel who had written after Napoleon's defeat of the Prussians at the Battle of Jena in 1806 that the triumph of the liberal political values of the French Revolution over those of reactionary conservatism marked the end of History. Hegel accepted that there was still a long way before these liberal ideals would be fully implemented in the world, but he saw Jena as the decisive turning point in ensuring that they were.

Fukuyama argued that the historical failure of Marxism's pretensions to bring about a more advanced society than bourgeois liberalism showed that Hegel had been right: the triumph of the liberal ideals of the French and American Revolutions over the Marxism of the Russian Revolution meant that nothing better than liberalism had been invented since 1806 and that liberalism is indeed the final form of human society. Russia's abandonment of Marxism and conversion to democracy was an important step on the road to the creation of Hegel's 'universal and homogeneous state' based on liberal principles. In that sense, Fukuyama was not arguing that history ended in 1989. It had taken two centuries from 1789 for liberal democracy to become the hegemonic political philosophy in Europe and he accepted that it might take centuries before all the world would be liberal democratic. In his later book, completed as the Soviet Union broke up, Fukuyama developed his argument further to explain why he thought liberal democracy would become universal and went on to consider the possibilities for any new rival to liberal democratic capitalism.[17]

Fukuyama admitted that the horrors of the 20th century have made people doubt that history has any direction. He argued, however, that the progress of natural science gives direction to history. He wrote that it is the only important human activity that is generally agreed to be advancing, even if its consequences are not necessarily good. Modern science had made possible not only the conquest of nature but, through technology, gave enormous capability for technologically advanced nations to militarily conquer other nations. Any state that wishes to remain independent must possess the technology to defend itself. Additionally, modern natural science gives enormous economic potential to countries that know how to use it. In order to be able to utilize that potential they have to go down the path called 'modernization'. Countries that have modernized come increasingly to resemble each other as economic logic dictates the forms of society they must have, with features like a centralized state, urbanization and universal education. According to Fukuyama, the lesson of the experience of Communism is that centrally-planned economies can reach the level of industrialization found in Europe in the 1950s, but they are unable to succeed as technologically innovative 'post-industrial' economies. Fukuyama admits that his economic interpretation of history resembles Marx's, except that it concludes with capitalism rather than socialism as the final outcome.

Fukuyama uses the same argument to explain why it is impossible to abandon technology and live in some Rousseauian idyll. Those who do that will be abandoning the means to defend themselves against those who do not. Even if the infrastructure of science and technology was destroyed in some global catastrophe, if any human beings survived, the knowledge of the scientific approach would survive too. Eventually, some group would start to develop science again.

A terrible weakness with Fukuyama's theory becomes apparent here: he simply doesn't take ecological issues seriously. His argument for why liberal democratic capitalism is going to conquer the world relies on the assumption that the mechanism of capitalist accumulation is going to continue in a linear fashion into the future. Fukuyama's approach to environmentalism is to ignore or parody its arguments, rather than address them seriously.

Fukuyama goes on to explain the appeal of democracy for people all around the world in terms of *thymos*, the 'struggle for recognition'. If people were purely self-interested rational calculators, they would not be prepared to put their lives on the line for abstract concepts like democracy. They would be content to live under authoritarian regimes, at least ones that were economically successful. Indeed, he believes that market-oriented authoritarianism is actually more effective at bringing about economic development than democracy. Fukuyama is struck by the way that authoritarian regimes in Spain and Portugal were replaced by democracy in the 1970s and the way that a similar transition occurred in South Korea and Taiwan at the end of the 1980s. Almost all industrialized societies now have democratically elected governments. In recent years, democratic values have increasingly been taken up by people with very different cultures from those of Western European countries where liberal democracy was invented and who were once claimed to be the only people culturally attuned to it. Fukuyama claims that the thymotic desire of people to have a say in how they are governed gives democracy universal appeal.

Fukuyama borrows his concept of *thymos* from Hegel, and ultimately from Socrates. Hegel believed that the establishment in France of a regime based on the recognition of the dignity of the individual was the beginning of the 'end of History'. Hegel saw the contradiction in traditional societies between lordship and bondage as a fatal weakness that would lead to a further stage of history – the 'universal and homogeneous state', one based on recognition of equal status for all its people. Marx, of course, later claimed that a liberal society itself contained contradictions that would lead to socialism and communism – his version of the universal and homogeneous state.

Fukuyama draws on Nietzsche in distinguishing between two kinds of thymia. There is a struggle for recognition based on equality, which Fukuyama calls *isothymia*. There is also a struggle for recognition based on superiority, which Fukuyama calls *megalothymia*. Nietzsche, as is well known, despised equality and celebrated superiority. Fukuyama argues that the strength of liberal democratic capitalism is that it balances both the urge for isothymia on the part of the mass and the urge for megalothymia on the part of the exceptional.

However, the source of recognition that people crave need not be the rights and dignity of the individual, as it is in liberalism. It can be a religion or a national identity. Fukuyama admits that it is possible that extreme nationalism or religious fanaticism will return as major forces in the world, but he regarded it as unlikely. The only part of the world that he believed was vulnerable to religious fundamentalism was the Middle East. He explained the rise of Islamic fundamentalism as a reaction against the humiliation of Islamic societies by the West. In his opinion, the most serious future threat to liberal democracy globally came from paternalistic authoritarianism of the kind seen in Singapore. East Asian countries had imported many Western values, but also drawn on patriarchal Confucian traditions of their own to fuel their economic growth. He thought that if the economic growth of America and Europe faltered relative to East Asia, the people of East Asian countries might come to reject the values of liberal democracy for Singapore-style authoritarianism (instead, the opposite seems to have happened after East Asia's model ran into serious trouble). Even so, he doubted that such an authoritarianism of deference could be accepted by people outside East Asia. According to Fukuyama, liberal democracy is the only political system left with appeal to people all around the world.

Fukuyama believes that in Western Europe nationalism is now being domesticated in the way that religion was a few centuries earlier. The nationalist seeks to assert his nationality by domination of others. As nationalism fades away, the irrational desire for domination is replaced by a rational desire for equal recognition. A world of liberal democracy, according to Fukuyama, would have much less incentive for war as all nations would recognize each other's legitimacy. Liberal democracies rarely have gone to war against each other. Fukuyama believes that a world of them would be largely peaceful. (He does not mention that the United States and some other Western countries have instead supported military coups to overthrow democratic governments they disliked.)

Are there any new threats to liberal democracy? Fukuyama believes that communism has been so discredited that any new threat from the left would have to be quite different and wear the clothes of liberalism. He considers the possibility of a 'superuniversalization' of rights, where the distinction between human and non-human is lost. In the days of Hegel and Kant, and in the original Christian tradition of European culture, human beings were considered superior to anything in nature because they were free and capable of moral choice. Modern science sees human behaviour in terms of the influence of genes and environment, not a matter of free moral choice. Since Darwin we have known that we are not separate from nature. It was our superior dignity that entitled us to the conquest of nature using the methods of natural science. Now natural science seems to have demonstrated that there is no essential difference between us and other animals.

Fukuyama draws this conclusion reluctantly and is evidently embarrassed by it. That is unsurprising, since a serious consideration of the point would lead to difficult questions about our relationship to the natural world and our treatment of it. The abandonment of the comfortable anthropocentrism that Fukuyama adheres to would again undermine his assumption that the capitalist conversion of the natural world into consumer goods is an unproblematic phenomenon.

Fukuyama, though, is more interested in the appeal from the right of Nietzschean nihilism. Nietzsche saw the only meaningful life as that of the warrior who is prepared to risk his life for glory. Fukuyama explains the current dissatisfaction with modernity in Western societies as the bored rage of Nietzsche's 'last man', the being at the end of history who has nothing significant left to struggle for. A few decades ago, many people thought that socialism would replace capitalism and lead to a more just and rational society. Today, there is no such faith that we can have a qualitatively better society than the liberal democracies that many people live in today. He sees the political struggles of today as being over the relatively small matters of the full expression of liberal democratic values. They are not for the *principle* of liberal democracy itself. Fukuyama points to what he sees as an irony in that those who struggled for the ideal of democracy on the streets of Beijing, Bucharest, Vilnius and Moscow were:

> ...the most free and therefore the most human of beings. They were former slaves who proved themselves willing to risk their lives in a bloody battle to free themselves. But when they finally succeed, as they eventually must, they will create for themselves a stable democratic society in which struggle and work in the old sense are made unnecessary, and in which the possibility of their ever again being as free and as human as in their revolutionary struggle had been abolished. Today, they imagine that they would be *happy* when they get to this promised land, for many needs and desires which exist in present-day Romania or China would be fulfilled. One day they too will all have dishwashers and VCRs and private automobiles. But would they also be *satisfied* with themselves? Or would it turn out that man's satisfaction, as opposed to his happiness, arose not from the goal itself, but from the struggle and work along the way?[18]

Fukuyama asks whether the danger is that having achieved a life of physical security and material plenty, we will be happy at one level, but dissatisfied on another level with the pointlessness of our existence and ready to drag the world back into the wars, injustice and revolutions of History. He gives the example of the crowds in the European capitals of 1914 who after decades of peace went on to the streets to cheer the news of the outbreak of war. However, he claimed that the terrible experiences of the two world wars have taught Europeans that the boredom of the last man is preferable to the excitement and horror of war.

Fukuyama sees liberal democracy as a good balance. On the one hand is the desire for equality that is required by democracy, but which cannot be achieved under capitalism. On the other hand is the desire by some individuals to be outstanding, which capitalism can tame and make compatible with civilization. It helps defend liberalism against its authoritarian opponents. Fukuyama believes that any attempt at too much isothymia will fail because people are naturally unequal. A society without people with megalothymic ambitions would have no great artists or scientists. More importantly, it would be unable to defend itself from another society whose people were more megalothymic.

One thing that is striking about Fukuyama's argument is how negative it is. He does not try to claim that capitalism best embodies the principles of democracy. He admits that some kind of democratic socialism could do that better. Rather, he argues that socialism lacks the capability for technological innovation necessary for its survival. Nor does Fukuyama argue that technological modernity satisfies people. He holds that people's real material needs are few, far below the levels of consumption found even in Communist Eastern Europe. The people of Eastern Europe were dissatisfied with their economic position, not because their material needs were not being met, but because they compared themselves with the people of Western Europe. Fukuyama's argument is not that modernity and capitalism are especially good things in themselves. Rather, they are unavoidable but at least allow space for individual liberty and democracy. Liberal democracy may not be perfect, but it is the best we can hope for.

Criticizing Fukuyama has virtually been a cottage industry.[19] Fukuyama makes so many contentious statements that it would take a book to deal with them all, so I will mention only some of the most important. It is possible to cast doubt on Fukuyama's argument for the universal appeal of democracy. He does not convincingly explain why a movement like Nazism could not recur, but essentially dismisses it as an aberration of an earlier stage of modernity. How would Fukuyama explain the rise of the extreme Right in many European countries in the last few years? Or why might not militarism return to Europe when the Second World War becomes as distant as the Napoleonic Wars were to the people of 1914?

Discussing contemporary liberal democracies, Fukuyama downplays the extent to which inequalities of gender, class and ethnicity mean that there is an absence of equality of opportunity. Fukuyama also overlooks the effect of inequalities of wealth. Are today's stable liberal democracies truly examples of the universal and homogeneous state?

Another problem lies in Fukuyama's implication that a post-industrial society cannot be socialist and that any isothymia greater than in contemporary Sweden is unsustainable. However, all that Fukuyama actually argues is that a centrally-planned economy could not deal with the degree of complexity required for a modern consumer economy, and that an economy without markets will tend to grossly misprice everything. He does not explain why some other alternative to contemporary capitalism is impossible.

But in my opinion the most fundamental problem with Fukuyama's argument lies in his unquestioned assumption that economic growth can be endless. It is through the mechanism of 'accumulation without end' that the post-industrial consumer society, and with it democracy, is to spread around the world. He does not even consider the possibility of any of the environmental problems inherent in such a vision.

The end of socialism

These issues are addressed by Anthony Giddens in *Beyond Left and Right*.[20] It is Giddens' attempt to reconfigure radical politics after the end of socialism. He is not content to restate a traditional liberal political philosophy, but instead tries to come up with a new political philosophy to address the contemporary world. He does not accept Fukuyama's claim that History has come to an end with the end of socialism.

Giddens starts with a paradox: the left and right have changed places. The left used to stand for change and progress, while the right stood for keeping things the way they were. Today, the Left has lost faith in its vision of Progress through history towards a socialist future. It now is reduced to seeking to defend many of its achievements from a Right that would seek to undo them. But the traditional conservative Right has disappeared in Europe too. Today the New Right takes up the classical liberal argument for the extension of the market into new areas of life. The Old Right was suspicious of markets and capitalism as undermining traditional society. The New Right calls for radical reforms to make life more market-based.

Giddens points to a contradiction in New Right ideology. It calls for the extension of the market and capitalism, which inevitably do away with traditional forms of life. Yet the New Right itself holds dear traditional family and gender relations. It is apparent that capitalist modernity has also led to recent social upheavals, particularly the emancipation of women as they have gone out to paid work, which have had consequences the New Right is unhappy about. So on the one hand the New Right upholds the view that market outcomes are always the best and on the other hand it wants to resist them when they threaten the traditional family.

Socialism was as much about Progress as conservatism was about resisting it. For two centuries, socialists believed that theirs was the way of the future. Now socialism itself is consigned to the past. Giddens sees socialism as having been about the idea that human beings can create a rational society, rather than one relying on the dead hand of tradition or the chaos of the market. Although socialism was often seen as being primarily about equality, Giddens argues that it was always more about the rational control of society and the subordination of history and nature to human will.

Giddens explains the ultimate failure of socialism in terms of what he calls its 'cybernetic model', that is the idea that the economy should be rationally planned from the centre. His view is different from the New Right argument that any kind of socialist planning would fail. Hayek argued that the fundamental fallacy underlying attempts at economic planning was the belief that all it was necessary to do was to work out the best way to allocate the given resources.[21] The problem he identified was that the information about the preferences of individual consumers was unknown, and that collecting enough information centrally would be impossibly difficult. In a market economy, a vast number of different products are available. Central planners are unable to obtain enough information to devise a plan of that complexity.

Giddens argues that some kinds of economic planning were successful in the phase of history that he calls 'simple modernization'. It was a time when people had relatively stable preferences. But as society 'detraditionalizes', people's wants become more complex and difficult to predict. The globalization of the world since the invention of the communication satellite increased the speed at which ideas and values move around the world. When that happened, the hope that socialism could overcome the irrationalities of capitalism foundered.

Giddens considers whether some kind of market socialism could keep the faith alive in place of central planning. It was proposed in the 1980s that Swedish workers should accumulate funds in businesses in such a way as to eventually eliminate shareholders. The companies would then become workers' cooperatives. The workers would elect their managers. Unlike ordinary shareholdings, workers' shares could not be bought or sold on the open market.

Giddens sees grave difficulties with an economic system based primarily on workers' cooperatives. If market pricing is necessary for efficient use of assets, that must also apply to capital. Without it, there would be the same problem of inefficiency found in centrally-planned economies. Capital stored in workers' cooperatives would tend to become risk averse and firms could stagnate like they did in the Soviet Union. Because each person's shareholding would be reduced if new workers were taken on in an existing cooperative, there would be little motivation to do so. There would be little mobility of labour because workers would not be able to take their shareholding with them. The result would be massive structural unemployment. 'There is no Third Way of this sort, and with this realization the history of socialism as the avant-garde of political theory comes to a close.'[22]

Turning to the welfare state, Giddens identifies a crisis caused by a number of different factors. Globalization has increased the competitive pressures on western economies and limited the welfare state's capacity for redistribution. The change in the role of women as they have gone out to paid employment and displaced men as family bread-winners has undermined the assumptions on which the welfare state is based. Increasing long-term structural unemployment has created a financial crisis and problems of welfare dependency. Giddens sees the social democratic model of the welfare state as now being on the defensive.

If the perspectives of right and left have been exhausted, as Giddens claims, it is because we now live in a different world. He characterizes the world today as one of 'manufactured uncertainty' where the nature of risk is different from what it was in earlier times. We are now faced with high-consequence risks which potentially affect people all across the world, such as global warming and the possibility of nuclear war, that are themselves the result of modernity. Although many risks of the past have diminished, we are continually faced with new uncertainties. This is the idea of Ulrich Beck's 'risk society'.[23] Giddens thinks that we should draw back from the ambitions of the Enlightenment for the domination of nature. But he argues that the social and natural world are now largely intertwined and there is no way for us to pull back from this reflexive engagement between society and nature. Reflexivity is the key idea for Giddens. Following Beck, he says that we are living in an age of 'reflexive modernization'. In simple modernization, industrial development seems a predictable process, scientific and technological advances are generally accepted and growth has a clear direction.

Reflexive modernization has its origins in globalization and the changes in society since the 1960s with the breakdown of traditional gender and sexual relations. Giddens sees globalization as the consequence of the development of instantaneous global communication. Activities are no longer as locally based as they were. Many personal decisions that were previously taken as givens are now open to question: what kind of diet to follow, whether to marry, whether to have children, for example. He sees all this as a part of a process of intensified detraditionalization: 'We are the first generation to live in a thoroughly post-traditional society, a term that is in many ways preferable to 'post-modern'.'[24] Capitalism, industrialization and democracy all broke down a previous traditional order, but led to the creation of new traditions of their own. These traditions themselves are now changing. Reflexive modernization is the process when traditional society has been destroyed by the rational critique that modernity brought to bear on it and the rational critique is applied to the assumptions of modernity itself.

Giddens claims that nature has come to an end in the same way as tradition. We no longer worry about what nature can do to us so much as about what we can do to nature. We are now forced to make conscious decisions about our relationship to what remains of a humanized nature. Following Beck, he rejects the Green idea that we can restore the traditional separation between humans and nature. However, Giddens claims that we are now in a 'post-scarcity economy'. Although there is still much scarcity in the world, he thinks that accumulation is widely seen as threatening or destroying valued ways of life. It has become counterproductive in its own terms; there is overdevelopment leading to suboptimal consequences.

Giddens criticizes Fukuyama's assumption of accumulation without end and his failure to consider ecological concerns. He also criticizes Fukuyama for being too optimistic about liberal democracy's ability to withstand the threat of nihilism. Giddens sees capitalism's tendency to destroy morals and values as a very serious problem. He thinks that Fukuyama is wrong to see liberal democracy's troubles lying far in the future. Disillusionment with the democratic process is already widespread and growing in Western countries.

Giddens suggests that the collapse of Communist states was not due to a weakness present in their origins, but due to changing conditions in the wider context of global society. He claims that democratization today is being driven by social reflexivity and detraditionalization. As people become better informed, they demand a greater role in taking decisions about their own lives. But democratization is not identical with support for the liberal democratic state. The state exists at the national level, but people now have points of reference that are more cosmopolitan and global. Giddens calls for a democratization of democracy itself.

He argues that the welfare state is still based around the society of simple modernization. It assumes full male employment, a policy for a time when women were systematically excluded from large parts of the labour market. Full employment also relied upon Keynesian national economic management, which is no longer viable in a globalized economy. Welfare states that guarantee the unemployed a fairly generous income indefinitely also create a situation where dependency on the state becomes a rational individual strategy, but ultimately undermines the legitimacy of the system with taxpayers. Most Western welfare states (except Britain) have also taken on pension commitments which he claims cannot be met. He also claims that welfare states have not in fact been effective at redistributing wealth between classes as the middle class have ended up taking a disproportionate share of the benefits.

Giddens sees the basic problem with the welfare state as being an assumption of a full-time job for every adult male under retirement age. The assumption is no longer justifiable. He believes that there should be a general reduction of working hours as part of a move away from 'productivism', the idea that paid employment bears moral meaning, defining the worth and social value of individuals. Under productivism, economic development substitutes for the goal of living a happy life in harmony with others.

Giddens argues that many of the problems with welfare state agencies put forward by New Right authors have parallels with the criticisms of official international development agencies made by Greens. Both are bureaucratic, inefficient and encourage dependency. His proposals for reform of the welfare state draw on Green ideas about alternative development: encouragement of informal economic activity (such as LETS), credit unions and other policies to encourage individual initiative and self-reliance.

Turning to ecological issues, Giddens sees affinities between the Green movement and conservatism, disguised by the way that Greens have identified themselves with the left. Green thought, after all, shares with traditional conservatism a suspicion of 'progress'. But Giddens is also aware of connections of Green thought to liberalism and socialism and its inherent radicalism. He sees Green thought as neither left nor right, its emergence reflecting the shifts of political orientation which his book documents.

His basic criticism of Green thought is that it is based on the concept of 'nature'. Giddens holds that ecological concerns have arisen only as nature, separate from human beings, is dissolving. Instead, he views contemporary ecological concern as another example of reflexive modernization:

> Problems of ecology cannot be separated from the impact of detraditionalization. Each raises the age-old question, 'how shall we live?' in a new guise – in a situation where the advance of science and technology, coupled to economic growth mechanisms, force us to confront moral problems that were once hidden in the naturalness of nature and tradition. The hazards associated with manufactured uncertainty bring home the need to deal with these problems – but if they are seen simply *as* 'natural dangers', their real character is misinterpreted.[25]

He explains that modern civilization is about control over things, including the physical environment, that were previously not under human control. However, control comes up against limits as it is generalized and globalized. Although environmental issues first appear in the negative form of problems, they can also be perceived more positively as related to the moral question 'how shall we live?' in a world of lost tradition and humanized nature.

Giddens criticizes Green ideas on several grounds. He thinks that the emphasis on radical or even revolutionary social change is inconsistent with the emphasis on continuity in Green thought. He believes that there is a confusion of protection of the biosphere with preservation of social and cultural traditions. There is an assumption that those who live close to nature are in harmony with it, yet he says nature only becomes friendly when it has come under human control; those who live close to nature often fear it. He does not think that mastery over nature is necessarily the same as destruction of the environment. He says the call for decentralization of society is in tension with the call for strong measures to protect the environment, because such measures could only be taken by a more powerful global authority than exists now. Small local communities are seen by Greens as emancipatory, but in fact they are often intolerant and oppressive.

Giddens believes that we cannot escape from our scientific and technological civilization. It creates high-consequence risks, but these are an inevitable outcome. The solution to these problems is not a withdrawal from modernity, but nor is it simply more science and technology.

Giddens asks '[w]hat should be salvaged from socialist critiques of capitalism and what discarded?'[26] Although he thinks that some of the basic ideals of socialism remain persuasive, it is necessary to take quite a different tack. He considers the main question now is not about how much regulation and how much market, but instead about how productivity can be disentangled from productivism. However, he does not believe it likely that there will be a general revolt against consumerism or that a halt will be called to economic growth. But he does think that the destructive aspects of untrammelled economic growth have become so obvious that nobody can ignore them.

Giddens rejects providentialism. Socialism, and particularly Marxism, believed that history had a direction. Giddens writes that we cannot any more expect some agent to come to our rescue, or believe that history has any necessary direction, and '[w]e must accept risk as risk, up to and including the most potentially cataclysmic of high-consequence risks; we must accept that there can be no way back to external risk from manufactured risk.'[27] However, Giddens sees unpredictability, manufactured risk and fragmentation as only one side of the coin of reflexive modernization. Global interdependence gives the possibility of a world where common interests and common risks can bring us together. Globalizing trends may lead to cosmopolitan tolerance and a new solidarity between peoples.

Unlike Fukuyama, Giddens seems to regret the passing of socialism's optimism about human progress. And he is unable to accept that contemporary liberal democracies are the best we can aspire to. Nor is he as optimistic as Fukuyama that the growth they depend upon can continue into the indefinite future or be generalized to the entire world. Giddens is all too aware of downsides to capitalism and growth.

The theory of reflexive modernization holds that modernity has destroyed the traditional social order that the Enlightenment first subjected to rational critique. Now that same critique is being reflexively turned on modernity itself. It seems to me that there is a structural similarity between Beck and Giddens' theory of reflexive modernization and Marx's theory of scientific socialism. After all, Marx and Engels claimed that socialism was subjecting capitalism to immanent critique, much as Beck and Giddens claim that reflexive modernization does to simple modernity. Scientific socialism was an immanent critique of the logic of the modernity of its day, claiming that there was a higher rationality beyond it that could more fully embody the ambitions of modernity. Giddens' theory makes much the same claim today, although with much less bold promises about what is possible.

Reflexive modernization is reflexive in a second sense. Under simple modernization, there is a linear cause-and-effect relationship that can be relied upon. In reflexive modernization, causes do not only have predictable effects in the same way, but the effects can feed back on the original causes. Beck originally applied this version of reflexivity to risk. As risks become increasingly high-consequence, they become increasingly reflexive. Giddens extends this notion to attempt to explain the failure of economic planning. It was because of detraditionalization and globalization that both Keynesianism and state socialism failed, he claims.

This argument is essentially the same as Fukuyama's about how Soviet socialism was unable to compete with the technological inventiveness of globalizing capitalism in the age of information technology. Giddens also claims that the revolutions of 1989 were facilitated by television. But how was detraditionalization at work in the Soviet Union's Brezhnevite 'years of stagnation'? Giddens doesn't explain.

In *Beyond Left and Right*, Giddens treats globalization as something that is unavoidable. Clearly, inventions like the jet airliner, the communications satellite and the Internet have shrunk the world and are still shrinking it. But international trade accounted for a larger proportion of world economic activity before the First World War than it does today.[28] Something prevented and for several decades largely reversed the globalization described so evocatively in *The Communist Manifesto*:

> The bourgeoisie, by the rapid improvement of all instruments of production, by the immensely facilitated means of communication, draws all, even the most barbarian, nations into civilisation. The cheap prices of its commodities are the heavy artillery with which it batters down all Chinese walls, with which it forces the barbarians' intensely obstinate hatred of foreigners to capitulate. It compels all nations, on pain of extinction, to adopt the bourgeois mode of production; it compels then to introduce what it calls civilisation into their midst, i.e., to become bourgeois themselves. In one word, it creates a world after its own image.[29]

The thing that reversed the globalization Marx and Engels described was national economic planning. It countered all the advances in communication and transportation technologies from 1914 to the 1970s. Only near the end of the 20th century did globalization win out again.

In his more recent book *The Third Way*, Giddens addresses this objection to his theory.[30] He argues that although it is true that the world economy today is no more globalized in terms of trade than a century ago, there is a very different situation from the one in the post-war Keynesian era. More importantly, we now have the new phenomenon of global financial markets. He also sees globalization as being about the way of life that is followed in a world of instantaneous communication. He accepts, however, that although globalization is often treated as a force of nature (as he himself had implied in *Beyond Left and Right*), it is not. States and corporations have promoted its advance. Influenced by the Asian crash, at another point he discusses mechanisms to limit the destabilizing influence of uncontrolled global speculation.

The Third Way, subtitled 'the renewal of social democracy', perhaps represents a recent shift in Giddens' thinking back towards social democratic politics. He now accepts the idea of being centre left, rather than 'beyond left and right'. The book is about re-inventing social democracy in a world where there is no alternative to capitalism. To democratize democracy, Giddens supports devolution of power to regions and the use of referenda, but also calls for a transfer of power upwards to the European Union and an extension of the role of the European Parliament. More ambitiously, he wants to create an elected world parliament along the lines of the European Parliament and similar assemblies to the European Parliament for other regions of the world. Discussing the welfare state, he places significantly less emphasis on Green ideas about LETS and credit unions than in his previous book and more emphasis on the New Labour themes of investment in education and training.

In his discussion of environmental issues, Giddens noticeably retreats from Green influence. Although he criticizes ecological modernization theory for its 'comfortable' assertion, following from the Brundtland report, that there is no necessary contradiction between economic growth and environmental protection, he also criticizes it for its emphasis on the precautionary principle:

> Yet the precautionary principle isn't always helpful or even applicable. Ecological risk often won't be normalized in this way, because in so many situations we no longer have the option of 'staying close to nature', or because the balance of benefits and dangers from scientific and technological advance is imponderable. We may quite often need to be bold rather than cautious in supporting scientific and technological innovation.[31]

Giddens is alarmingly comfortable about taking risks. The passage quoted above is found in his discussion of the BSE crisis. Giddens argues that much of the criticism of the British government that presided over the emergence of the crisis was unfair. If a potential risk is publicized and then turns out to have been exaggerated or non-existent, critics can claim that there has been scare-mongering. But if a government is cautious about making an announcement or believes the risk is low, then they will be accused of a cover-up.

However, in that specific case the government told the public that there was *no* risk. Although they announced action in 1989 to reduce the then theoretical risk of human infection by removing brains and spinal cords of slaughtered cattle, it turned out subsequently that this measure was not enforced. The behaviour of the government was not properly precautionary; their prime motive seems to have been to reassure the public and protect the industry from loss of confidence. It was only when human infections were an established fact that serious action was taken.

The case of the release of genetically modified organisms (GMOs) into the environment reveals a similar attitude. Although some governments have tried to take a precautionary approach, others have been happy to proceed with the release of GMOs despite concerns about safety and environmental impacts. The attitude of many biotechnologists and politicians has been arrogant and complacent. The assumption seems to have been that no danger deserves to be taken seriously until it has actually happened. For instance, the public was told that there was no possibility of genetically modified (GM) pollen travelling more than 50 metres to contaminate other crops. It turned out that GM pollen could travel large distances. GM maize has already caused significant and irreversible genetic contamination of indigenous maize in Mexico. No testing of the safety of GM foods was done before their release because politicians accepted the biotechnology companies' claim that genetically engineered crops were 'substantially equivalent' to conventional crops. The test of the safety of GM food is being done now on millions of consumers.

Being bold, rather than cautious, really means choosing to take risks on the bet that disasters will not occur. But if you take such risks many times, you can be sure that disasters will befall you.[32]

Most chillingly, Giddens claims that nuclear weapons, by making large-scale wars unthinkable, are demilitarizing society. But Giddens is writing from the assumption that the outcome of the Cold War we experienced – our survival – was almost inevitable because nobody would consider starting a nuclear war. It was revealed after the Cold War that during the Cuban missile crisis, unknown to the Americans, there were already Soviet nuclear missiles present in Cuba. The local commanders had orders to launch them against US cities in the event of an American attack on Cuba. Had Kennedy followed the advice of his generals and invaded Cuba, the consequence would have been a full-scale nuclear war that would have destroyed civilization. There were also several incidents during the Cold War when early warning systems falsely indicated a surprise nuclear attack by the other side. On some occasions, the launch of nuclear missiles was only minutes away. If you consider the different ways the Cold War could have gone, the outcome in the history we live in was by no means inevitable or even likely. We were lucky to survive.[33] Who can be sure that we will be so lucky in future conflicts between nuclear powers?

If you are prepared to take very high consequence risks that may result in the literal end of history, you are engaged in a global version of Russian roulette. Even if the risk of extinction from each risk is low, if you take such a risk a sufficiently large number of times then you are almost certain to destroy yourself in the end. The reason why we survived the Cold War is because of the anthropic principle: we are here because we are here. If we hadn't survived, we wouldn't be around to discuss it. Giddens' implicit argument that very high consequence risks can be worthwhile because we have survived so far is based on a fallacious line of reasoning. It is like a player of Russian roulette saying that the game isn't as dangerous as people make out because he's pulled the trigger many times and hasn't shot himself yet.

Why should we accept the risks involved in reflexive modernization? If reflexivity creates limits to control, why not try to stay safely within them, rather than 'explore the risk environment'? If globalization is not a force of nature, why embrace it?

The end of progress

A counterpoint to Giddens' arguments can be found in the work of Richard Norgaard. He has reached rather different conclusions about the lessons to be drawn from the demise of Communism.[34] Norgaard sees the failure of the Soviet Union as significant because it was the first major power to collapse while diligently pursuing modernity. Its version of progress ended up destroying people's creativity and initiative in bureaucracy, wasted soil in an effort to modernize agriculture, and polluted water and air to accelerate industrial development. In the end its efforts stretched everything beyond breaking point. Norgaard claims that democratic capitalist nations are wrong to interpret its failure as a victory for their version of modernity, 'not realizing that the differences in versions only amount to how quickly the breaking point is reached.'[35] For Greens, as Jonathon Porritt memorably put it in 1984, 'the debate between the protagonists of capitalism and communism is about as uplifting as the dialogue between Tweedledum and Tweedledee'.[36] Capitalism and communism both were forms of 'industrialism', differing only as how best to divide the proceeds from exploiting the Earth.

Norgaard believes that the call for sustainability is a recognition that something has gone wrong with progress, but that 'sustainable development', as commonly understood, requires more data, more sophisticated use of science, more controls on technology, better institutional design and appeals to existing values. The logic of sustainable development seems to be that modernity has gone wrong because people have not been fully in control:

> In this schema, development might become unsustainable if technology and social order do not advance sufficiently quickly to uncover new resources and to make enough poor quality resources available. The solution to unsustainability is to accelerate technological change and adapt society to these changes. Ironically, indeed irrationally, in this view of environmental history, if development is unsustainable, the driving forces of development – technology and social change – should be accelerated. The idea that changing ever faster is the path to sustainability underlines the contradiction in combining the terms 'sustainable' and 'development' in the first place.[37]

Norgaard argues that the crisis of modernity lies in its false understanding of science. Modernism, according to Norgaard, is based on a set of five philosophical assumptions: atomism, mechanism, universalism, objectivism and monism. These assumptions have been the basis of Western science. Society has accepted particular scientific ways of understanding and tried to act rationally on these understandings to the exclusion of other ways of understanding: 'The particular scientific ways of knowing by themselves are neither bad nor good, but the beliefs which makes these ways dominant create both an overdependence on particular ways of understanding and blindspots through the exclusion of other ways of knowing.'[38] Norgaard thinks that the problem lies in the belief that all problems can be solved in a deterministic fashion. It has become clear that instrumental reason can be highly effective, but its use has not created the Utopia that was expected. Norgaard writes: 'We have become so effective at dividing and conquering that problems that can be treated in this manner are no longer problems.'[39] But these assumptions are not a good basis for thinking about complex systems, particularly systems that involve people.

Norgaard's solution is a co-evolutionary approach. Conventional approaches to development seek to humanize nature. Norgaard's approach takes as the starting point that nature and society co-evolve. He gives the example of the co-evolution of pests and pesticides. Despite the continuous introduction of ever newer and more expensive pesticides, the level of losses to pests today is about the same as it was before the first synthetic pesticides were introduced. The story is proof of the old maxim that 'when a man invents a better mousetrap, nature invents a better mouse.' Norgaard argues that both social and environmental determinism ignore the two-way flow between nature and society. Norgaard sees the period from the Industrial Revolution until recently as an era where for a long time it was possible for societies to develop with relatively few environmental constraints.

Norgaard considers the disastrous impact of attempts to bring modernization to the Amazon. He argues that the imposition of the knowledge systems of Western 'experts' (he writes as a former adviser to the World Bank) fails because they do not understand the interaction of the particular social and ecological systems as well as the locals do. Instead, they impose their theories about how development occurs.

A problem which Norgaard highlights is that our systems of knowledge co-evolve with the world. For example, how we understand agricultural systems affects our decisions about agriculture. The decisions taken affect the agro-ecosystem and also the ideas about agriculture that we have. Because what we know is both within the system we are trying to understand and affects what we are trying to understand, our knowledge co-evolves with its environment. Norgaard claims that this means that there is no absolute knowledge, because knowledge only has meaning relative to how well it explains the state, dynamics and evolution of a system; there is no meaning to the idea that knowledge accumulates. Particularly in areas like economics and ecology, it is apparent that there is a reflexive loop between the understanding and the 'object' of study. Norgaard writes: 'This view of the nature of knowledge and our interactions with systems helps explain why there are always new problems needing new solutions. It is not the case, as is often argued, that we are constantly generating new problems [just] because we cannot foresee all of the consequences of our actions.'[40] There is a certain similarity between Norgaard's analysis and the ideas of Beck and Giddens. But where they see reflexivity only requiring a re-orientation of modernity and a stepping back from some of its grander ambitions, Norgaard sees the problem of reflexivity as dooming further pursuit of the project.

Norgaard explains the problem of operationalizing sustainability in terms of scale. We can start at the local level and ask whether a region's agricultural and industrial practices can continue indefinitely or whether they will destroy the local resource base and environment. This first level ignores whether there might be net material or energy inputs to the region being supplied from outside. The second issue Norgaard identifies is how to weigh the degradation of some aspects of the environment against investment in environmental improvements and investment in capital. Third, if a region is dependent on external non-renewable resources, there are a number of questions to answer. How long might they last before being exhausted? Are there renewable substitutes? If the region is dependent on external renewable resources, are these being managed sustainably? Fourth, is the region contributing as much to the knowledge, organizational and technological bases of other regions as it is dependent on them? How might we determine whether new technologies and better education can compensate for depletion of resources and environmental degradation? Fifth, does the region have the capability to adapt to climate change and surprises imposed on it by others? Sixth, is the region contributing to global environmental problems, forcing other regions to change their behaviour? Seventh, are the regions evolving along mutually compatible paths or will they, for example, destroy each other through war?

Norgaard states that, from a conventional environmental science perspective, keeping track of material and energy flows would be a necessary start to putting sustainable development into practice. He claims that keeping track of the flows, particularly for a number of regions with complex economies, would be nearly impossible. He writes that one of the challenges of sustainable development, at least with the data requirements of Western scientific environmental management, would be to keep track of the flows without tying up the entire labour force.

Norgaard is raising the spectre of Hayek's notorious 'information problem'. But for Norgaard, leaving everything to the market is no solution. Markets depend on having the correct system of property rights. The design of an appropriate system of property rights would not only require an equivalent degree of prescience to omnipresent planning, but also presume a static world.

What is Norgaard's answer? His co-evolutionary approach would involve smaller political units, a flattening of bureaucratic hierarchies and more public participation – the standard Green ways to ensure that information about specific local circumstances is used in decision making. It would also involve moves towards greater regional self-sufficiency and less global trade because Norgaard sees the global market and cultural homogenization as ultimately risk-increasing by reducing the diversity of local strategies. When I interviewed him, Norgaard told me that he was concerned by the way that free trade and deregulation mean that increasingly decisions are taken not at a regional or national level, but at an individual level or a global level: 'a juxtaposition of extremes that I think are very strange.'

Norgaard would divide the world into a large number of self-governing units. He told me he was envisaging units of a few million people. Rather ironically, Norgaard and other Greens propose this kind of division essentially because they see sustainability as easier to deal with if you divide the problem up. Norgaard's solution to the complexity of the present world is to drastically decentralize decision making. He told me that he did not want to come up with a single global definition for sustainability: 'I'm looking for a lot of local definitions. And setting up technologies and economies that don't have as much interaction.'

However, one consequence of that kind of decoupling would be rather like the effect of central planning: to drastically simplify the economy. The complexity of modern economies depends on the complex flows of resources around the world. Without such flows, it would be easier to keep track of the sustainability of each region. But without trade, the people of many regions would be unable to support themselves. Should sustainability start at the local level or at the global level? The regions of the world are so interdependent that it would be very difficult to attempt to disentangle them now.

Norgaard himself recognizes that regions are affected by the actions of other regions. Issues like climate change and ozone depletion obviously require global coordination. Norgaard argues that more emphasis on the local should not mean less emphasis on the global. Frustratingly, he does not describe how to bring about this trick of simultaneous decentralization and globalism.

There are a number of other criticisms that could be made of Norgaard's arguments. Fukuyama and Giddens both cite examples of countries like Burma and Tanzania that in the post-colonial era pursued the path of economic autarky. Indeed, it was Schumacher's work in Burma in the 1950s that inspired many of the ideas in his Green classic *Small is Beautiful*.[41] However, the policies of national self-sufficiency and village socialism pursued by these and other countries (which Norgaard mentions approvingly) eventually led to economic failure.

A further problem is that although large projects and advanced technologies do indeed often create environmental devastation, there is no guarantee that a large number of small scale projects using relatively inefficient low technology will not create an equal or greater amount of environmental devastation. The deforestation brought about by villagers in Africa and India collecting fuelwood springs to mind here. World population is six times what it was 200 years ago and the sheer number of people is a major problem in itself. Solutions that worked when the population was much smaller will not necessarily work now. We have little idea of how even to sustainably feed the billions of the 21st century.

A deeper problem with Norgaard's ideas lies in the consequences of his espousal of Richard Rorty's postmodernist relativism and his consequent rejection of universal values. There is an obvious paradox in such thinking which Fukuyama points to.[42] Postmodernists like Rorty tend to hold rather conventional liberal attitudes. Rorty, for example, makes it clear that he does not approve of totalitarian regimes or atrocities like ethnic cleansing. Yet postmodernists are also committed to demonstrating that there is no philosophical basis for these judgements. They are a matter of sentiment, cultural influence and pragmatism. What if the moral environment is not an American university, but Hitler's Germany or Milosevic's Serbia? The philosophy of postmodernists leaves no moral grounds on which to criticize participation in something like 'ethnic cleansing' in such a context.

Norgaard himself gives the examples of the Islamic revolution in Iran and the crushing of the Tiananmen Square protests in China to show how the world is not converging on a single set of values. But he does not acknowledge that those alternative value systems can be very unpleasant for those who live under them.

The paradox is that postmodernists believe in a pluralism of moral values that owes much to liberalism. But they are so committed to this pluralism that they are unable to argue against totalitarian or fundamentalist philosophies that themselves deny any kind of diversity.

Norgaard told me that he was looking for a lot of local definitions of sustainability. A further paradox in his position is that sustainability itself is a value based on an ethical appeal to conceptions of universal justice. How can such a moral claim carry weight if you deny that there are universal values?

Globalism or localism?

That returns us to the previous objection to Norgaard's ideas: if almost everything is decentralized to the local level (even the definition of sustainability), then how can problems of a truly global nature be tackled? What is to prevent beggar-my-neighbour parochialism? If the definition of sustainability is to be a matter for each region to decide, chaos is likely to result.

But if we instead follow Giddens' route of reflexive modernization, then there is the problem that as everything becomes increasingly globalized and interconnected, any kind of control becomes increasingly impossible as everything become just too complicated to manage. Giddens holds that high consequence manufactured risk is an unavoidable consequence of modernity. But even if it is unavoidable to some extent, why embrace it? Why not have more concern about the downsides?

Giddens and Norgaard put forward almost opposite answers, but both seem unsatisfactory. Neither seems to bring us sustainability. Unlike Fukuyama, Giddens at least recognizes environmental issues as a matter of serious concern, but his endorsement of a continuation of many of the trends that have brought us to this position seems perverse. Norgaard's is the classic radical Green viewpoint. The problem is seen as the imposition of Enlightenment values on the world. If indigenous local cultures are allowed to return and world trade is done away with, the problems it has brought will largely go away. But are local cultures really better in their approach to the environment? There are many examples of environmental destruction brought about by traditional cultures. The most notorious example is the Polynesian deforestation of Easter Island, precipitating the collapse of their entire society, but it is only one of many. It is believed that the first human inhabitants of Australia and the Americas hunted most of the large animal species on those continents to extinction. Many agrarian societies, such as the Sumerian, Mesopotamian and Indus Valley civilizations, are believed to have brought about their own downfall through overexploitation of the land. Contrary to the romantic myth, ours is not the first society to devastate its environment, although it is the first to do it on a global scale.[43]

When the Taleban attempted to enforce traditional Pashtun cultural values and undo the modest Westernization that Afghanistan had experienced, they devoted a great deal of effort to taking away the rights of women, but none to tackling the very serious problems of desertification and rapid population growth in Afghanistan.

Is there a middle way between Giddens and Norgaard? Many Greens would not go down the postmodernist road. Although the environmental movement has been extremely critical of modernity, it has a more ambiguous relationship with the broader Enlightenment tradition. In some ways, the Green movement has hoped to revitalize leftism by disowning modernity and returning to the pre-Marxist radical Enlightenment tradition.

The concept of sustainability has historically emerged out of a critique of modernity and the trajectory environmentalists see it taking us on towards disaster. Yet, at the same time, the concept of sustainability is rooted in faith in human perfectibility, the possibility of reform and, perhaps most tellingly, the values of equality and solidarity. The concept of sustainable development is even more split in its loyalties, torn between environmentalist criticism of industrial society and support for 'development', the more politically correct post-1945 term for Progress.

Sustainability is an idea which combines postmodernist pessimism about the domination of nature with almost Enlightenment optimism about the possibility to reform human institutions. With worldwide disillusionment about attempts to engineer better societies after the collapse of socialist ideology, the goal of sustainability sounds increasingly ambitious for the pessimistic times we live in.

Sustainability and the limits to control

When planners and regulators fail it is not just because they are unable to foresee some of the consequences of their policies. Those who attempt to push the path of society in a particular direction are faced with the more fundamental problem that they are dealing with a target that is not merely difficult to predict, like the weather, but which is reflexive and responds intelligently to predictions in such a way as to be able to make them self-fulfilling or self-confounding. Peter Medawar used this argument to explain why economic prediction is so unsuccessful.[44] Could policies to bring about sustainability be successful in the long term? Sustainability policies would have to be capable of making long term predictions about the behaviour of human society as well as of the physical environment.

Another fundamental problem with any kind of long term historical prediction which Karl Popper identified is the impossibility of predicting the future course of science.[45] If we could predict its course, we would also know the contents of future science. Future scientific knowledge will make possible new technologies, which we do not know of, and which will have unpredictable social and environmental consequences. (Incidentally, the same basic argument easily refutes Fukuyama's claim that liberal democracy is the final form of human society.) Economists have used Popper's argument to criticize environmentalists for failing to allow for scientific progress in their view of the future. Environmentalists have responded that scientific progress is unpredictable: we cannot simply assume that scientific advances will come along to get us out of environmental problems. The difference between weak and strong sustainability was about the extent to which technology can substitute for natural capital. But future social evolution is even more unpredictable than future technology. Attempting to achieve sustainability sounds like a goal even more difficult to achieve than successful socialism.

Politics after socialism

As Giddens points out, one of the tremendous ironies of present times is the way that, since Marxism went into decline, leftists have taken up arguments that once belonged to conservatives. In this case, at the beginning of the modern age Malthus' claim of natural limits was conservative and Engels' argument that there were no limits was progressive. Today, Greens attack economic growth with an analysis derived from Malthus, and free market economists defend it with an argument they have borrowed from Engels.

The role of the Left has traditionally been to criticize the present society and suggest a better one. The role of the Right has been to defend present social arrangements and argue against change. In recent years, the Left has increasingly been defending its historical achievements, and the Right has increasingly been seeking to do away with them. The Left has stopped being progressive and the Right has stopped being conservative in the earlier senses of those words. The vision of the Left is increasingly informed not so much by the socialist vision of the future, but by the Green one. The Right finds itself, as the proponent of capitalism, cast as the defender of Progress. The Right has ceased to be conservative and instead it seeks to remake society in the interests of capitalism. The Green position is odder still. It recycles the traditional conservative and Romantic scepticism of progress. However, in some ways Green ideology returns to the pre-Marxist roots of socialism. Green ideology generally retains certain elements of progressive Enlightenment thinking – the support for liberty, equality and fraternity. It lacks the faith in human rationality that was the driving force of the Enlightenment. Instead, it considers the instrumental rationalism that drove modernism to have been a disaster. Without faith in the ability of science or the state to transform society for the better, it instead puts its faith, like anarchism, in bringing about the transformation of society from the bottom up.

Green thought rejects the myth of Progress, but in other ways it is not so different from other Western belief systems. Trevor Blackwell and Jeremy Seabrook have explored the structural parallels between the Christian, Marxist and Green myths.[46] In the beginning there was harmony on Earth (the Garden of Eden, a classless society, human beings living in harmony with nature). Then that harmony was lost (The Fall, the invention of private property, the domination of nature). The story involves suffering (Christ's death on the Cross, the sufferings of the proletariat, the ruin of the planet), followed by redemption (the Resurrection, the development of class consciousness, the renunciation of the industrialist way of life), a moment of truth (the Day of Judgement, the revolution, the *avoidance* of apocalypse) and finally a resolution (Heavenly afterlife, communism, survival). The green myth differs from the others in that it is more modest, offering not the end of history after the struggle, but the continuation of existence. It also offers no clear redemptive agency. Nonetheless, its structure is largely that of the standard Western myth.

Blackwell and Seabrook claim that originally capitalism borrowed from the Christian myth, adding only the idea that the soul could be saved through work that created wealth. They claim that in recent times it has turned itself into a religion too. It has abandoned the Christian elements of its story and claims that paradise lies in the rich societies here and now. Francis Fukuyama's subsequent claim that contemporary liberal democracy marks the End of History[47] seems to embody their interpretation of the new capitalist myth.

Blackwell and Seabrook argue that the Green myth has a great deal of potential as a new myth to appeal to the entire human race. It is surely quite telling that Fukuyama did not directly respond to the Green challenge. He was able to argue against the feasibility of abandoning technology, but he had no answer to the challenge to anthropocentrism.

The road to sustainability

Environmentalists these days often use the measuring stick of sustainability. It is very hard to defend an activity once it has been condemned as 'unsustainable'. Attempts to bring about 'sustainability' are faced with several serious problems, however. Most immediately, there are powerful vested interests that favour unsustainability. Socialists had to fight the vested interests of capitalists. For environmentalists, the present generation has a vested interest in putting itself before the claims of future generations. Those who live in particularly unsustainable ways – the affluent consumers – have a strong vested interest in resisting change immediately. What is more, the poor of the South often want wealth quickly and are tempted to ignore the long term consequences.

The second stage to face in attempting to achieve sustainability is defining what we mean by the word. It has not been particularly difficult to come up with definitions. The difficult bit is getting agreement on any given definition. It is even harder to find a definition that can readily be operationalized. Any operational definition of sustainability is ultimately based on more or less arbitrary decisions about the extent to which new knowledge and technology will be able to substitute for various natural resources. Yet it is fundamentally impossible to predict with any accuracy what future technologies will be available.

The decision about whether a particular activity is sustainable depends further on knowledge about how many other similar examples of the activity are taking place. A million cars in the world might have been sustainable; a billion cars are not. This means that it is also necessary to agree on a distribution key for the use of the environmental space available. Attempting to achieve sustainability in one country is almost useless if other countries continue to act unsustainably. Sustainability seems to demand global agreements about the use of the environmental space.

The logic of competition and free trade will tend to oppose considerations of sustainability, so there would be a need for global enforcement mechanisms as well as national policies towards sustainability. On the other hand, the pursuit of sustainability could turn into a latter day version of central planning if everything was decided at a global level. Some kind of a division of labour between different scales of decision making would have to be worked out.

Even so, it would never be possible to be sure that sustainability had been achieved. Proving that something is sustainable is impossible. There is always the possibility that there is something that has been overlooked. The effects of DDT on bird life is a good example of something that only became apparent after it had happened and would have been difficult to predict with the available knowledge. Today, environmental science is much further advanced, but there still remains the possibility that some apparently harmless activity will turn out to be highly unsustainable. We can eliminate or bring under control all activities that are known to be unsustainable. It is much more difficult to deal with activities that are only suspected of being unsustainable. It is impossible to prevent all potential sources of unsustainability.

The central idea of Progress was that rationality could be used to master nature and to build a better society. Sustainability is a rather similar idea in that its implementation also requires the use of rationality and science. The main difference is that it is less optimistic about our capacity to 'master' nature. But the belief that we will actually be able to achieve something like sustainability seems to be based on optimism that it is possible to predict or direct the future and that it will prove possible to persuade people to act not just rationally, but with altruism towards future generations. It could be said that the search for sustainability is the continuation of modernity by other means.

There is a paradox at the heart of the concept of sustainability. Sustainability has come to prominence as the spirit of post-Enlightenment optimism about human progress has faded, to be replaced with concern about the environment and its consequences for future human generations. Upon reflection, it turns out that achieving sustainability is a goal that would require an enormous capacity to predict the future and handle uncertainty. The idea of sustainability itself has arisen out of increasing pessimism about the capacity of human institutions even to handle much less challenging problems.

Is there an alternative?

What are we to do if there are limits to rationality and planning? As this awful realization sank in over the past 30 years, many turned to neoliberal economic theory. It offers the seductive message that markets left to themselves will sort things out and make government planning unnecessary. However, if that was really true, there would never have been a Great Depression. As Eric Hobsbawm observes, it took nearly half a century before folk memory of the catastrophe had faded and liberal economics made a comeback. He is astonished that this spectre of his youth returned to stalk the world in his old age.[48] (Perhaps neosocialism will be all the rage in the 2030s...)

It is a common observation that many people like simple answers to complicated problems. As the billionaire financial speculator George Soros has pointed out, the appeal of neoliberalism is rather similar to those of communism and fascism: it reduces everything to a simple totalizing solution.[49] Like Marxism, it relies on a supposedly scientific theory that is in fact an axiomatic structure whose conclusions are contained in its assumptions and not based on empirical evidence. Marxism deduced that since markets are imperfect, state planning would be perfect. Neoliberalism deduces that since regulations are faulty, unregulated markets are perfect. In reality, both markets and planning are imperfect. Soros identified untrammelled capitalism as the greatest threat to human freedom in the post-Cold War world.

Developments such as the WTO and the proposed General Agreement on Trade and Services, which subordinate environmental and social considerations to the maximization of international trade and investment, are propelling us in the direction of increasing unsustainability. Meanwhile, the extremely rapid flow of funds around the world that has been made possible by the removal of capital controls is increasing the instability of the global economy.

But some radical Green ideas about decentralization can also be seen as based on a simplistic reaction to the failures of state planning. It is quite correct that decisions should be taken at the appropriate level – the famous principle of subsidiarity – and that nearly all existing states are too centralized. But it is also apparent that many of the problems (particularly environmental problems) we face can only begin to be dealt with through international or global coordination. Robyn Eckersley seems to be right in her view that Greens commonly place too much emphasis on decentralization and not enough on the creation of supranational structures to handle large scale problems. She argues that a better arrangement would be a multi-layered federal system of governance from the local to the global based on different scales and capable of meeting different objectives.[50]

We cannot escape from having to make impossibly difficult decisions by advocating that they should be left to markets or local communities who will magically sort them out. These ideas have received currency because of the catalogue of disastrous decisions taken by governments during the 20th century, but the solutions they offer are illusory. The idea that because one system is imperfect, the opposite system would be perfect is both fallacious and very dangerous.

The same kind of fallacy is to be found in postmodernist theories which imply that because absolute knowledge is impossible, any kind of knowledge is impossible. It is very important not to fall into the trap of thinking that because we cannot be sure that sustainability is possible, there is no point in doing anything to try to become more sustainable.

What to do about reflexivity?

Giddens and Norgaard make the same diagnosis of the fundamental cause of the limits to modernity; they are due to the reflexivity of both nature and society. But while Norgaard sees these limits as marking the end of modernity, Giddens sees a new kind of modernity opening up where we can learn to stop worrying and love manufactured risk. Norgaard's solution is not only to attempt to disentangle nature and society, but also to attempt to disentangle different societies in order to free the world from the domination of Western modernity. Giddens, by contrast, argues that we cannot disentangle nature and society and that it is only through continuing globalization that we can create communities capable of cultural tolerance and global solidarity.

I have already discussed problems with the consequences of both positions. Giddens' reflexive modernization seems too sanguine about manufacturing new risks. Norgaard's co-evolutionary approach runs the danger of allowing narrow parochialisms to compete and create a 'tragedy of the commons' scenario.

Could we somehow disentangle the good and bad aspects of modernity? As I wrote near the beginning of this book, there are two Enlightenment traditions; one flowing from Jean-Jacques Rousseau and the other flowing from Adam Smith. While Smithian rationalism has been the dominant influence for the past two centuries, Rousseau's respect for the natural world has been sidelined. Just as recognition of human fallibility underlies the liberal conception of freedom in society, it could also underlie our relationship with nature. Soros writes that after 200 years' experience of the Age of Reason we should as reasonable people accept that rationality has its limits. He concludes that where reason has failed, fallibility may yet succeed.[51]

The end of sustainability?

The trouble is that bringing about sustainability would depend on creating a rational society, one where people's desire for riches could be subsumed to the need to maintain a habitable world for future generations.

What would it be like in a more sustainable world? Environmental limits would be accepted and lived within. There would be a recognition that even extravagant benefits from new technologies are not worthwhile if they involve the risk of serious or irreversible environmental impacts – in other words, the precautionary principle would be followed in practice and not just in rhetoric.

However, in a world of competing states, each has an incentive to go for the maximum growth and become dominant. The societies that fail to grow, as Fukuyama points out, end up losing their influence to those that do grow. So each state has an incentive to follow the path of modernity in the short to medium term, even if it is likely to lead to global disaster in the long term.

We would also have to consider social sustainability. A world with the great inequalities of wealth that we have now is inherently unstable. The pressure from below to raise the living standards of the poor majority may be suppressed for a long time, but it is hard to imagine such inequality being effectively enforced forever. In a world where the environmental limits are already being exceeded, any move to allow improvements in the condition of the poor majority is going to require the rich minority to reduce their consumption of environmental space still more drastically than even the need for physical sustainability would imply. There are a number of problems with doing that. The rich show very little sign of being prepared to cut back on their use of resources for the sake of sustainability. Americans, for example, regard any attempt to increase the price of gasoline to international levels as an attack on their way of life. Europeans may appear more enlightened, but it is worth remembering the protests calling for reductions in the tax on petrol that took place in many European countries in 2000. It might not be too cynical to draw the conclusion that people are all in favour of sustainability only so long as it does not involve any personal inconvenience.

The story of the collapse of communism is not encouraging, either. What greatly impressed most Eastern Europeans about the West was not so much the political freedom as the consumer goods to be found on the other side of the Iron Curtain. The failing that ultimately destroyed the communist system was that its rate of economic growth could not keep up with the West's. That simple fact underlies nearly everything that we have been hearing for the past decade about the superiority of capitalism over socialism. It rests on the triumph of consumerism. But as far as sustainability is concerned, consumerism is a large part of the problem. As far as capitalism is concerned, consumerism is essential.

As many Green authors have pointed out, wealth and materialism do not bring true happiness. It is a truth that was pointed out much earlier by Buddha and then by Jesus. Yet over two millennia of this knowledge have failed to prevent consumerism from more recently displacing Christianity and Buddhism as the religion of both Europe and East Asia. Now that we live in a world where many of us are faced with enormous material temptations, some people resist but most cheerfully give in. Consumerism is an addiction that most people afflicted with do not want to be cured of, any more than most wealthy cocaine addicts really want to be cured.

The capitalist triumphalism of today will brook little compromise after the defeat of socialism. The justification for deregulation, free trade and economic globalization is that it increases growth. Concern about sustainability is dismissed as a barrier to trade. The former Thatcherite John Gray has recently argued that today's era of capitalist globalization will be at least as short lived and end as catastrophically as the globalizing *belle époque* of 1870–1914. He predicts that the social destructiveness of globalization and the economic instability it creates will lead to crisis.[52] We can perhaps hope that the end of the present long economic cycle will see a change of economic fashion much as the crises after 1929 and 1973 did. Unfortunately, what is driving globalization is not just economic fashion but new technology. It might be politically possible to institute exchange controls, but it would be very difficult to do away with television and the Internet.

As Giddens says, improved communications technologies lead to ideas and fashions spreading ever faster around the world. When people's ideas are based on tradition they remain relatively fixed for generations and can be planned for. As communications improve, ideas and fashions bounce around the world so quickly that planning can no longer keep up. The idea is an interesting twist on Marx's famous observation that capitalism involves the continual revolutionizing of social relations. This insight of Giddens may seem quite innocent, but it implies that improving communications technologies could undermine any attempt at sustainability in much the same way that he claims they undermined economic planning. It is not simply the increasing flow of goods and services that are measured in international trade statistics that constitutes globalization. It is also constituted by the increasing flow of information and people.

There is a paradox here. The pursuit of sustainability requires a global moral and political community. Such a community can be contemplated today only because we have such powerful communications technologies. On the other hand, these technologies promote rapid social change; that sort of continual revolutionizing of society is not conducive to following a path of sustainability because it makes it impossible to predict people's ideas and values.

Eric Hobsbawm concluded his history of the 20th century with the observation that although accurately predicting the future is impossible, it is reasonable to suppose that the growth model of capitalism cannot continue indefinitely. So, he claimed, despite the demise of socialism, something will have to replace capitalism in the future.[53]

The basic argument of my book has been that the language of sustainability returns us to many of the unfashionable ideas about fairness and solidarity that were associated with socialism in the past, although also dealing with concerns about nature, risk, growth, and technology that were not issues for socialism. The solutions that socialism offered have been discredited and meanwhile new problems have emerged to which there are no easy answers.

Sustainability is a rather different idea from modernity. It is about maintaining things, while modernity is about constant change. It is about the control of human society in order to protect nature, while modernity is about human control of nature. But sustainability is like socialist modernity (and unlike capitalism) in that it is about the conscious regulation of social development. No matter how much people may have wanted to regulate social development, they have to a large extent failed in the long run. Many Greens claim that it is because they tried to do it in too grand and centralized a fashion – if it is done in a small scale, decentralized fashion then it may succeed. But what is to guarantee that these small scale structures will look to the long term broader interest and cooperate, rather than short term parochial interests and compete for advantage?

There appear to be reasons in principle why we cannot have sufficient information or foresight to design institutions that can successfully deal with very complicated reflexive problems. Despite all this, there is a lot that could be done to make our civilization more sustainable than it presently is. Just because we don't know how to create a truly sustainable society, that doesn't mean that we can't do things to become less unsustainable.

There are many ideas that have been discussed in this book that could move the world in the direction of sustainability: reform of the world trading system, ETR, development of 'factor ten' technologies, the environmental space concept, contraction and convergence, the precautionary principle and the strong sustainability rule.

We know something about the principles that would underlie sustainability and it is possible to suggest measures that would move us in its direction, but reflexivity means that it is impossible to draw up a detailed blueprint of a sustainable society or even of the route to get to it. We can be sure that any attempt to bring about sustainability will meet enormous resistance from many people and vested interests. But there is not much choice about the matter. The alternative to the pursuit of sustainability is to continue along the present path of unsustainability, leading to disaster.

References

Introduction

[1] World Council of Churches (1974) Report of Ecumenical Study Conference on Science and Technology for Human Development, Geneva: World Council of Churches

[2] International Union for Conservation of Nature and Natural Resources (1980) *World Conservation Strategy: Living Resources Conservation for Sustainable Development*, Gland, Switzerland: IUCN

[3] World Commission on Environment and Development (1987) *Our Common Future*, Oxford: Oxford University Press

[4] ibid, p 8

[5] Tim O'Riordan (1988) 'The Politics of Sustainability' in *Sustainable Environmental Management: Principles and Practice*, edited by R. Kerry Turner, London: Belhaven

[6] Michael Jacobs (1991) *The Green Economy*, London: Pluto

[7] WCED (1987), op cit, p 43

[8] Herman E. Daly (1992) *Steady-State Economics*, Second Edition, London: Earthscan, p 248

[9] Richard B. Norgaard (1994) *Development Betrayed*, London: Routledge

[10] Ulrich Beck (1992) *The Risk Society*, London: Sage

[11] Anthony Giddens (1994) *Beyond Left and Right*, Cambridge: Polity

1. Progress and its Discontents

[1] Richard B. Norgaard (1994) *Development Betrayed*, London: Routledge

[2] William Leiss (1972) *The Domination of Nature*, New York: George Braziller

[3] Bacon, quoted in Leiss (1972) op cit, p 55

[4] René Descartes (1637) *A Discourse on Method*, London: Everyman, 1992

[5] John Locke (1689) *Two Treatises of Government*, London: Everyman, 1993

[6] Adam Smith (1776) *The Wealth of Nations*, Oxford: Oxford University Press, 1993

[7] Jean-Jacques Rousseau (1755) *Discourse on Inequality*, Oxford: Oxford University Press, 1994

[8] Thomas Malthus (1798) *An Essay on the Principle of Population*, Oxford: Oxford University Press, 1993, p 11

[9] Kenneth Smith (1951) *The Malthusian Controversy*, London: Routledge & Kegan Paul

[10] Michelle Perrot (1983) 'Malthusianism and Socialism' in *Malthus Past and Present*, edited by Jacques Dupâquier, Antoinette Fauve-Chamoux and Eugene Grebenik, London: Academic

[11] Karl Marx (1875) 'Critique of the Gotha Programme' in Karl Marx and Friedrich Engels, *Selected Works*, London: Lawrence & Wishart, 1968, p 324

[12] Friedrich Engels (1844) 'Outlines of a Critique of Political Economy' in Karl Marx and Friedrich Engels, *Collected Works,* London: Lawrence & Wishart, 1987, vol 4, pp 439–40

[13] ibid, p 440

[14] ibid, p 439

[15] Ted Benton (1989) 'Marx and Natural Limits: An Ecological Critique and Reconstruction', *New Left Review,* 163: 51–86

[16] Marx, quoted in Benton (1989) op cit, p 83

[17] Engels, quoted in Benton (1989) op cit, p 82

[18] Rainer Grundmann (1991) 'The Ecological Challenge to Marx', *New Left Review* 187: 103–120

[19] ibid, p 109

[20] ibid, p 119

[21] Mary Shelley (1818) *Frankenstein,* Oxford: Oxford University Press, 1994

[22] Shelley, quoted in Brian Easlea (1983) *Fathering the Unthinkable,* London: Pluto, pp 30–31

[23] Mary Shelley (1826) *The Last Man,* London: Hogarth, 1985

[24] John Stuart Mill (1848) *Principles of Political Economy,* Harmandsworth: Penguin, 1985, pp 113–116

2. From Muir to Meadows

[1] John Muir (1894) *The Mountains of California,* San Francisco: Sierra Club, 1988, p 257

[2] Juan Martinez-Alier (1987) *Ecological Economics,* Oxford: Basil Blackwell

[3] Donald Worster (1985) *Nature's Economy,* Cambridge: Cambridge University Press

[4] Roderick Nash (1989) *The Rights of Nature,* Madison: University of Wisconsin Press

[5] Aldo Leopold (1949) *A Sand County Almanac,* New York: Ballantine, 1970

[6] ibid, p 262

[7] ibid, p 240

[8] ibid, p 190

[9] Rachel Carson (1962) *Silent Spring,* New York: Houghton Mifflin

[10] ibid, p 243

[11] Richard B. Norgaard (1994) *Development Betrayed,* London: Routledge

[12] Barbara Ward (1966) *Spaceship Earth,* New York: University of Columbia Press

[13] Kenneth Boulding (1966) 'The Economics of the Coming Spaceship Earth' in *Environmental Quality in a Growing Economy,* edited by H. Jarrett, Baltimore: Johns Hopkins Press

[14] Marshall McLuhan and Quentin Fiore (1967) *The Medium is the Massage,* New York: Bantam

[15] E.J. Mishan (1967) *The Costs of Economic Growth,* London: Staples

[16] John Kenneth Galbraith (1958) *The Affluent Society,* New York: New American Library

[17] Paul Ehrlich (1968) *The Population Bomb*, New York: Ballantine

[18] Paul R. Ehrlich and Anne H. Ehrlich (1991) *The Population Explosion*, New York: Simon & Schuster

[19] John Maddox (1972) *The Doomsday Syndrome*, London: Macmillan

[20] John Holdren and Paul Ehrlich (1974) 'Human population and the global environment', *American Scientist* (62) 282–92

[21] Donella H. Meadows, Dennis L. Meadows, Jørgen Randers and William W. Behrens III (1972) *The Limits to Growth*, New York: Universe Books

[22] ibid, p 23

[23] ibid, p 24

[24] H.S.D. Cole, Christopher Freeman, Marie Jahoda and K.L.R Pavitt (1973) *Thinking About The Future: A Critique of 'The Limits to Growth'*, London: Chatto & Windus

[25] Herman E. Daly (1977) *Steady-State Economics*, San Francisco: Freeman

[26] Nicholas Georgescu-Roegen (1971) *The Entropy Law and the Economic Process*, Cambridge, Massachusetts: Harvard University Press

[27] Gerald Barney, director (1981) *Global 2000 Report to the President*, New York: Penguin, p 1

[28] Norman Myers (1979) *The Sinking Ark*, New York: Pergamon

[29] Mark Green and Gail MacColl (1983) *There He Goes Again: Ronald Reagan's Reign of Error*, New York: Pantheon

3. Sustainability Emerging

[1] E.F. Schumacher (1973) *Small is Beautiful*, London: Blond & Briggs

[2] World Council of Churches, quoted in Elizabeth Dowdeswell (1994) 'A global view' in *Partnerships in Practice*, London: Department of the Environment

[3] Dennis Pirages, editor (1977) *The Sustainable Society*, New York: Praeger

[4] International Union for Conservation of Nature and Natural Resources (1980) *World Conservation Strategy: Living Resources Conservation for Sustainable Development*, Gland, Switzerland: IUCN, Section 1.2

[5] ibid, Section 1.3

[6] ibid, Section 1.4

[7] World Commission on Environment and Development (1987) *Our Common Future*, Oxford: Oxford University Press

[8] ibid, p 4

[9] ibid, p 8

[10] ibid, p 8–9

[11] ibid, p 5

[12] ibid, pp 28–29

[13] ibid, pp 49–50

[14] ibid, p 43

[15] ibid, p 44

[16] ibid, p 45

4. From Rio to Kyoto and Later Disappointments

[1] Intergovernmental Panel on Climate Change (1990) *Climate Change: The IPCC Assessment* , Geneva: World Meteorological Organization

[2] Michael Grubb, Matthias Koch, Koy Thomson, Abby Munson, Francis Sullivan (1993) *The 'Earth Summit' Agreements: A Guide and Assessment*, London: Earthscan

[3] United Nations Conference on Environment and Development (1992) 'The Rio Declaration on Environment and Development', Rio de Janiero: UNCED Secretariat

[4] Grubb et al (1993) op cit

[5] ibid

[6] ibid

[7] Norman Myers (1998) 'Lifting the veil on perverse subsidies', *Nature* 392: 327–328

[8] South Centre, quoted in Grubb et al (1993) op cit, p 26

[9] Donella H. Meadows, Dennis L. Meadows and Jørgen Randers (1992) *Beyond the Limits: Global Collapse or a Sustainable Future*, London: Earthscan

[10] Pratap Chatterjee and Matthias Finger (1994) *The Earth Brokers*, London: Routledge

[11] Martin Khor (1992) Editorial, *Third World Resurgence*, 24–25, p 4

[12] Stephen Schmidheiny (1992) *Changing Course*, Cambridge, Massachusetts: MIT Press

[13] Herman E. Daly and John B. Cobb (1990) *For the Common Good*, London: Green Print

[14] World Trade Organization Ministerial Conference (2001) 'Doha Ministerial Declaration', Doha: WTO

[15] Al Gore (1992) *Earth in the Balance*, London: Earthscan

[16] Intergovernmental Panel on Climate Change (1995) *Climate Change 1995*, Cambridge: Cambridge University Press

[17] Intergovernmental Panel on Climate Change (2001) *Climate Change 2001*, Cambridge: Cambridge University Press

[18] United Nations Environment Programme (2002) *Global Environment Outlook 3*, London: Earthscan

5. What Does 'Sustainable Development' Mean?

[1] Tim O'Riordan (1988) 'The Politics of Sustainability' in *Sustainable Environmental Management: Principles and Practice*, edited by R. Kerry Turner, London: Belhaven

[2] ibid

[3] Nicholas Hildyard (1993) 'Foxes in charge of the chickens' in *Global Ecology*, edited by Wolfgang Sachs, London: Zed

[4] Michael Jacobs (1991) *The Green Economy*, London: Pluto

[5] Jacobs (1991) op cit, p 60

[6] Lewis Carroll (1872) 'Alice Through the Looking-Glass' in *The Penguin Complete Lewis Carroll*, Harmandsworth: Penguin, 1982, p 196

[7] World Commission on Environment and Development (1987) *Our Common Future*, Oxford: Oxford University Press, p 43

[8] David Pearce, Anil Markandya and Edward B. Barbier (1989) *Blueprint for a Green Economy*, London: Earthscan

[9] Amartya Sen (1999) *Development as Freedom*, Oxford: Oxford University Press

[10] Michael Carley and Ian Christie (1992) *Managing Sustainable Development*, London: Earthscan

[11] United Nations Development Programme (1996) *Human Development Report 1996*, New York: Oxford University Press

[12] World Bank (2000) *World Development Report 2000–2001: Attacking Poverty*, New York: Oxford University Press

[13] Economist (2001) 'Not by their bootstraps alone', *The Economist*, 12 May, p 74

[14] Martin W. Lewis (1992) *Green Delusions*, Durham, North Carolina: Duke University Press

[15] Paul Ekins (1999) *Economic Growth and Environmental Sustainability*, London: Routledge

[16] Wolfgang Sachs (1999) *Planet Dialectics*, London: Zed

[17] Richard A. Easterlin (1996) *Growth Triumphant*, Ann Arbor: University of Michigan Press

6. Taking Sustainability into Economics

[1] David Pearce, Anil Markandya and Edward B. Barbier (1989) *Blueprint for a Green Economy*, London: Earthscan

[2] ibid

[3] ibid pp 37–38

[4] Wilfred Beckerman (1995) *Small is Stupid*, Oxford: Duckworth

[5] Partha Dasgupta (1993a) 'Optimal versus Sustainable Development' in *Valuing the Environment*, edited by Ismail Serageldin and Andrew Steer, Washington DC: World Bank

[6] ibid, p 36

[7] Andrew Steer (1993) Discussant Remarks in *Valuing the Environment*, edited by Ismail Serageldin and Andrew Steer, Washington DC: World Bank, pp 67–68

[8] Partha Dasgupta (1993b) Floor Discussion in *Valuing the Environment*, edited by Ismail Serageldin and Andrew Steer, Washington DC: World Bank, p 70

[9] Ismail Serageldin and Andrew Steer (1994) *Making Development Sustainable: From Concepts to Action*, Washington DC: World Bank

[10] John Pezzey (1989) *Economic Analysis of Sustainable Growth and Sustainable Development*, Washington DC: World Bank

[11] United Nations Economic Commission for Europe (1990) Bergen Ministerial Declaration on Sustainable Development, Bergen, UNECE

[12] Serageldin and Steer (1994) op cit

[13] Herman E. Daly and John B. Cobb (1990) *For the Common Good*, London: Green Print, pp 195–7

[14] Herman E. Daly (1991) 'Elements of Environmental Macroeconomics' in *Ecological Economics: The Science and Management of Sustainability*, edited by Robert Costanza, New York: Columbia, pp 44–5

[15] Horst Siebert (1982) 'Nature as a life-support system', *Journal of Economics*, 42 (2): 133–42

[16] R. Weterings and J.B. Opschoor (1994), *Towards Environmental Performance Indicators Based on the Notion of Environmental Space*, Rijswijk, The Netherlands: Advisory Council for Research on Nature and the Environment, pp 3–4

[17] National Institute for Public Health and Environmental Protection (1988) *Caring for Tomorrow: National Environmental Outlook 1985–2010*, The Hague: National Institute for Public Health and Environmental Protection

[18] Maria Buitenkamp, Henk Venner, Teo Wams, editors (1993) *Action Plan Sustainable Netherlands*, Amsterdam: Vereniging Milieudefensie

[19] ibid, p 18

[20] Duncan McLaren, Simon Bullock and Nusrat Yousuf (1998) *Tomorrow's World: Britain's Share in a Sustainable Future*, London: Earthscan, p 11

[21] Gro Harlem Brundtland (1994) 'The challenge of sustainable development and consumption patterns' in *Symposium Report: Sustainable consumption*, edited by Sylvi Ofstad, Liv Westby and Tone Bratelli, Oslo: Ministry of Environment, p 26

[22] David Pearce (1995) *Blueprint 4: Capturing Global Environmental Value*, London: Earthscan, p 115

[23] ibid, p 116

[24] Amory B. Lovins (1977) *Soft Energy Paths*, Harmandsworth: Pelican

[25] Ernst von Weizsäcker, Amory B. Lovins, L. Hunter Lovins (1997) *Factor Four: Doubling Wealth – Halving Resource Use*, London: Earthscan

[26] William Nordhaus (1990) 'Count before you leap: economics of climate change', *The Economist*, 7 July, pp 21–24

[27] Stephen Tindale and Gerald Holtham (1996) *Green Tax Reform*, London: Institute for Public Policy Research

[28] Ernst-Ulrich von Weizsäcker (1994) *Earth Politics*, London: Zed

[29] European Commission (2002) 'European Policy Brief', PETRAS website, http://www.soc.surrey.ac.uk/petras/reports.html

[30] Joseph A. Schumpeter (1943) *Capitalism, Socialism and Democracy*, London: Allen & Unwin

[31] Tindale and Holtham (1996) op cit

[32] United Nations Development Programme (1996) *Human Development Report 1996*, Oxford: Oxford University Press

[33] ibid, p 126

[34] R. Heuting, P. Bosch and B. de Boer (1992) *Methodology for the Calculation of Sustainable National Income*, The Hague: Central Bureau of Statistics

[35] Robert Goodland and Herman Daly (1993) 'Why Northern income growth is not the solution to Southern poverty', *Ecological Economics*, 8: 85–101

[36] Daly and Cobb (1990) op cit

[37] Martin Ryle (1988) *Ecology and Socialism*, London: Century Hutchinson

[38] Daly and Cobb (1990) op cit

[39] ibid

[40] Tim Jackson and Nick Marks (1994) *Measuring Sustainable Economic Welfare: a pilot index for the UK 1950 – 1990*, Stockholm Environment Institute/New Economics Foundation

[41] Friends of the Earth (2001) 'Measuring Progress', Policy and Research Unit, Friends of the Earth website, http://www.foe.org.uk/progress/

[42] Herman E. Daly (1977) *Steady-State Economics*, San Francisco: Freeman

[43] Herman E. Daly (1977) *Steady-State Economics*, Second Edition, London: Earthscan, 1992, p 117

[44] ibid, p 119

[45] Eric Drexler (1990) *Engines of Creation*, London: Fourth Estate

[46] Derek Wall (1990) *Getting There: Steps Towards a Green Society*, London: Green Print

[47] Tim Huet (1997) 'Can Coops Go Global? Mondragon Is Trying', *Dollars and Sense*, Nov/Dec, http://www.dollarsandsense.org/issues/nov97/mon.html

7. Putting a Price on the Planet

[1] Herman E. Daly and John B. Cobb (1990) *For the Common Good*, London: Green Print

[2] ibid, p 142

[3] Aubrey Meyer and Tony Cooper (1995) 'A Recalculation of the Social Costs of Climate Change', Global Commons Institute, London

[4] Norman Myers (1998) 'Lifting the veil on perverse subsidies', *Nature*, vol 392, pp 327–8

[5] Aisling Irwin (1995) 'Green economist faces picket', *Times Higher Education Supplement*, 24 November

[6] Fred Pearce (1995) 'Global row over value of human life', *New Scientist*, 19 August

[7] Samuel Fankhauser and Richard Tol (1995) Appendix D to Meyer and Cooper, op cit

[8] Intergovernmental Panel on Climate Change (1995) 'Summary for Policy-makers of the Report of Working Group III', Geneva: World Meteorological Organization

[9] R. Kerry Turner (1991) 'Environment, economics and ethics' in *Blueprint 2: Greening the World Economy*, edited by David Pearce, London: Earthscan

[10] Global Commons Institute (1994) 'The Unequal Use of the Global Commons', paper for IPCC workshop, Nairobi, 18–23 July

[11] Klaus Meyer-Abich (1993) 'Winners and Losers in Climate Change' in *Global Ecology*, edited by Wolfgang Sachs, London: Zed

[12] Wilfred Beckerman (1995) *Small is Stupid*, Oxford: Duckworth, p 61

[13] ibid, p 62

[14] Paul R. Ehrlich and Anne H. Ehrlich (1991) *The Population Explosion*, New York: Simon & Schuster

[15] David Pearce, Anil Markandya and Edward B. Barbier (1989) *Blueprint for a Green Economy*, London: Earthscan, pp 51–2

[16] Amartya Sen (1987) *On Ethics and Economics*, Oxford: Basil Blackwell

[17] J. Burgess, J. Clark and C.M. Harrison (1998) 'Respondents' evaluations of a contingent valuation survey: a case study based on an economic valuation of the wildlife enhancement scheme, Pevensey Levels in East Sussex', *Area*, vol 30(1), pp 19–27

[18] Michael Jacobs (1991) *The Green Economy*, London: Pluto

[19] ibid

[20] Turner (1991) op cit

[21] Aldo Leopold (1949) *A Sand County Almanac*, New York: Ballantine, 1970

[22] Turner (1991) op cit, p 221

8. The Ethics of Sustainability

[1] John Rawls (1971) *A Theory of Justice*, Cambridge, Massachusetts: Harvard University Press

[2] Aldous Huxley (1932) *Brave New World*, London: Chatto & Windus

[3] Rawls (1971) op cit, p 178

[4] ibid, p 291

[5] ibid, p 287

[6] John Rawls (1993) *Political Liberalism*, New York: Columbia University Press

[7] David J. Richard (1971) *A Theory of Reasons for Action*, Oxford: Clarendon

[8] Brian Barry (1989) *Theories of Justice*, London: Harvester-Wheatsheaf

[9] Beckerman (1995) op cit, p151

[10] John Pezzey (1994) 'Concern for Sustainability in a Sexual World', Centre for Social and Economic Research on the Global Environment, London

[11] Pezzey (1994) op cit

[12] Michael Jacobs (1991) *The Green Economy*, London: Pluto

[13] William D. Nordhaus and Joseph Boyer (2000) *Warming the World: Economic Models of Global Warming*, Cambridge, Massachusetts: MIT Press

[14] Wifred Beckerman (1995) *Small is Stupid*, Oxford: Duckworth

[15] Anthony Giddens (1994) *Beyond Left and Right*, London: Polity

[16] Robyn Eckersley (1992) *Environmentalism and Political Theory*, London: UCL Press

[17] Marcel Wissenburg (1998) *Green Liberalism: The free and the green society*, London: UCL Press

[18] Robert Nozick (1974) *Anarchy, State and Utopia,* New York: Basic Books

[19] Wissenburg (1998) op cit, p 123

[20] Rawls (1993) op cit, p 274

[21] ibid

[22] Wissenburg (1998) op cit, pp 153–4

[23] ibid, p 212

[24] Mark Sagoff (1988) *The Economy of the Earth,* Cambridge: Cambridge University Press

[25] Eckersley (1992) op cit, p 24

[26] Luke Martell (1994) *Ecology and Society,* Cambridge: Polity

[27] Isiah Berlin (1958) *Two Concepts of Liberty,* Oxford: Clarendon

[28] Isiah Berlin (1969) *Four Essays on Liberty,* Oxford: Oxford University Press, p xlv

[29] ibid, p xlvi

[30] ibid, pp xlvi–xlvii

[31] World Commission on Environment and Development (1987) *Our Common Future,* Oxford: Oxford University Press, p 43

[32] ibid, p 8

9. The End of Sustainability?

[1] Edmund Burke (1790) *Reflections on the Revolution in France,* Oxford: Oxford University Press, 1993

[2] Karl Marx and Friedrich Engels (1848) *The Communist Manifesto,* Oxford: Oxford University Press, 1992, pp 7–8

[3] ibid, p 6

[4] John Kenneth Galbraith (1958) *The Affluent Society,* New York: New American Library

[5] *Encyclopædia Britannica* (1911) eleventh edition, Cambridge: Cambridge University Press, vol 27, p 72

[6] ibid, vol 28, p 314

[7] Eric Hobsbawm (1994) *Age of Extremes: The Short 20th Century 1914–1991,* London: Michael Joseph

[8] ibid

[9] ibid

[10] Timothy Garton Ash (1990) *We The People,* London: Granta

[11] Hobsbawm (1994) op cit

[12] Timothy Garton Ash (1989) *The Uses of Adversity,* London: Granta

[13] Hobsbawm (1994) op cit

[14] Martin Summers, ed (1992) *Economic Alternatives for Eastern Europe,* London: New Economics Foundation

[15] Carl Boggs (1995) *The Socialist Tradition,* New York: Routledge

[16] Francis Fukuyama (1989) 'The End of History?' *The National Interest,* Summer 1989, 3–18

[17] Francis Fukuyama (1992) *The End of History and the Last Man*, London: Hamish Hamilton

[18] ibid, p 312

[19] Timothy Burns, ed (1994) *After History? Francis Fukuyama and His Critics*, Lanham, Maryland: Littlefield Adams

[20] Anthony Giddens (1994) *Beyond Left and Right: The Future of Radical Politics*, Cambridge: Polity

[21] F.A. Hayek (1945) 'The Use of Knowledge in Society', *American Economic Review* 35, 519–530

[22] Giddens (1994) op cit, p 69

[23] Ulrich Beck (1992) *The Risk Society*, London: Sage

[24] Giddens (1994) op cit, p 83

[25] ibid, p 206

[26] ibid, p 247

[27] ibid, p 249

[28] Paul Hirst and Graham Thompson (1996) *Globalization in Question*, Cambridge: Polity

[29] Karl Marx and Friedrich Engels (1848) *The Communist Manifesto*, Oxford: Oxford University Press, 1992, p 7

[30] Anthony Giddens (1998) *The Third Way: The Renewal of Social Democracy*, Cambridge: Polity

[31] ibid, p 61

[32] Anthony Clayton and Nicholas Radcliffe (1996) *Sustainability: A Systems Approach*, London: Earthscan

[33] Jeremy Isaacs and Taylor Downing (1998) *The Cold War*, London: Bantam

[34] Richard B. Norgaard (1994) *Development Betrayed*, London: Routledge

[35] ibid, p 185

[36] Jonathon Porritt (1984) *Seeing Green: The Politics of Ecology Explained*, Oxford: Basil Blackwell, p 44

[37] Norgaard (1994) op cit, p 34

[38] ibid, pp 9–10

[39] ibid, p 70

[40] ibid, p 95

[41] E. F. Schumacher (1973) *Small is Beautiful*, London: Blond & Briggs

[42] Francis Fukuyama (1994) 'Reflections on the End of History, Five Years Later', in *After History: Francis Fukuyama and His Critics*, edited by Timothy Burns, Lanham, Maryland: Littlefield Adams

[43] Clive Ponting (1992) *A Green History of the World*, Harmandsworth: Penguin

[44] Peter Medawar (1984) *Pluto's Republic*, Oxford: Oxford University Press

[45] Karl Popper (1957) *The Poverty of Historicism*, London: Routledge & Kegan Paul

[46] Trevor Blackwell and Jeremy Seabrook (1988) *The Politics of Hope*, London: Faber & Faber

[47] Fukuyama (1992) op cit

[48] Hobsbawm (1994) op cit

[49] George Soros (1997) 'The Capitalist Threat', *The Atlantic Monthly*, February, http://www.theatlantic.com/issues/97feb/capital/capital.htm

[50] Robyn Eckersley (1992) *Environmentalism and Political Theory*, London: UCL Press

[51] Soros (1997) op cit

[52] John Gray (1997) *False Dawn: The Delusions of Global Capitalism*, London: Granta

[53] Hobsbawm (1994) op cit

Bibliography

Ash, Timothy Garton (1989) *The Uses of Adversity*, London: Granta

Ash, Timothy Garton (1990) *We The People*, London: Granta

Barney, Gerald, director (1981) *Global 2000 Report to the President*, New York: Penguin

Barry, Brian (1989) *Theories of Justice*, London: Harvester-Wheatsheaf

Beck, Ulrich (1992) *The Risk Society*, London: Sage

Beckerman, Wilfred (1995) *Small is Stupid*, Oxford: Duckworth

Benton, Ted (1989) 'Marx and Natural Limits: An Ecological Critique and Reconstruction', *New Left Review*, 163: 51–86

Berlin, Isiah (1958) *Two Concepts of Liberty*, Oxford: Clarendon

Berlin, Isiah (1969) *Four Essays on Liberty*, Oxford: Oxford University Press

Blackwell, Trevor and Jeremy Seabrook (1988) *The Politics of Hope*, London: Faber & Faber

Boggs, Carl (1995) *The Socialist Tradition*, New York: Routledge

Boulding, Kenneth (1966) 'The Economics of the Coming Spaceship Earth' in *Environmental Quality in a Growing Economy*, edited by H. Jarrett, Baltimore: Johns Hopkins Press

Brundtland, Gro Harlem (1994) 'The challenge of sustainable development and consumption patterns' in *Symposium Report: Sustainable consumption*, edited by Sylvi Ofstad, Liv Westby and Tone Bratelli, Oslo: Ministry of Environment

Buitenkamp, Maria, Henk Venner, Teo Wams, editors (1993) *Action Plan Sustainable Netherlands*, Amsterdam: Vereniging Milieudefensie

Burgess, J., J. Clark and C.M. Harrison (1998) 'Respondents' evaluations of a contingent valuation survey: a case study based on an economic valuation of the wildlife enhancement scheme, Pevensey Levels in East Sussex', *Area*, 30(1): 19–27

Burke, Edmund (1790) *Reflections on the Revolution in France*, Oxford: Oxford University Press, 1993

Burns, Timothy, ed (1994) *After History? Francis Fukuyama and His Critics*, Lanham, Maryland: Littlefield Adams

Carley, Michael and Ian Christie (1992) *Managing Sustainable Development*, London: Earthscan

Carroll, Lewis (1872) 'Alice Through the Looking-Glass' in *The Penguin Complete Lewis Carroll*, Harmandsworth: Penguin, 1982

Carson, Rachel (1962) *Silent Spring*, New York: Houghton Mifflin

Chatterjee, Pratap and Matthias Finger (1994) *The Earth Brokers*, London: Routledge

Clayton, Anthony and Nicholas Radcliffe (1996) *Sustainability: A Systems Approach*, London: Earthscan

Cole, H.S.D., Christopher Freeman, Marie Jahoda and K.L.R Pavitt (1973) *Thinking About The Future: A Critique of 'The Limits to Growth'*, London: Chatto & Windus

Daly, Herman E. (1977) *Steady-State Economics*, San Francisco: Freeman

Daly, Herman E. (1991) 'Elements of Environmental Macroeconomics' in *Ecological Economics: The Science and Management of Sustainability*, edited by Robert Costanza, New York: Columbia

Daly, Herman E. (1992) *Steady-State Economics*, Second Edition, London: Earthscan

Daly, Herman E. and John B. Cobb (1990) *For the Common Good*, London: Green Print

Dasgupta, Partha (1993a) 'Optimal versus Sustainable Development' in *Valuing the Environment*, edited by Ismail Serageldin and Andrew Steer, Washington DC: World Bank

Dasgupta, Partha (1993b) Floor Discussion in *Valuing the Environment*, edited by Ismail Serageldin and Andrew Steer, Washington DC: World Bank

Descartes, René (1637) *A Discourse on Method*, London: Everyman, 1992

Dowdeswell, Elizabeth (1994) 'A global view' in *Partnerships in Practice*, London: Department of the Environment

Drexler, Eric (1990) *Engines of Creation*, London: Fourth Estate

Easlea, Brian (1983) *Fathering the Unthinkable*, London: Pluto

Easterlin, Richard A. (1996) *Growth Triumphant*, Ann Arbor: University of Michigan Press

Eckersley, Robyn (1992) *Environmentalism and Political Theory*, London: UCL Press

Economist (2001) 'Not by their bootstraps alone', *The Economist*, 12 May, p 74

Ehrlich, Paul (1968) *The Population Bomb*, New York: Ballantine

Ehrlich, Paul R. and Anne H. Ehrlich (1991) *The Population Explosion*, New York: Simon & Schuster

Ekins, Paul (1999) *Economic Growth and Environmental Sustainability*, London, Routledge

Encyclopædia Britannica (1911) eleventh edition, Cambridge: Cambridge University Press

Engels, Friedrich (1844) 'Outlines of a Critique of Political Economy' in Karl Marx and Friedrich Engels, *Collected Works*, vol 4, London: Lawrence & Wishart, 1987

European Commission (2002) 'European Policy Brief', PETRAS website, http://www.soc.surrey.ac.uk/petras/reports.html

Fankhauser, Samuel and Richard Tol (1995) Appendix D to Aubrey Meyer and Tony Cooper, 'A Recalculation of the Social Costs of Climate Change', Global Commons Institute, London

Friends of the Earth (2001) 'Measuring Progress', Policy and Research Unit, Friends of the Earth website, http://www.foe.org.uk/progress/

Fukuyama, Francis (1989) 'The End of History?', *The National Interest*, Summer 1989, 3–18

Fukuyama, Francis (1992) *The End of History and the Last Man*, London: Hamish Hamilton

Galbraith, John Kenneth (1958) *The Affluent Society*, New York: New American Library

Georgescu-Roegen, Nicholas (1971) *The Entropy Law and the Economic Process*, Cambridge, Massachussets: Harvard University Press

Giddens, Anthony (1994) *Beyond Left and Right*, Cambridge: Polity

Giddens, Anthony (1998) *The Third Way: The Renewal of Social Democracy*, Cambridge: Polity

Global Commons Institute (1994) 'The Unequal Use of the Global Commons', paper for IPCC workshop, Nairobi, 18–23 July

Goodland, Robert and Herman Daly (1993) 'Why Northern income growth is not the solution to Southern poverty', *Ecological Economics*, 8: 85–101

Gore, Al (1992) *Earth in the Balance*, London: Earthscan

Gray, John (1997) *False Dawn: The Delusions of Global Capitalism*, London: Granta

Green, Mark and Gail MacColl (1983) *There He Goes Again: Ronald Reagan's Reign of Error*, New York: Pantheon

Grubb, Michael, Matthias Koch, Koy Thomson, Abby Munson, Francis Sullivan (1993) *The 'Earth Summit' Agreements: A Guide and Assessment*, London: Earthscan

Grundmann, Rainer (1991) 'The Ecological Challenge to Marx', *New Left Review*, 187: 103–120

Hayek, F.A. (1945) 'The Use of Knowledge in Society', *American Economic Review*, 35: 519–530

Heuting, R., P. Bosch and B. de Boer (1992) *Methodology for the Calculation of Sustainable National Income*, The Hague: Central Bureau of Statistics

Hildyard, Nicholas (1993) 'Foxes in charge of the chickens' in *Global Ecology*, edited by Wolfgang Sachs, London: Zed

Hirst, Paul and Graham Thompson (1996) *Globalization in Question*, Cambridge: Polity

Hobsbawm, Eric (1994) *Age of Extremes: The Short Twentieth Century 1914–1991*, London: Michael Joseph

Holdren, John and Paul Ehrlich (1974) 'Human population and the global environment', *American Scientist*, 62: 282–92

Huet, Tim (1997) 'Can Coops Go Global? Mondragon Is Trying', *Dollars and Sense*, Nov/Dec, http://www.dollarsandsense.org/issues/nov97/mon.html

Huxley, Aldous (1932) *Brave New World*, London: Chatto & Windus

Intergovernmental Panel on Climate Change (1990) *Climate Change: The IPCC Assessment*, Geneva: World Meteorological Organisation

Intergovernmental Panel on Climate Change (1995) *Climate Change 1995*, Cambridge: Cambridge University Press

Intergovernmental Panel on Climate Change (1995) 'Summary for Policy-makers of the Report of Working Group III', Geneva: World Meteorological Organisation

Intergovernmental Panel on Climate Change (2001) *Climate Change 2001*, Cambridge: Cambridge University Press

International Union for Conservation of Nature and Natural Resources (1980) *World Conservation Strategy: Living Resources Conservation for Sustainable Development*, Gland, Switzerland: IUCN

Irwin, Aisling (1995) 'Green economist faces picket', *Times Higher Education Supplement*, 24 November

Isaacs, Jeremy and Taylor Downing (1998) *The Cold War*, London: Bantam

Jackson, Tim and Nick Marks (1994) *Measuring Sustainable Economic Welfare: a pilot index for the UK 1950–1990*, Stockholm Environment Institute/New Economics Foundation

Jacobs, Michael (1991) *The Green Economy*, London: Pluto

Khor, Martin (1992) Editorial, *Third World Resurgence*, 24–25

Leiss, William (1972) *The Domination of Nature*, New York: George Braziller

Lewis, Martin W. (1992) *Green Delusions*, Durham, North Carolina: Duke University Press

Leopold, Aldo (1949) *A Sand County Almanac*, New York: Ballantine, 1970

Locke, John (1689) *Two Treatises of Government*, London: Everyman, 1993

Lovins, Amory (1977) *Soft Energy Paths*, Harmandsworth: Pelican

Maddox, John (1972) *The Doomsday Syndrome*, London: Macmillan

Malthus, Thomas (1798) *An Essay on the Principle of Population*, Oxford: Oxford University Press, 1993

Martell, Luke (1994) *Ecology and Society*, Cambridge: Polity

Martinez-Alier, Juan (1987) *Ecological Economics*, Oxford: Basil Blackwell

Marx, Karl and Friedrich Engels (1848) *The Communist Manifesto*, Oxford: Oxford University Press, 1992

Marx, Karl (1875) 'Critique of the Gotha Programme' in Karl Marx and Friedrich Engels, *Selected Works*, London: Lawrence & Wishart, 1968

McLaren, Duncan, Simon Bullock and Nusrat Yousuf (1998) *Tomorrow's World: Britain's Share in a Sustainable Future*, London: Earthscan

McLuhan, Marshall and Quentin Fiore (1967) *The Medium is the Massage*, New York: Bantam

Meadows, Donella H., Dennis L. Meadows, Jørgen Randers and William W. Behrens III (1972) *The Limits to Growth*, New York: Universe Books

Meadows, Donella H., Dennis L. Meadows and Jørgen Randers (1992) *Beyond the Limits: Global Collapse or a Sustainable Future*, London: Earthscan

Medawar, Peter (1984) *Pluto's Republic*, Oxford: Oxford University Press

Meyer, Aubrey and Tony Cooper (1995) 'A Recalculation of the Social Costs of Climate Change', Global Commons Institute, London

Meyer-Abich, Klaus (1993) 'Winners and Losers in Climate Change' in *Global Ecology*, edited by Wolfgang Sachs, London: Zed

Mill, John Stuart (1848) *Principles of Political Economy*, Harmandsworth: Penguin, 1985

Mishan, E.J. (1967) *The Costs of Economic Growth*, London: Staples

Muir, John (1894) *The Mountains of California*, San Francisco: Sierra Club, 1988

Myers, Norman (1979) *The Sinking Ark*, New York: Pergamon

Myers, Norman (1998) 'Lifting the veil on perverse subsidies', *Nature*, 392: 327–328

Nash, Roderick (1989) *The Rights of Nature*, Madison: University of Wisconsin Press

National Institute for Public Health and Environmental Protection (1988) *Caring for Tomorrow: National Environmental Outlook 1985–2010*, The Hague: National Institute for Public Health and Environmental Protection

Nordhaus, William (1990) 'Count before you leap: economics of climate change', *The Economist*, 7 July, pp 21–24

Norgaard, Richard B. (1994) *Development Betrayed*, London: Routledge

Nozick, Robert (1974) *Anarchy, State and Utopia*, New York: Basic Books

O'Riordan, Tim (1988) 'The Politics of Sustainability' in *Sustainable Environmental Management: Principles and Practice*, edited by R. Kerry Turner, London: Belhaven

O'Riordan, Tim (1993) 'The Politics of Sustainability' in *Sustainable Environmental Economics and Management: Principles and Practice*, edited by R. Kerry Turner, London: Belhaven

Pearce, David (1995) *Blueprint 4: Capturing Global Environmental Value*, London: Earthscan

Pearce, David, Anil Markandya and Edward B. Barbier (1989) *Blueprint for a Green Economy*, London: Earthscan

Pearce, Fred (1995) 'Global row over value of human life', *New Scientist*, 19 August

Perrot, Michelle (1983) 'Malthusianism and Socialism' in *Malthus Past and Present*, edited by Jacques Dupâquier, Antoinette Fauve-Chamoux and Eugene Grebenik, London: Academic

Pezzey, John (1989) *Economic Analysis of Sustainable Growth and Sustainable Development*, Washington DC: World Bank

Pezzey, John (1994) 'Concern for Sustainability in a Sexual World', Centre for Social and Economic Research on the Global Environment, London

Pirages, Dennis, editor (1977) *The Sustainable Society*, New York: Praeger

Ponting, Clive (1992) *A Green History of the World*, Harmandsworth: Penguin

Popper, Karl (1957) *The Poverty of Historicism*, London: Routledge & Kegan Paul

Porritt, Jonathon (1984) *Seeing Green: The Politics of Ecology Explained*, Oxford: Basil Blackwell

Rawls, John (1971) *A Theory of Justice*, Cambridge, Massachussets: Harvard University Press

Rawls, John (1993) *Political Liberalism*, New York: University of Columbia Press

Richard, David J. (1971) *A Theory of Reasons for Action*, Oxford: Clarendon

Rousseau, Jean-Jacques (1755) *Discourse on Inequality*, Oxford: Oxford University Press, 1994

Ryle, Martin (1988) *Ecology and Socialism*, London: Century Hutchinson

Sachs, Wolfgang (1999) *Planet Dialectics*, London: Zed

Schmidheiny, Stephen (1992) *Changing Course*, Cambridge, Massachussets: MIT Press

Schumacher, E.F. (1973) *Small is Beautiful*, London: Blond & Briggs

Schumpeter, Joseph A. (1943) *Capitalism, Socialism and Democracy*, London: Allen & Unwin

Sen, Amartya (1987) *On Ethics and Economics*, Oxford: Basil Blackwell

Sen, Amartya (1999) *Development as Freedom*, Oxford: Oxford University Press

Serageldin, Ismail and Andrew Steer (1994) *Making Development Sustainable: From Concepts to Action*, Washington DC: World Bank

Shelley, Mary (1818) *Frankenstein*, Oxford: Oxford University Press, 1994

Shelley, Mary (1826) *The Last Man*, London: Hogarth, 1985

Siebert, Horst (1982) 'Nature as a life-support system', *Journal of Economics*, 42 (2): 133–42

Smith, Adam (1776) *The Wealth of Nations*, Oxford: Oxford University Press, 1993

Smith, Kenneth (1951) *The Malthusian Controversy*, London: Routledge & Kegan Paul

Soros, George (1997) 'The Capitalist Threat', *The Atlantic Monthly*, February,
http://www.theatlantic.com/issues/97feb/capital/capital.htm

Steer, Andrew (1993) Discussant Remarks in *Valuing the Environment*, edited by Ismail
Serageldin and Andrew Steer, Washington DC: World Bank

Summers, Martin, ed (1992) *Economic Alternatives for Eastern Europe*, London: New
Economics Foundation

Tindale, Stephen and Gerald Holtham (1996) *Green Tax Reform*, London: Institute for
Public Policy Research

Turner, R. Kerry (1991) 'Environment, economics and ethics' in *Blueprint 2: Greening
the World Economy*, edited by David Pearce, London: Earthscan

United Nations Conference on Environment and Development (1992) 'The Rio
Declaration on Environment and Development', Rio de Janiero: UNCED Secretariat

United Nations Development Programme (1996) *Human Development Report 1996*,
Oxford: Oxford University Press

United Nations Economic Commission for Europe (1990) 'Bergen Ministerial Declaration
on Sustainable Development', Bergen, UNECE

United Nations Environment Programme (2002) *Global Environment Outlook 3*, London:
Earthscan

Wall, Derek (1990) *Getting There: Steps Towards a Green Society*, London: Green Print

Ward, Barbara (1966) *Spaceship Earth*, New York: University of Columbia Press

Weizsäcker, Ernst-Ulrich von (1994) *Earth Politics*, London: Zed

Weizsäcker, Ernst-Ulrich von, Amory B. Lovins, L. Hunter Lovins (1997) *Factor Four:
Doubling Wealth – Halving Resource Use*, London: Earthscan

Weterings, R. and J.B. Opschoor (1994) *Towards Environmental Performance Indicators
Based on the Notion of Environmental Space*, Rijswijk, The Netherlands: Advisory
Council for Research on Nature and the Environment

Wissenburg, Marcel (1998) *Green Liberalism: The free and the green society*, London:
UCL Press

World Bank (1992) *World Development Report 1992: Development and the Environment*,
New York: Oxford University Press

World Bank (2000) *World Development Report 2000–2001: Attacking Poverty*, New
York: Oxford University Press

World Commission on Environment and Development (1987) *Our Common Future*,
Oxford: Oxford University Press

World Council of Churches (1974) 'Report of Ecumenical Study Conference on Science
and Technology for Human Development', Geneva: World Council of Churches

World Trade Organization Ministerial Conference (2001) 'Doha Ministerial Declaration',
Doha: WTO

Worster, Donald (1985) *Nature's Economy*, Cambridge: Cambridge University Press

Index